Teatime in the Northwest

THE NORTHWEST'S BEST TEA ROOMS AND
RECIPES FOR TASTY TEA TIME TREATS.

By

Sharon & Ken
Foster-Lewis

SPEED GRAPHICS
SEATTLE, WASHINGTON

About the authors

Ken and Sharon Foster-Lewis live on a quiet corner of Camano Island in Washington State.

Ken hails from Liverpool, England where his life experience was as varied as jumping out of airplanes with the British Parachute Regiment and working as a dancehall bouncer during The Beatles' early days. He has also lived in New Zealand, where his adult daughters Jennifer and Amanda and grandson Connor live.

Sharon grew up on the Oregon Coast and received her education at Linfield College and University of Oregon before moving to Alaska. She met Ken in Alaska in 1978 where she was working for the airline on which he was a passenger.

They own and operate TeaTime, a national wholesale distributor of tea and tea-related gifts and are working on a new book. A shared love of nature, history, animals and travel carried them around the world before settling in the home Ken built for them overlooking the teatime sunset on the sparkling waters of Puget Sound.

 Contact Chuck Hill at Speed Graphics, 17919-2nd Ave. NW, Shoreline, WA 98177. (206) 546-8523.

Printed in the United States of America.
ISBN 0-9617699-7-1

To Mom and Dad and Emily-Mum,
who cheered us on from both sides of the world.

Acknowledgements

The old Ed Sullivan Show (on black and white television) used to feature an entertainer whose talent it was to keep a long row of plates spinning while they balanced precariously on the top of long sticks. When he'd get the whole row of plates spinning, the ones at the far end would start to wobble and he'd rush down and twirl the stick a little more. He did it all by himself and got all the applause for not breaking any. We, however, were fortunate while writing this book in having a tremendous amount of assistance and support. Special thanks go to these "stick twirlers" for not letting any of our plates hit the ground:

Chuck Hill, for immediately understanding the dream and bringing it to reality with encouragement and good humor.

Ian Clyde, for the generosity of his tea wisdom and Scottish good sense.

Ross Bulmer, for allowing us to travel for research without worrying about starving cats, dogs, deer and hedgehogs at home.

Our readers who advised us of tea rooms opening, and who expressed in many kind ways their appreciation for our efforts. In particular, **Maureen Wilson** and **Lily Yamamoto**, who we hope someday to meet, for sending along tea room information on a regular basis.

Dear latte-saturated, coffee-chugging friends like **Valerie Herlocker** and **Mary Higgins** for keeping their eyes open for new tea rooms in their travels. Good neighbors **Susan Creighton** and **Claire Winget** for pep talks and tea.

Mom, for learning how to play card games with actual cards instead of her computer so we could ride it hard and leave it in the stable wet. My brother Greg for buying her the cards.

Julee and **Sue** and the staff of the Perennial Tea Room for their consistent enthusiasm, and support.

Credits

Front cover photograph © 1998 by **Chuck Hill.** Food styling and preperation on front cover photo by **Anne Nisbet**.

Special thanks to **The Perennial Tea Room** for providing the classic teapot and accessorites used in the front cover photograph. The pattern is Rose and Ivy from Heirloom English bone china.

Special thanks to **Kamian J. Dowd** for providing teapots from her collection for use on the back cover and to **Terri Hutyler** for providing props used in the cover photograph.

Photograph of Sharon and Ken Foster-Lewis on the back cover © 1996 **Unlimited Exposure**, Stanwood, WA (360) 629-6383

TABLE OF CONTENTS

A note about this new edition

I came across an old file the other day. In it was a letter I had written to a bookstore shortly after our first edition of Teatime in the Northwest was released. One phrase stood out, "Tea is quietly blooming in the Northwest . . ." I smiled, because just over a year later there is absolutely nothing "quiet" about the amazing growth in popularity of tea in our region.

This edition has doubled our first one with over 120 places to go for tea (or to have tea come to you with our new sections on Tea Parties and Tea Caterers) in Washington, Oregon and Southern British Columbia. We have included a new section for tea lovers escaping the Northwest winter chill in Hawaii, and the recipe section for treats to enjoy with tea at home has also been expanded.

We have learned from tea room owners (by far the most hospitable group you're likely to meet anywhere) that there are now roving bands of tea lovers about — individually or with friends — "tea touring" with our book. Last year Maverick Tours began operating their Victoria Tea Tour charters in the Northwest and to our delight our book is their guide!

By the very nature of the way tea is prepared, you are forced to slow down. Judging by the response to the first book, shaking off the "grab and go" mind-set has been a rewarding experience for many of us in the latte-saturated Northwest, and with any luck at all, we will never, ever see a drive-through tea room.

So whether you're in the mood for being pampered and steeped in elegance or maybe just looking for a quiet spot to really connect with an old friend or collect your thoughts, it's in here for you. From the ivy-mantled, hushed-toned tinkle of silver on porcelain tea rooms to the upbeat, cheerfully countrified tea rooms these 120 places for tea are as diverse as the Pacific Northwest itself. That "quiet blooming" of tea has become an opulent and colorful mixed bouquet for your enjoyment.

Sharon & Ken

Introduction

I admit it now. Years ago, when my English mother-in-law, Emily Bell Lewis, entered the guest room I had carefully decorated for her first visit, looked around, and pronounced it "homely," I may have been at a loss for words. And when Emily was rummaging hopefully through my cupboard looking for tea and came upon a teabag, which she dangled in front of her face for a moment, I really think now that it was my rich imagination and new bride insecurity that made me think she was eyeing it as though it were a dead mouse.

I soon learned, to my relief, that "homely" meant cozy, warm, and comfortable to an Englishwoman. I also learned there is a whole world of tea to be explored and enjoyed.

It was a year or two later, when Ken and I were on a hike through the foothills of the Himalayas in Nepal that I really began to think of tea as more than a simple beverage. We were honored to be invited into a private home near our trail. Through our bi-lingual Sherpa guide, Sonam, we learned that we were invited to share tea, chai, with the household. We had no shared language with which to converse, and yet the sense of companionship and graciousness experienced over that chipped porcelain cup of tea with yak butter bridged our two cultures. Nothing else embodies the true essence of hospitality like sharing tea. While sitting on a simple bench set by the open fire of that mud-floored dwelling, I learned that tea is by nature "homely."

A Brief History of Tea

All the tea in China

. . . At the fifth cup I am purified;
The sixth cup calls me to the realms of the immortals.
Lu T'ung

Like the thick fogs that often shroud our Pacific Northwest coastline, so too has the origin of tea been clouded through time by myth and legend.

Scholars seem to agree that in the year 2,737 BC. there existed an enlightened Chinese emperor, Shen Nung, on whose silk-clad shoulders rest at least one of the accepted versions of the origin of tea. Shen Nung was revered as "The Divine Cultivator" and "The Divine Healer" and was a person whose advanced knowledge of hygiene predisposed him to boil his drinking water. One day while working in his garden, several glossy, green leaves with serrated edges drifted into his cauldron of hot water. Glancing up, he noted that it came from a tree bearing a lovely pure white flower. Shen Nung discovered as he bent over his cauldron that a delicate and pleasant aroma was emitted as the water gently boiled, and so he filled a ladle and tasted it. Now thoroughly pleased with the recuperative properties of this tasty, refreshing brew he immediately issued instructions to his subjects to carefully cultivate the plant, today known as Camellia sinensis, a distant cousin of those harbingers of spring gardening, our camellia bushes.

Drink tea that your mind may be lively and clear.
Wang Yu Cheng
Sung Dynasty

India and Japan also lay claim to the discovery of tea, and it is safe to say that the plant was growing in those areas too as it is native to semitropical and tropical climates as well as in the rarefied air above 5,000 feet. If left untrimmed, the plant grows to treelike proportions of 40 feet and more and lives 70 years. It did not take early cultivators long to see the advantage for harvesting if kept trimmed to a bush of 3 or 4 feet. By 350 AD a thriving tea cultivation society had emerged.

By the 5th century AD tea had become as popular a trade commodity as vinegar, rice, and noodles, making its way along established trade routes to Persia by sure-footed caravan. The subtle shift had begun from considering tea as a medicinal and natureopathic substance to a pleasurable social beverage and major bartering tool.

By 780 AD, enterprising tea merchants sought a forum to promote their product. In commissioning Lu Yu to create the masterpiece essay Ch'a Ching or The Classic of Tea they had found a means to put forth detailed instructions that served to unify the cultivation, preparation, and enjoyment of tea. Until its publication, information on all aspects of tea had been passed on orally. The book had far-reaching effects, some of which were not anticipated by the tea merchants. Government revenue officials, tirelessly on the trail of ways to augment their coffers, levied the first tea tax. It is an excellent indication of how deeply ingrained tea had become to the culture that the unified cry of outrage by the tea-drinking populace was actually heeded by the officials who rescinded the tax for 13 years.

Lu Yu was an orphan found wandering by a Buddhist monk. Not at all enamored of the austerity surrounding his adopted father's calling, Lu Yu did what young boys have wanted to do for centuries; he ran away and joined a circus as an acrobatic clown. While performing in the provinces he shared his ebullient energy and talents with countless people, one of whom became a benefactor. Through this mentor Lu Yu was introduced to books and provided with an education. So it was that Lu Yu, orphan and clown, became a scholar, author, cultural celebrity and friend to an emperor before retiring to the life of a mountain hermit where he died in peaceful introspection in the year 804.

We shape clay into a pot, but it is the emptiness inside that holds whatever we want.
Tao-te Ching

So poetic and detailed are the instructions set forth in Lu Yu's essay that they have survived for more than 1,200 years and today form a basis for the beautiful ritualized Japanese Tea Ceremonies, "Cha-no-yu". It has been said that the beauty and simplicity described in Lu Yu's tea ceremony captured the very essence of the religious thought of the day.

"The cup that cheers" - Tea and Europeans

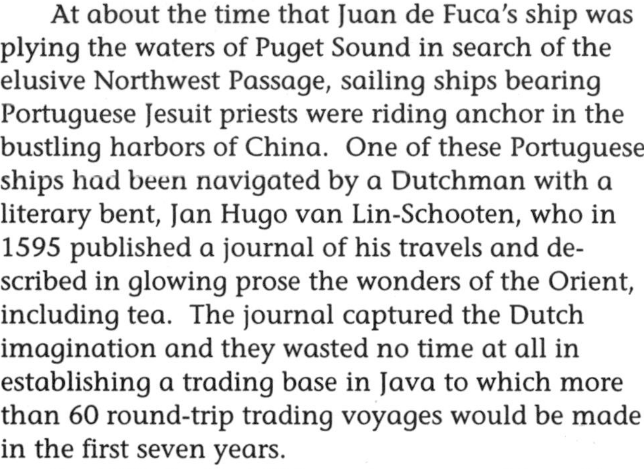

> *We had a kettle; we let it leak.*
> *Our not repairing it made it worse.*
> *We haven't had any tea for a week . . .*
> *The bottom is out of the Universe.*
>
> Rudyard Kipling

At about the time that Juan de Fuca's ship was plying the waters of Puget Sound in search of the elusive Northwest Passage, sailing ships bearing Portuguese Jesuit priests were riding anchor in the bustling harbors of China. One of these Portuguese ships had been navigated by a Dutchman with a literary bent, Jan Hugo van Lin-Schooten, who in 1595 published a journal of his travels and described in glowing prose the wonders of the Orient, including tea. The journal captured the Dutch imagination and they wasted no time at all in establishing a trading base in Java to which more than 60 round-trip trading voyages would be made in the first seven years.

By 1610 the first Chinese teas were shipped to Europe by the Dutch. By the mid-1600s, tea had been introduced to Britain, France, Germany, Holland, Scandinavia, Russia and America. The Germans and French were quick to shrug off the new beverage, returning instead to the comfortable familiarity of their ales and wines. The other countries adopted tea as a beverage of daily consumption, but in England tea virtually entered the national bloodstream and was embraced with the same passion they held for the playwright of the day, William Shakespeare.

Revered in Britain as a cure-all and health elixir, tea was restricted to the aristocracy and kept under lock and key for its first 50 years there due to its high price. Tea was first offered to the public in London in 1657 at an Exchange Alley coffee house and tobacco shop owned by Thomas Garway. A handbill (or "broadside" as they were called) passed out by Garway to promote sales imbued tea with medicinal and moral powers of almost magical proportions. Reminiscent of later day TV "infomercials", the virtues attributed to tea were "boosted memory, cured fever, rid colic, eased brain, and strengthened stomach muscles".

The Dutch held what amounted to a monopoly on trading tea for some time, but after a combination of bloodshed, upheaval, and diplomacy, The

British East India Trading Company grasped control of much of the tea trade from the Dutch. By 1700 tea was being imported directly to England on its own ships, and so the prices dropped. More than 500 coffee houses in London were then able to offer tea as well. Eager horticulturists even tried to grow the evergreen tea plants in England, but found no cooperation from the climate there to do so. Nonetheless, tea had finally made the transition from being the exclusive nectar of emperors, tsars, and kings, to the daily table of the common man.

Tea, Toil, and Trouble in the Colonies

Late in the 1700s British tea merchants commissioned American shipbuilders to develop and build a class of sailing ship designed specifically for the tea trade. The clippers, as they were called, were three-masted, graceful and fast. Capable of transporting one million pounds of tea each trip, their speed dramatically reduced the voyage time. Fortunes were now being made and lost not only in the commerce of tea but also in gambling on the outcome of the annual 88 to 102 day duration race from the harbor in Canton around the Cape of Good Hope past the Azores and into the English Channel. Finally the clipper ships were towed up the Thames and the precious cargo rushed to waiting London auction houses.

The celebrated tea clipper Cutty Sark

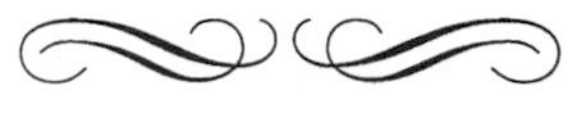

There are few hours in life more agreeable than the hour dedicated to the ceremony known as afternoon tea.

Henry James, *Portrait of a Lady*

Meanwhile on the other side of the Atlantic, dissatisfaction was growing in the colonies at the same rate as the taxes being levied upon them. While many British taxes on goods bound for America had been repealed, the three pence per pound of tea stayed intact. The relationship between America and England would not. In 1773 American colonial housewives united under the name "Mistresses of Families." In what amounted to a boycott, this powerful consumer group vowed to rid tea from their tables until the rapidly increasing taxes were repealed. It was also suspected that England was keeping the best tea for themselves and sending inferior product to the colonies. The colonial womens' scandalous "uprising" set tongues wagging in the gentile parlors of London tea parties, and planted seeds for an even larger uprising in three years that would lead to the loss of the colonies.

The high taxation and shortsightedness of the English government was not limited to the colonies, however. In England the duties added to the tea by the government had raised the cost for a pound of tea to four times the average man's weekly wage, and the taxes levied on tea reached 120%, with much of the revenue earmarked to save the financially beleaguered and generally mismanaged British East India Company.

And freedom's teacup
still o'erflows
With ever-fresh
libations,
To cheat of slumber all
her foes
and cheer the wakening
nations!
Oliver Wendell Holmes
Ballad of the Boston Tea Party

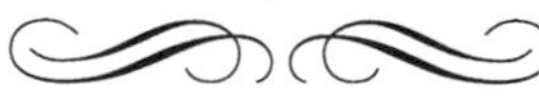

Smuggled Goods

High duty and high demand for tea combined to make smuggling a lucrative vocation in England. The intricate coves and hidden inlets that make the southern England coastline so charming were the perfect setting for the clandestine off-loading of tea. Small vessels plied the moonlit waters to meet the large commerce ships, most of them Dutch, silently riding the swell offshore. The lucrative business of tea courier caused a farm labor shortage in the south of England as a network of swift and strong young men conducted the business of transporting tea to shore by small boats and then on to secret caches as diverse as church crypts and castles throughout the countryside. At one point, 50% of the tea off-loaded to English shores was contraband. Most of the able-bodied young smugglers that were lucky enough to be caught alive by the revenue officials were conscripted into the navy.

Meanwhile in the colonies, another group of able-bodied young men under the name of "The Sons of Liberty" were determined to make a more dramatic and visible statement against tea taxation. On December 16, 1773, disguised as American Indians, they swarmed onto ships off-loading tea and dumped 340 large chests of tea into Boston Harbor. The British Parliament was swift in meting out punishment by enacting strict laws designed to penalize the rebellious colonists and to limit their political freedom. In the colonies the cauldrons of revolution simmered and bubbled like the tea kettle, and the First Continental Congress convened. The country mobilized for its fight for independence. Tea had started a revolution.

Finally by 1784 the tax on tea in England was reduced to 12.5% and the benefits that had been derived from smuggling were effectively negated. By now, it was far too late to repair the damaged relationship with the colonies that had broken away to form an independent nation.

The American coastal explorer, Captain Gray, had developed in the meantime a lucrative trade with our Pacific Coast Indian tribes to obtain the lush pelts of otter, mink, and beaver. These furry denizens of our Northern waters became the valuable link that allowed trade directly with the Chinese for tea. The doors to trade in the Orient swung open for the young country and tea began being imported directly to North America on its own ships.

The Duchess of Bedford's Stomach Growls

Afternoon tea began as an English institution in 1840 when Anna, the 7th Duchess of Bedford's stomach began to growl. The Duchess, a society trend setter who apparently could not get by on the two big meals a day, took to having tea and a snack of sandwiches and cakes served around four or five in the afternoon. Legions of closet-snackers looking for an afternoon lift followed the trend setting duchess and the custom spread throughout the country. The tea time was adopted by manual workers and farmers in the form of "high tea," a more substantial meal that often included meats and cheeses and more robust fare. This was often the laborers' main meal of the day.

The term "high tea" came about because it was often served at the dining table (or high table) as opposed to a "low tea" (which later became known as "afternoon tea") served on a lower tea table in the parlor or by the fire.

In 1848, in what amounts to early industrial espionage, an English gentleman with the providential name of Fortune disguised himself in the garb of a Chinese merchant. Carried in a curtained sedan-chair under cover of darkness, and sleeping in monasteries, Robert Fortune surreptitiously garnered tea cultivation knowledge, soil samples, and processing methods in areas of China that were off-limits to foreigners. His acquired knowledge unlocked the secrets to tea and enabled the British to establish large tea plantations, known as "gardens" that thrive to this day throughout India.

Queen Victoria herself declared tea to be the national beverage of England, and she even outfitted her vacation retreat with a small scale table and plush chairs with the names of each of her children embroidered on the back so they too could participate in afternoon tea. Other teatime indulgences emerged in the general marketplace. Pottery makers sensed the demand and began competing with each other for novel teapot designs that were both utilitarian and ornamental. Suddenly merchants' shelves were awash with teatime paraphernalia.

In 1864, an enterprising manager of A.B.C.-Aerated Bread Company in London encouraged her employer to allow her to open a tea room in some unused space. It was her intention to serve tea and refreshments in the afternoon. Business thrived. Society's approval of tea had thus created the first public place where a proper lady could actually go unchaperoned. While they still would not win the right to vote for another 40 years, tea drinking ladies were heady with this new found freedom. Tea rooms blossomed everywhere.

Tea . . . the cup that cheers but not inebriate.
William Cowper

Tea Rooms of the Pacific Northwest

Today, those initial endeavors have engendered a harvest of public tea rooms in Oregon, Washington, and British Columbia. As varied as the inhabitants of this beautiful area, the tea room roster in this book will have a special place to delight every reader. From the ivy-mantled, hushed tone, tinkle of silver on porcelain tea rooms to the fun, eclectic and funky tea rooms, the Northwest has a special place for you to linger over "the cup that cheers."

Lu Yu Explains Tea

Imagine, if you will, that Lu Yu is given one day back on 20th century earth and he must spend it in the Pacific Northwest. Closing his eyes and randomly dialing numbers in a phone booth, he calls your home. It's Saturday morning, you have some free time, so you arrange to pick him up since he doesn't drive.

Lu Yu is easy to spot near the phone booth in the colorful silk brocade jacket which he has gathered around him to ward off the misty Northwest chill. As he shifts from foot to foot to stay warm, you note with concern the small splash his sandals make in the puddle. "The first stop will be Eddie Bauer and Nike," you ruminate thoughtfully, "then a good cup of tea to set things right." (Fortunately, you had the presence of mind this morning to bring along your copy of Teatime in the Northwest.) "An 8th century tea philosopher should enjoy a good 'cuppa'."

Tea tempers the spirit and harmonizes the mind, dispels lassitude and relieves fatigue; awakens thought and prevents drowsiness.
Lu Yu

The shelves of the cheery tearoom are a feast for the eyes! The colorful tins and shiny boxes glisten in the morning light with colors to rival the richness of Lu Yu's silk jacket, (which you feel a little guilty thinking would look good with your black slacks). After apologizing for the weather on the drive over, you realize that with the topic of tea you've struck a pleasant chord for conversation.

"So many teas . . ." his eyes caress the crowded shelves with delight, lingering over the myriad of green teas like one recognizing an old friend. He makes his choice, and the pot is delivered to your table. With his waterproof Eddie Bauer jacket draped casually over the back of his chair, and the aromatic beverage creating a mystic aura over your table, Lu Yu once again takes on the mantle of an 8th century tea philosopher. As you make a mental note to remove the price tags and extra button packet hanging from his new jacket, he begins:

"All teas come from the leaves of one bush, the Camellia sinensis. It is in the processing of the tea leaves that the three different teas are created." His new Nikes squeak on the floor under the table and appear to startle him.

"Three different teas? There must be thousands," you assert, perhaps a little too strongly. You may not be a tea philosopher, but you do know your retail tea merchants' shelves. "Perhaps Lu Yu is a little out of touch with what's happened in the last 12 centuries," you decide to yourself.

"Three teas," he patiently restates, his voice underlining the importance of this very basic piece of tea information, "black tea, green tea, and oolong. It is the processing that determines their differences. There are dozens of varieties of each of these three, usually named for the region in which they are grown, and then literally thousands of different tea blends."

The goodness is a decision for the mouth to make.
Lu Yu
The Classic of Tea

"What is this 'process' that the tea leaf undergoes?" you query, realizing this person really does know his tea.

Lu Yu inhales the aroma of the tea. He fumbles a moment with the handle on the cup, decides to simply avoid it, and holds it gently in his two hands like one would a small bird. The warmth is a welcome comfort to his cold palms. "The process is either three or fourfold depending on the type of tea. First, withering removes as much moisture as possible from the leaves. Then they are rolled or manipulated to partially rupture the leaf tissue. This step releases naturally-occuring enzymes that begin the process of fermentation. It is the degree of fermentation that determines which of the three tea types you are producing. That is what distinguishes them from each other," he says matter-of-factly.

Suddenly you flash back to a wine appreciation class you took from a local wine expert. "Fermentation?" you ponder, "Like in the production of a good wine?"

"No," he says simply and patiently like speaking to a child. "Like in the production of a good tea. The term fermentation actually is a slightly misleading technical term for the process of oxidation - the exposure of the leaves and the released enzymes to air. Finally, they are dried or fired, which stops the fermentation process and dries the leaves evenly." "Naturally" he adds, "there are numerous variations on this general process depending on the source of the leaves and also the country in which the final tea is manufactured. Darjeeling, Keemun, Assam and Ceylon are all black teas for example. Black teas are subjected to all four of the steps, Oolongs are lightly withered and rolled and only partially fermented before being dried."

"And your favorite, the green tea?" you probe.

"Ah, green tea," he rolls his eyes skyward in remembered delight, "green tea is not fermented at all. The leaves are steamed or heated rather than withered, then rolled and dried. The leaves remain green because they do not oxidize. A green tea is light and clear with a delicate, very flavorful taste." He smiles and nods toward the pot between us, "But I must say I am enjoying this black tea! As I say in my book, 'the goodness is a decision for the mouth to make'. You have read my book, haven't you?"

Avoiding his stare over the rim of his cup you assure him that it was your fond intention to read the whole book, and one day soon you certainly would, that you had been a bit busy lately. You are relieved to notice that this seems to satisfy Lu Yu.

" What a delightful experience it has been for me to see how far tea has come in 1,200 years." he actually smacks his lips after tipping his cup for the last taste and rises. "But now I really must be getting back. Do you have any other questions for me before I go?"

"Well, I read somewhere that you actually were an acrobatic clown in a travelling circus in China. Is this true?" You had been longing to ask that question all through the morning but did not want to seem impertinent nor to interupt the wondrous flow of tea knowledge. Slipping the embroidered silk jacket from his shoulders, he folds it gently, caressing the fine brocade, and hands it to you with a slight bow saying "Please accept this humble gift as appreciation of your kind hospitality," and with a smile, Lu Yu executes two perfect backflips out the door of the tearoom and disappears into the Pacific Northwest mist.

I am in no way interested in immortality, but only in the taste of tea.
Lu T'ung

Types of Teas

My Aunt Marwayne knows the night sky. With unbridled delight she will rock back on her heels, throw her gray head back, and enthuse, "Oh look, there's Venus in Taurus! Ah, Jupiter's moving through Gemini." From the sky she can tell the seasons of the year. From the sky she can tell the seasons of a person's life. The night sky in her company seems a friendly place, populated by stars with which you are on a first name basis. I admire that wealth of knowledge and the comfort of that familiarity.

Before I got to know much about tea I had a general feeling it must all be pretty much like the teabag variety. My expectations were minimal, and the brew I made met these limited expectations nicely. It would be brownish. It would burn my tongue if I wasn't careful. It was okay. The idea of subtle varietal differences in tea had not entered my thoughts.

The following varieties of the three main types of tea (Black, Oolong, and Green) are provided simply as a starting point for your own exploration. Within these varieties are literally thousands of variations based on country of origin and even the blending techniques of various tea companies. Experimentation will help you find your personal favorites, and even to create your very own blends:

The first European teacups evolved from Oriental tea bowls and were without a handle. To avoid burned fingers, Europeans pourred a sip of tea into the saucer to cool. A single handle was added to the cup in the mid-18th century.

Black Teas

Assam - from northeast India, this is a robust and hearty tea with a strong malty flavor and rusty color, grown at low altitude, and used in Irish Breakfast Tea. Good served with milk.

Ceylon - from Sri Lanka, golden color, a strong full taste and delicate fragrance. Good served throughout the day.

Darjeeling - makes an excellent after-dinner tea, rich in flavor, with a flowery bouquet. This tea is grown high in the foothills of the Himalayas of north India, and is an expensive tea.

Earl Grey - a 19th century British statesman the Second Earl Grey, was given this recipe in appreciation from the Chinese for his diplomatic work. Typically drunk in the afternoon, Earl Grey has a pungent, flowery fragrance and delicacy owing to Oil of Bergamot sprayed on the tea.

English Breakfast - often either a blend of Indian and Ceylon teas or a Keemun based blend, this popular morning tea is full-bodied, strong, and aromatic. Its rich flavor is enhanced with milk.

Keemun - a fine quality Chinese tea originating in the Anhui Province of southern China, this is a full-bodied tea with a haunting nut-like quality to its taste. Serve with milk for maximum enjoyment.

Lapsang Souchong - the leaves are smoked over embers to create this rich exotic tea. Redolent of campfires, its distinctive aroma reminds both Ken and me of the smell of Admiral Nelson's ship moored in Portsmouth, England. We don't know why, but we find a tarry, nautical quality to this unusual tea experience.

He loved happiness like I love tea.
Eudora Welty

Oolong Teas

Formosa Oolong - almost all Oolong comes from Taiwan. This tea has a refreshing, fruity aroma and sparkling nature, and has been anointed "the philosopher's drink". Oolongs are created in other countries, but Formosa Oolong has been given the nod by most tea experts as the best.

Green Teas

Gunpowder - when Europeans first arrived in Zhejiang Province of China and were shown the pellets of rolled young or medium-age leaves that constitute this tea, it is said that they named it because of the resemblance to lead ball shot. Low in caffeine, it has a delicate yet penetrating flavor.

Gyokuro - one of Japan's most highly revered green teas made from only the tender top buds. Mild and sweet, as its name "Pearl Dew" would imply, it is one of Japanese teas that have become known collectively as "the white wines of teas."

Hyson - green tea from China or India; fragrant, light, and mellow.

Mattcha - Japan's ceremonial powdered tea, less than 1% is exported.

Hoochow - the first of the annual crop of green tea from China, a light and sweet tea.

In the early 1900s, Mr. Thomas Sullivan, a tea merchant in New York City accidentally created the teabag. Attempting to stimulate sales by mailing samples of the tea wrapped in silk cloth to potential customers, many who received it simply poured boiling water over the bag rather than opening it as the vendor had originally intended. Hemp gauze soon replaced the silk to make the teabag cost effective.

When is tea not tea?

While the question may sound like a riddle emanating from the head of the Mad Hatter's table, it does require some consideration.

It is important to remember that true tea is a beverage created by the infusion of boiling water and the leaves of only one specific plant, the Camellia sinensis. Western cultures, however, have embraced the term 'tea' to encompass healthful herbal, root, fruit, tree bark, and seed brews in rapidly growing varieties and blends. Well-known examples, all of which are caffeine-free, are chamomile, rose hip, burdock, ginseng, cardamom, and a wide array of mints. The French call these refreshing herbal infusions "tisanes" to distinguish them from tea.

Imbued by traditional folklore of all cultures, (and more recently medical research), to possess beneficial properties, the herbal infusions constitute a whole separate world of steeped beverages. The varieties deserve study, respect, appreciation and experimentation. There are many excellent books on the topic.

Chai

The word cha is the original word for tea in China. In India, where milk and spices were added, the word became chai (rhymes with high). Now at least four Northwest companies are creating Chai. Three Oregon companies: Oregon Chai and Xanadu Teas in Portland, and Sattwa Chai in Newberg are succeeding in introducing the spicy tea drink to the North American taste buds, as is The Chai Guy (a.k.a. Jan Drabeck) in Seattle, Washington.

As Chaimeister Jan Drabek asserts, "Chai is like chocolate chip cookies or lemonade, everyone has their own way of doing it." Usually Chai is created from varying combinations of the following: black tea, hot milk, vanilla, honey, ginger, cinnamon, clove, nutmeg, cardamom, sometimes crushed almonds and even pepper (yes, pepper). A highly individual drink, it varies from household to household in India. Invigorating, refreshing and rich, many predict that Chai will gain converts from the latte crowd in rapidly growing numbers. See our recipe section for a version of chai made from individual herbs and spices.

How to brew a perfect pot of tea

The custom of pouring the milk into the cup before the hot tea dates back to seventeenth century England. Until then, the British had only known pewter and earthenware mugs for drinking ale, and were afraid that hot tea poured into newly introduced fine porcelain cups would crack them. The custom continues to this day as a matter of personal choice. Queen Elizabeth adds milk after the tea is poured.

Bring freshly drawn, cold water to a rolling boil in your kettle, allowing about 3/4 cup water per serving. Do not allow the water to boil too long as this tends to diminish the end flavor through insufficient aeration. Never reheat water. By the way, if you do not like the taste of your tap water for drinking, you will not like it any better in tea. In that case, use commercially bottled waters.

Use a spotless ceramic or glass teapot that has been warmed by filling with hot tap water for a few minutes. Drain that water completely out of the teapot.

Into the warmed teapot place one rounded teaspoon of a good quality loose tea per six-ounce cup that you are making.

Pour the boiling water over the tea in the teapot, stir, and allow to brew for five full minutes. Time the brew. The single most common cause for poor tea is not following this step and erroneously attempting to judge the brew by its coloration. Use this time to get your cups, milk, sugar, and/or lemon slices ready.

Separate the spent leaves from the brew. This is especially easy if your teapot has a removable leaf basket, use a strainer, or decant into a warmed serving pot. Stir the brew to even it out.

Serve it fresh. If you like your tea less strong, add hot water after the tea has brewed. Brewing another pot, if everyone wants more, is the tastiest idea.

"Sun Tea" advice

Iced tea was invented at the St. Louis World's Fair by an enterprising British tea vendor on a hot day when he became tired of watching customers pass his booth to get free samples of ice-cold soft drinks and lemonade.

Make special ice cubes for your iced tea by freezing a raspberry, blackberry or mint leaf in each cube.

Maybe it's because the Northwest doesn't see as much sun as other parts of the country that we're immediately charmed by a beverage made with solar power. Maybe it's the memories for many of us of our first sip of the brew in the 1960s with gentle folk music playing in the background. Whatever the reason, "sun tea" followers attach the same seasonal significance to placing the jar on the windowsill that many bird lovers attach to the return of the swallows. Summer just can't be far behind.

Health care professionals recently have raised several unsettling questions regarding the possibility of bacteria forming during the regular "sun tea" brewing conditions. Tea authorities recently have pointed out that the flavor of the tea will never be at its height since the water never really gets hot enough for maximum flavor. As charming a ritual as a jar of water and teabags on a sunny windowsill may seem, all signs seem to indicate that there is now a better way.

Harney & Sons Fine Teas recommends the following: for 1 quart of tea, place 7 tea bags or 3 T. loose tea in a heatproof 1 quart container. Bring 1 cup of cold water to a rolling boil and pour over the tea. Stir, cover, and let stand for 15 minutes. Add 3 cups of cold water and stir. Remove the tea bags or strain the loose tea and serve over ice. Adding a cinnamon stick, lime or orange slices, or a split vanilla bean while the tea steeps lends a light natural flavor.

So give the sunny windowsill back to your cat so she can watch the return of the swallows to your yard, and raise a healthy glass to summer.

A Home Tea-Tasting

My friend Valerie had what seemed to me to be a 'dream job' during summer break in high school. She was a Cookie Dipper, the person responsible for the cream filling in the sandwich cookies. Not only did she look perky in her little white cotton Cookie Dipper hat, but she could actually nibble on her work all day. She was prepared for my envy. I cleaned shrimp on a dock and wore a hairnet and big black rubber boots. Very few people envied that. With a sigh she would give me the litany of drawbacks of her job, although in retrospect I think Valerie was just being kind because I smelled like fish. "First, of course, you could never quite look at a sandwich cookie the same way again, having known them so intimately," she'd sigh dramatically. Then there was the little matter of the ten pounds she always had to rush to lose so she could zip her cheerleader outfit in September. Valerie proved to me that often 'dream jobs' do not hold up well under close scrutiny.

Love and scandal are the best sweeteners of tea.
Henry Fielding

Most of us lack the educated palate that would allow us to be a professional tea-taster. On closer inspection, the job would seem to have considerable drawbacks anyway. For instance, the tea is sprayed unceremoniously onto the back of the mouth with an atomizer, rather than sipped from delicate china cups and lingered over thoughtfully. Then there's the matter of the required 15 minute breaks twice a day. Exactly what would you do while everyone else had a coffee break?

Having, therefore, eliminated it as a career choice, it would seem that the best way to participate in a tea-tasting is simply for the sheer fun of it. A weekend brunch is the perfect chance to gather some friends, and educate yourselves about the subtle differences in the character of various teas. Here are a few suggestions:

Get comfortable ahead of the tasting with a few of the terms used by tea professionals. (Those of you who are wine lovers will recognize some terms common to the understanding and appreciation of both beverages.) Check the glossary in the back of this book for the most often used descriptive terms.

. . . it took her a long time to prepare her tea; but when ready it was set forth with as much grace as if she had been a veritable guest to her own self.
A New England Nun (1881)

Select 4-6 teas of distinctly different character. Some recommendations might be: Black Tea: English Breakfast or Irish Breakfast, Lapsang Souchong, Darjeeling, Oolong, Formosa Oolong; Green Tea: Gyokuro or Gunpowder. Serve each tea from a different teapot.

Learn something beforehand about the teas you will serve. Frequently the makers of the tea will have some promotional material on the various teas. Begin by pouring one flavor for all to taste. Lead your guests in a discussion of the varying properties of the tea.

Offer lemon, sugar, and milk; but ask them please to taste the tea first to get the real tea properties before adding anything.

Use demitasse cups, or fill the cups only partially. Place a large, attractive bowl in the center of the table so that each guest can discard the tea after tasting. Empty the bowl frequently - it's not pretty when full.

Rinse the cups between tastings or supply new cups for each brew. Unlike a wine-tasting, tea's flavor is often enhanced by some snacks and sweets that you can offer between tastings.

Variations as your tastings become more advanced would be 'blind' tasting where your guests would make educated guesses as to the type of tea and even country of origin. Another idea would be to purchase the same tea, i.e. English Breakfast from a variety of suppliers and evaluate the blends.

Peering through the leaves into the future

Old West outlaw and gunslinger Jesse James was married to a tea leaf reader. History does not chronicle if Mrs. James saw bad omens in her teacup the morning that her husband was ambushed, or whether Mr. James, in a hurry to go out and rob some more banks simply dismissed her dire predictions. He was, after all, a coffee drinker. This simply proves that history, like tea leaf reading, is more of an art than a science.

It is widely suspected that fortune telling from tea leaves began with the Chinese, and like the beverage itself, spread from China throughout civilization. Cultural variations developed, with Scottish ladies adding much to the lore. In the highland of Scotland, the tea leaf reader was called the "spae-wife" (or "spy-wife") because every morning she could spy into the day's events.

To read tea leaves, make the tea in a pot that has no strainer. Pour the brewed tea into a cup, preferably one with a plain white interior. The person with the question drinks the tea, holding in mind a question or a wish, until only a teaspoonful of tea remains. The person with the question then takes the cup by the handle in his or her left hand and swirls the remaining liquid and leaves three times to the left (counterclockwise). Gently, holding the questions or wish in mind, he or she then turns the cup upside down in the saucer. The tea and many of the leaves will fall out. Wait a moment for the cup to drain.

The reader then picks the cup up and turns it right side up. The first pattern or impression the reader receives on turning the cup over and looking at the leaves remaining is the response to the questioner's query or wish. Sometimes combinations of images and symbols will have formed, and the skillful reader will be able to discern the meaning.

The handle of the cup represents the questioner. Like a written page, the reading begins at the left of the handle and proceeds around the entire cup. Patterns farthest from the handle are events at a

One pound of tea makes over 200 cups.

Matrons, who toss
the cup, and see
The grounds of fate in
grounds of tea.
Alexander Pope

physical distance from the questioner. Patterns close to the rim represent the here and now, and the bottom of the cup is the future. If the questioner is in a confused state of mind, or generally a muddled thinker, then the patterns will be difficult to discern.

The following pictures are linked through folklore to specific meanings:

Tea will always be the favored beverage of the intellectual.
Thomas DeQuincey

Bird	-	good luck
Cat	-	treachery
Cow	-	prosperity
Dog	-	a close friend
Ring	-	marriage
Anchor	-	success or voyage
Cross	-	trouble and suffering
Letters	-	initials of significant people
Star	-	good luck
Triangle	-	inheritance
Flower	-	love and honor
Clover	-	good luck
Tree	-	success, happiness
Ladder	-	gradual rise, advancement
Clouds	-	doubts
Crown	-	good luck
Windmill	-	hard work pays off
Wings	-	an important message is coming

I would like to propose a toast. May your cup always hold cows in crowns and birds in trees and may your windmill always blow away your clouds. Cheers!

TEA ROOMS OF OREGON

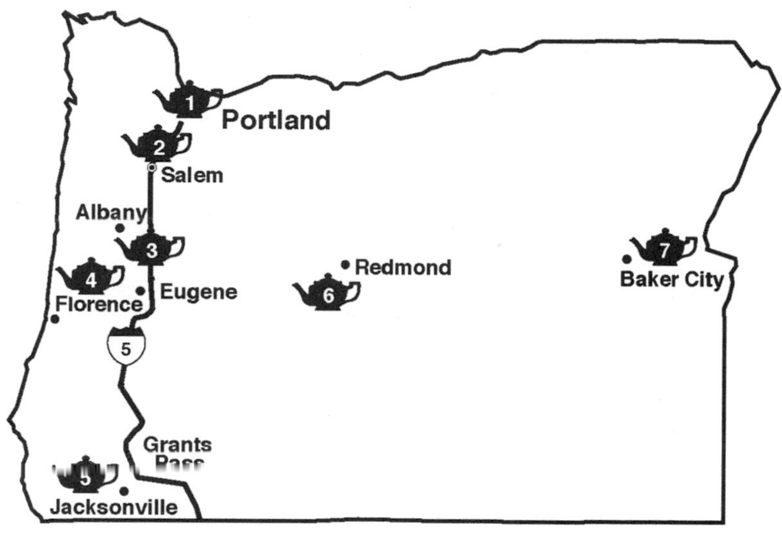

1. PORTLAND AREA
   Annie Fenwick's Bakery
   & Tea Room
   The British Tea Garden
   The Garden Gate Tea Room
   The Gate Lodge Restaurant
   at the Pittock Mansion
   The Heathman Hotel
   Lady Di's Country Store
   Stratford House Tea Parlour
   The Tao of Tea
   Tea Time on Hawthorne

2. NORTH WILLAMETTE VALLEY
   Angelina's French Country
   Tea Room
   Barbara Ann's Tea Room
   Lavender Tea House
   Tudor Rose Tea Room

3. SOUTH WILLAMETTE VALLEY
   Flinn's Tea Parlour

4. Lovejoy's at Pier Point

5. ROGUE VALLEY
   Country Cottage Cafe
   & Tea Room
   Tea Cottage
   Yvonne's Espresso and
   Tea House

6. Wild Rose Tea Room

7. Bella - Resort Street
   Fine Spirits & Tea Room

ANGELINA'S FRENCH COUNTRY TEA PARLOUR

2137 Highway 99E
Aurora, OR 97022
Phone (503) 678-3303

In the 1820s and 30s the ambitious Hudson Bay Company sought to gain a legitimate claim on the fertile Willamette Valley of Oregon by directing French-Canadian trappers to settle there. The French Prairie Loop, as it came to be called, today encompasses the charming little town of Aurora where tea is served by reservation at Angelina's French Country Teas.

Owner Marilyn Grimm has a personal connection to France that goes beyond the rich local history of this charming community. The granddaughter of a French tea lover, Marilyn's earliest memories of 'grandmere' are entwined in peaceful teatimes shared with her. Continuing those timeless traditions with her own teenaged daughter, Angela, the two found the absolutely perfect setting to share the French ancestral flair for style and elegance in a lovingly restored 125-year-old country farmhouse on the Registry of Historic Homes, that with only one short exception, has always been the domicile and haven of women.

Time has gently distorted the original window panes overlooking the walnut grove surrounding the house, giving a timeless, other-worldly softness to the fog-shrouded acreage. Inside, yards of soft white chiffon drape the vintage wrought iron chandeliers, and the original fireplace overflows with the brilliance of lighted white candles reflected in antique mirrors. Garlands of ivy and everlasting hydrangeas form a counterpoint to the elegance of white on white table covers of vintage lace and fresh flowers.

Up a narrow winding wooden staircase is Emma's Room, named for one of the previous owners of this charmed dwelling. Decorated in period accessories and gentle dresses, Emma's Room is the perfect enclave for children to enjoy a tea prepared just for them. In the main tea room the attention to detail is meticulous. From the water bottle with fresh flowers frozen around it to the French country hat shaped petit-fours and ribbon tied sandwiches embellished with flowers, the afternoon tea is elevated to an art form. Private label teas, blended for Angelina's are imported from France and served by your hostesses in long lace dresses and white gloves. No one leaves their tea without a long stemmed white rose and a personally written thank you on a white paper doily from Marilyn and Angela that reads in part, "Seek moments of beauty in every day..." It is safe to say that for many, the experience of tea at Angelina's, namesake of the oldest tea parlor in Paris, will be the most beautiful experience of this day and many more to come.

Tea served with reservations only, on Wednesday, Friday, Saturday, and Sunday at 4 p.m. Call for details of special events and delectable French teas by mail order.

Annie Fenwick's Bakery & Tea Room

Annie Fenwick's

336 North Main Street
Gresham, OR 97030
Phone (503) 667-3768

Jan Heedum smiles when you call her "a Renaissance woman." She has, after all, heard it before. An accomplished water color artist, wood carver, gardener, writer, wedding planner, cook and business woman; Jan even found the time to home-school four daughters. Even with all that, Jan still humbly describes her life before opening Annie Fenwick's as "just a Mommy." It's exactly that synergy of exuberant energy, style and humility that defines Annie Fenwick's. Unpretentious and comfortable, like Jan herself, this bakery/ tea room combination has graced the unexpectedly quaint Main Street of Gresham since 1993.

The scones, from a secret recipe, are legendary in their variety . . . Apple Cream, White Chocolate, Brandied Orange Currant among them. Legendary too, are the special tea events each year that can include a six-foot leprechaun serving an Irish tea on Saint Patrick's Day to the strolling Victorian carolers heralding Jan's arrival in the tea room with her annual flaming Plum Puddings at Christmas. (Be sure to ask her to share some of her Plum Pudding fire stories with you.) Father Christmas, resplendent in a flowing white beard and Victorian gold tunic may even visit your table. Once a year in summer Annie Fenwick's hosts a White Tea that is served to overflow crowds, many in white gloves and flowered hats. It's no surprise that Jan's goal is to be discovered by "Victoria" magazine for a feature article, and it must be just a matter of time so authentically does she capture that era. Since Annie Fenwick's does no advertising, it's good to call ahead for each year's schedule of special teas.

The high-ceilinged storefront operation is divided into two distinctly different areas. In the casual bakery area you can sit at bistro tables beneath the gentle breeze of a paddled ceiling fan to enjoy a hearty lunch or bakery snack with your tea. The menu is varied, from the hearty English sausage "bangers" or Cornish pasty in combination with various side dishes, to an elegant luncheon salad or Cream Tea. A child's menu is also offered.

In the grander tea room, set apart from the bakery by a wooden screen festooned with grape vines and Boston ferns, Jan's daughter deftly serves alternating trays of savory and sweet finger foods. All the serving trays are artfully adorned with nasturtiums from Jan's own gardens. Set amid the Regency period English antiques, the full-skirted round tables are as festively elegant as girls in party dresses. The atmosphere beckons you to linger over a pot of delicious tea as long as you like. Jan recommends an hour or two to really savor the attention you will receive here. You'll feel pampered for the rest of the day. Reservations are recommended, and visit a cash machine first, since Annie Fenwick's does not accept charge cards.

Surprisingly, Jan has never desired to travel abroad. When asked how she could so faithfully recreate the very essence of an English tea room without having visited one, Jan's eyes crinkle into a delicious smile as she answers, "I have a very rich imagination." So who is the namesake Annie Fenwick? Like the unforgettable scones, she too is Jan's creation, "I just liked the name," she laughs.

Annie Fenwick's is open Tuesday through Saturday, 11:00 a.m. to 5:00 p.m.

BARBARA ANN'S TEA ROOM

116 W. Main
Carlton, OR 97111
Phone (503) 852-4440

We have long been proponents of the travel philosophy that avoids freeways, motorways, autobahns or whatever you want to call them all over the world in favor of the gentle country back roads. Regrettably we don't always practice what we preach when it comes to visiting family and friends in Oregon, and often find ourselves grumbling at trucks on I-5 in a high speed, "how much farther is it" race for our Camano Island home. Recently, however, we diverted along rural back roads for one of the most refreshing and relaxing drives we have had in a long time through the heart of Oregon's wine country. Up the rich west side of the verdant Willamette Valley, we found Barbara Ann's Tea Room in peaceful little Carlton, Oregon.

Time stands still in Carlton, worlds away from that fast freeway pace. The one block long Main Street business district is fronted with charming brick buildings, well-tended plant boxes, convenient park benches and ample parking. Antiques grace many store windows, and country arts and crafts boutiques enliven the mix. Rapidly becoming an area of 'gentleman farms' and horse acreage, Carlton reflects that comfortable blend of old and new. Locals consider Barbara Ann's their "village tea room", and you are as welcome in your jeans and loafers as in your flowered hat and gloves. Unpretentious and comfortable, this 1920s building was once the local movie theater, and the two rooms that comprise the business are decorated with vintage hats, books and accessories. The gift area is a showcase for local products and Barbara Ann's own private label tea blends.

The service by Barbara Ann or her assistant Kathleen is comfortable and warm, as is the food which takes advantage of local produce to create traditional English fare like Shepherd's Pie, Bangers and Mash, pot pies, sausage rolls, baked apple garnishes, homemade soups, savory or sweet scones, and delightful olive spread tea sandwiches on a local hazelnut bread.

The tea roster is extensive, offering more than 20 choices, all served in vintage pots with individual silver strainers, and charmingly mismatched china cups and saucers.

Just like a good pot of tea, the back roads of Oregon will demand that you slow your pace. With a stop at Barbara Ann's for tea you may find, like we did, the longer route may be the most refreshing in every possible sense of the word.

Winter hours (September through December) Monday through Saturday 11a.m. to 5 p.m., Spring/Summer hours (February through August) 11 a.m. to 5 p.m., Tuesday through Saturday. Call for special event or holiday schedule or retail mail order teas.

Black tea accounts for 90% of all tea consumed in North America.

A cup of coffee has 50% more caffeine than a cup of brewed tea.

BELLA – RESORT STREET FINE SPIRITS & TEA ROOM

2040 Resort Street
Baker City, OR 97814
Phone (541) 523-4299

The proprietor of Bella in Eastern Oregon's historic Baker City is Beverly Calder. This renaissance woman attended college in western Oregon before embarking on a career centered on fine food, fine wine and the hospitality industry. In her early twenties Beverly worked in the seafood business, landed a job at the prestigious Salishan Lodge restaurant as assistant wine manager, then became wine director for Portland's elegant Atwater's Restaurant atop the U.S. Bank Building.

So what does this all have to do with tea? WELL! Along the way to becoming an expert on fine wines, Beverly picked up many other skills related to fine dining. Her cooking skills are superb, her spirit indomitable and her homemade pastries and desserts are divine. Moving to Baker City from the wine country of the Willamette Valley, she quickly became a favorite with local residents who enjoy her enthusiasm for all things outdoors and her community spirit.

But what does all this have to do with TEA!?! WELL! Beverly just couldn't resist opening a wine shop to bring the taste of the grape to Baker City and when the historic McCord home (residence of the town's first mayor) became available she jumped in with both feet. Bella maintains the original 1874 Victorian floor plan of the home utilizing each space as a retail gift shop, wine cellar, tasting room and formal parlour. Each room is uniquely furnished with murals, gold leaf trim, faux wall and floor treatments and period lighting. It's beautiful!

In the formal parlour Bella guests enjoy fine loose teas prepared in French press pots and selections of Beverly's delectable scones, shortbreads, biscotti, fruit tarts and specialty cakes, such as the Cherries Jubilee Truffle Torte. Formal High Tea is served in two seatings on Saturdays and has become a favorite with Baker City residents and travelers through the area.

The shop also offers imported cheeses, freshly roasted coffees, fine quality bulk teas, and chocolates in addition to the selection of wines that represents the greatest values of the "Old World" along with treasures of the new.

Hours at Bella are 10 a.m. to 7 p.m. Call for reservations for Saturday High Tea.

BRITISH TEA GARDEN

725 S.W. Tenth Avenue
Portland, OR 97205
Phone (503) 221-7817

The twelve-foot long banner high on the whitewashed wall of the British Tea Garden proclaims "There will always be an England." Standing at the entry, letting your eyes adjust, it may be hard to convince your senses that you have not just walked right into the heart of it.

First there is the sound of lyrical Welsh and Liverpool voices as the owners Carmel Ross, and mother and daughter team Judith and Sarah Bennett banter gaily with the customers, "Cuppa tea, luv?" Your nose will be delighted to detect authentic British fare; "bangers and mash," flaky warm pastries, simmering vegetable soup, Shepherd's Pie and bubbling Welsh Rarebit all blending with any number of freshly brewed teas. As you survey the long, narrow, high-ceilinged room your eyes will spy a myriad of familiar yet hard to find British grocery items such as Branston Pickle, Cadbury's wonderful chocolate bars, jams and marmalades, sauces and mixes and teas in delicious variety. Teapots, functional and decorative, porcelain teacups, tea books, tea cozies, and other gift items lead your eyes to the massive wood mantle over the large, non-functioning but dramatic focal point fireplace. A photograph of a middle-aged Queen Elizabeth looks down on you. And what about the sense of taste? You will fool your taste buds too. They will be convinced that your brain forgot to mention you were taking a trip to England. It's all here near the main library in downtown Portland.

Started in December 1992 as a gift shop, the tea room evolved from customer requests for a pot of tea. It has now expanded to include a pleasant outdoor courtyard and 15 inside tables all dressed in their best floral chintz with toppers of pink and midnight blue. It has become so popular with locals that they now offer a takeout menu and a mail-order catalog with more than 300 types of teas from around the world. Special event teas are planned throughout the year which in the past have included Sherlock Holmes' Tea, Tea Leaf Readings, and a popular Celtic Harpist. It's best to call to see what special events are planned, because much is conveyed word of mouth.

Just like the parts of Great Britain from which these ladies hail, there is not a trace of pretense here. The atmosphere is comfortable and relaxing, the

Continued next page.

service personal and friendly, the food is excellent and attention is paid to the nice details of presentation. Among the house specialities, a cognac-laced pate of chicken and pork; Steak or Chicken and Mushroom Pie; and nine or ten different British desserts. The "Garden Set Tea" is an excellent value complete with your choice of one of seven different types of finger sandwich, a scone with Devonshire clotted cream and jam, a freshly baked tart, and a pot of tea. The homemade Soup of the Day is a hearty meal in itself with the house special Cheese Bread accompaniment.

The British Tea Garden is open Monday, 10:00 a.m. to 5:00 p.m., Tuesday through Friday, 10:00 a.m. to 6:00 p.m., Saturday, 10:00 a.m. to 5:00 p.m., and Sunday noon to 4:00 p.m.

COUNTRY COTTAGE CAFE & TEA ROOM

2315 Upper River Road Loop
Grants Pass, OR 97526
Phone (541) 476-6882

President Herbert Hoover loved the Rogue River. When criticized that the week in 1930 he spent fishing there was a "waste of time", he engendered the everlasting goodwill of folks who enjoy the pastime when he retorted, "The hours a man spends fishing do not count against his total lifespan." I like the response so much I think I'll adopt it for Afternoon Tea.

David and Dianne Linderman opened their Country Cottage Cafe and Tea Room in 1994 as the culmination of a shared dream to present gourmet cuisine and authentic English teas in a relaxed country setting. Dianne's appreciation of tea began early. The daughter of a London-born father, High Tea remains the family tradition reminiscent of the hardy meals she enjoyed while visiting relatives in England.

In this lovely rural setting you are invited to take a walk through the herb garden. Daily Specials reflect the abundant herbs and produce grown on site. Particular attention is paid to the preparation of the tea, delivered in the pot to your table with warmed milk. The menu offers four delightful choices for tea lovers, with the hearty Cottage Tea consisting of delicious tea sandwiches, fresh warm scones with hand-whipped cream and preserves, Brown Sugar Shortbread, a sweet surprise, and fresh local fruit with your tea. Dianne's philosophy that "no one should leave the table unless he is full," is apparent in her servings.

So take your time and truly savor this delightful tea experience. After all, (and you may quote me) I have decreed that the hours you spend taking Afternoon Tea do not count against your total lifespan!

Tea is offered Tuesday through Saturday, 11:00 a.m. to 3:00 p.m.

FLINN'S TEA PARLOUR

222 West First Avenue
Albany, OR 97321
Phone (541) 753-4926 Toll free (888) 878-4787
e-mail joytek@proaxis.com

It's unfortunate but true that we often dismiss places based on what we can see or smell from the freeway. Albany is one of those places that pays handsome rewards for the little effort it takes to leave the freeway and your preconceptions and explore.

Albany boasts more historic homes than any other Oregon city, with 350 lovingly restored Victorians. These homes bear powerful testimony to the prosperity and civility of Albany in the early 1900's when it was a commerical hub for the export of Willamette Valley produce and wheat. As many as 30 freight trains a day left Albany in 1910, for example, laden with the valley's bounty. Today more than 170 different crops are grown in the valley, and 95% of the nation's filberts come from this region. Within a 20 mile radius of the city are eight remaining covered bridges nestled in a rolling countryside that puts Madison County to shame.

On West First Avenue in historic downtown, teatime has returned to Albany with Flinn's Tea Parlour. Every Saturday by reservation only, a three or five course tea is served in true Victorian opulence. Owners Larry Joyner and Kaye Munford replicate historic recipes to complement their own signature dishes and Larry's freshly baked breads at this old world tea experience. The three course tea usually offers cumpets, Dundee bread, and walnut honey bread followed by tea sandwiches of bacon and avocado, oyster flan, and blue pear squares, finished by a sweet course of tea cookies and applesauce cake. Flinn's also creates a Living History Dinner Theater periodically with such original performances as "Don't Drink the Ginger Ale!" (billed as "The true life poisoning of Minnie Monteith Vandran"). Here's your chance to hiss the villains of Albany's rich past after a delightful meal. Every Christmas Flinn's offers Heritage Tours and merrymaking. Call or e-mail for current schedules of events.

A visit to historic Albany will hopefully change the way you judge other cities along your route. There's alot more here than meets the eye and nose.

Teas served by reservation only. Tea served Saturday, noon to 3:00 p.m., or by special arrangement for parties. High Tea served Saturday, 6 to 9 p.m. Reservations are required.

The Garden Gate Tea Room
at Jaye's Bouquets

16434 S.E. Division
Portland, OR 97236
Phone (503) 761-8861

Like working women everywhere, Jaye Billings longed for luxury. Not the dripping-in-diamonds kind of luxury, mind you, what she longed for was the luxury of time. Those mythical days of leaning on a rose entwined garden gate and talking with a dear neighbor while the bees hummed appealed to her gentle sensibilities. But like all working women know, ultimately all the 'woulda-coulda-shoulda's' reared their heads and her clock would signal that it was time again to dash off to the flower shop and crafter's boutique she has owned and operated for over twenty years.

This past year it dawned on Jaye that she could be instrumental in providing a cozy spot where people could slow down a little. Setting aside about a third of her store, she decorated in rich burgundy and deep hunter green, fresh flowers and lace. She covered six pretty little tables with skirts and toppers, twined ivy through a picket fence and encouraged silk flowers to climb an arbor entry. The Garden Gate was open. Among the first visitors were ladies just like her, friends who wanted to catch up with each other over a pot of good tea; grandmothers with granddaughters; and a harried lady who threw open the door making a bee-line to the tea room alcove saying over her shoulder, "Just keep the tea coming...I've got to balance my checkbook and the kids are driving me crazy at home." A couple of hours later, it was more than her checking account that was in balance.

The Garden Gate offers more than 60 kinds of tea, with a constantly changing variety of gourmet pastries and rich goodies, muffins and scones. A light lunch tea with soothing hot soup, a scone, and a rich dessert has been especially popular. Special theme teas with tea speakers, herbalists, flower arrangers, Little Girl Teas with Miss Molly Manners, and Mother-Daughter Teas are all on the schedule, which you can obtain by calling. Linger a little at The Garden Gate, it'll do you good. 'Woulda-coulda-shoulda' can wait.

Tea is served Monday through Saturday, 9 a.m. to 5:30 p.m., soup tea, 11 a.m. to 1:30 p.m.

THE GATE LODGE RESTAURANT

at the Pittock Mansion
3229 N. W. Pittock Dr.
Portland, OR 97210
Phone (503) 823-3627

The Pittock Mansion in Portland. The Gate Lodge Restaurant is just around the back!

It is impossible to separate the history of the Pittock family from the history of Portland when it was little more than a clearing in the forest.

Henry Lewis Pittock, English-born, embarked on a wagon train cross-country to Oregon in 1853 when he was 17. Eight years later, starting with nothing but a well-developed work ethic, he had taken ownership of the fledgling Oregonian newspaper and the hand and heart of an American bride, bright-eyed and cultured Georgiana Burton. Together they invested in the future of the Northwest with real estate, railroads, pulp and paper mills, sheep ranching, banking and steamboats. They also started a family. Georgiana's own civic vision and kind heart are credited with founding the Ladies Relief Society to assist needy women and children, as well as originating the annual Rose Festival and establishing the Martha Washington Home as a respectable residence for single, working women.

Mr. Pittock was a member of the first party to climb Mount Hood, and he is quoted on one of his expeditions as saying, "The man who sits down never reaches the top." Henry Pittock apparently sat very little, and in 1914, at the age of 79, moved his family into what is now referred to as The Pittock Mansion. Situated on 46 acres with an expansive view 1,000 feet above downtown Portland, the mansion featured such advanced technology as central vacuums and intercoms.

Georgiana preceded her husband in death by one year in 1918, and their children and grandchildren resided there for the next 40 years. When the estate fell into disrepair, exacerbated by the Columbus Day storm of 1962, the City of Portland stepped in. With enthusiastic community support, they purchased the property for $225,000 and set about an extensive 15 month restoration. Viewing the Pittock Mansion is a must, especially during the Christmas holiday season when it is decorated. It is open to the public for a modest fee 7 days a week from noon to 4:00 p.m. It is closed on major holidays, "a few days in late November for holiday decorating", and the first three weeks of January for major maintenance. Mansion tour information can be acquired by calling 503-823-3624.

Tea is served in three rooms of the restored Gate House, vacated by long-time gardener, custodian, and chauffeur James Skene and his family in 1953.

Continued next page.

The four story restaurant, located along the winding lane to the mansion, was the result of the Junior League of Portland's inspiration, in cooperation with highly acclaimed Yours Truly Caterers.

Hours are 11:30 a.m. to 3 p.m., Monday through Saturday with reservations taken for 11:30 a.m., noon, 1:30 p.m. and 2:00 p.m., January 24 through November 30. The hours are extended during December, when the lavishly decorated restaurant is open daily with seatings at 11:00 a.m., 11:30 a.m., 1 p.m., 1:30 p.m., 3 p.m. and 3:30 p.m. The restaurant is closed January 1 through January 23. Call for details of special events or to arrange a bridal luncheon or baby shower of your own.

THE HEATHMAN HOTEL

1001 S. W. Broadway
Portland, OR 97201
Phone (503) 241-4100

There is a cute little house on the island where we live, and I keep hoping that someone will be out working in the garden when I pass so I can roll down my window and thank them for the beauty of their yard. The truth is, to pass this house I need to drive about five miles out of my way and then turn onto a dead end spur road, but it's worth it for the lift it gives my spirits. What distinguishes this little yard from countless others is that there is always something different going on regardless of the time of year. Season to season a glorious ever-changing montage of foliage and flowers greets passersby. Orchestrated by some unseen garden maestro, the bloom fades on the spring bulbs as the summer flowers burst into extravagant bloom, followed by rich autumn tones and well-planned winter shapes and textures. To assume it's effortless since I never see human life when I pass may not be fair. Perhaps they struggle with weeds and rabbits, short hoses and snacking deer like we do. Maybe someday I'll ring their doorbell and thank them for this celebration of the seasons. Or maybe I will just continue to admire its effortlessness.

The Heathman Hotel in downtown Portland is to Northwest teatime what our island garden maestro is to landscape. There is always something fresh and seasonal happening to teas at the Heathman. The richly appointed Tea Court surroundings bespeak its 1920's vintage heritage. Opulent crystal chandelier overhead and French landscapes gracing the original eucalyptus paneling set the tone for an elegant tea. The servers, effortlessly accomplished in period lace aprons, offer thirteen reserve teas as well as sherry and port to complement an ambitious and elegant seasonal menu. It could include toasted walnut crostini and crumbled bleu cheese with Oregon pear.

Tea is served daily on fine English bone china, guaranteed in the words on the menu to "transport you elegantly to another place in time, and deliver you back refreshed." Good things are definitely worth a little side trip.

Hours for tea at The Heathman are daily, from 2:00 - 4:00 p.m.

LADY DI'S COUNTRY STORE

420 Second Street
Lake Oswego, OR 97034
Phone (503) 635-7298

Once there was a time, not too long ago, when Lake Oswego was a weekend retreat for Portlanders seeking peace and quiet. Cute little shingled cottages hugged the shoreline or peeked out of the peaceful evergreen forest. Residents sipped their iced tea while gazing at the lake from Adirondak chairs and counted their blessings. Today Lake Oswego is a bustling bedroom community for Portland, and the cute little cottages have been enlarged and remodelled to the point that it's now the lake that peeks out at you from between carefully landscaped upscale homes. The list of blessings to be counted has expanded, however, to include Lady Di's Country Store.

Lady Di's began as a retail clothing store for the fine wool knits and tweeds from the owner's native England as well as Scotland and Ireland. British gift items were added and with their acceptance and popularity, British foods and teas soon followed. Delightfully short on prim and properness, the owner gaily banters with a growing roster of regulars. Many of whom are sure to stop by on the days that May, the owner's delightful 89-year-old mother, is holding court in the tearoom. A popular and colorful fixture at Lady Di's, May works the shop three or four days a week, dispensing wisdom and good cheer on a wide variety of subjects.

Pastel cloths and fresh flowers adorn several small tables set aside for lingering with a pot of fresh tea. Crumpets, cream scones, jam tarts, mince pie, fruitcake, and biscuits can be selected from a simple baked goods menu that changes regularly.

For a little taste of England in an equally lush, green setting, a stop for shopping and tea at Lady Di's rewards and cheers the soul.

Lady Di's is open Tuesday through Saturday from 10:00 a.m. to 5:00 p.m.

While there's tea, there's hope.
Sir Arthur Pinero

LAVENDER TEA HOUSE

340 N.W. First St.
Sherwood, OR 97140
Phone (503) 625-4479

"I don't pick colors." While he cheerfully immerses himself in decorating projects, and never rushes me in the decorating department, Ken intones this mantra when it comes to selecting paint and wallpaper for the house he built for us. Still I drag him along to the paint chip displays and wallpaper books hoping to involve him in a substantive color dialogue. I am reminded of Myrna Loy in the wonderfully dated "Mr. Blanding Builds His Dream House" describing the color for her kitchen to the painter. She goes into rich detail, straining for him to understand, "The softest yellow like the richest buttercream frosting, like the center of a newly opened narcissus, the color of freshly churned butter, the color of filtered sunlight on a summer morning." Nodding with seeming sensitivity, he bellows to his crew, "A gallon of yellow!"

"How 'bout these?" Hopefully I hold up the chip of rose beige paint that I have painstakingly coordinated with the wallpaper sample and the piece of the flooring I carry with me for these outings. Ken says, "Right then, a gallon of yellow it is!"

Choosing the colors for the newest tea room in historic Sherwood, Oregon, was easy for Dianna Soller and her daughter/partner Tonie Calabrese. It had to be the color of their favorite perennial, Lavender, the name of their new joint venture, a comfortable tea room. Lavender is the culmination of many shared interests and hobbies of this mother-daughter team. Both ardent gardeners, the ladies harvest and dry their perennials and herbs for wreaths, swags and floral arrangements. Experimenting with tea blends from their harvest, they have taught numerous tea classes at a local herb nursery before opening the tea room in the winter of 1997.

Located in the historical part of cozy little Sherwood, across from the park, the snowy white 1892 Victorian is easy to spot with its lavender trim and wood oval signboard. Two rooms are set for tea, decorated with vintage finds and antiques, European laces and everlasting flowers and candles. Decorated in soft pastels with lace filtering the windows' light, the feeling is of a gentle visit to a dear friend's home. With the wrap-around porches of the era, outdoor seating will be available when weather permits, either on the covered porch or beneath the fragrant boughs of an ancient cedar tree in the backyard. Small tea sandwiches or their signature ham or turkey sandwiches (with a secret spread) share the first year's menu with homemade soups, biscotti, and a variety of scones, including lavender ones. In the spring a marvelous swath of perennials and herbs are planned for the property, many of which will be harvested for culinary and decorative use.

Luckily Dianna and Tonie are nature lovers. A tree that was planted too close to the house eras ago and can now be touched from the kitchen window has extended its vigorous roots, embracing the floor system of this charming cottage. The result is a quirky slant to the floors, and what Dianna cheerfully describes as "a hill" in the kitchen. No doubt with these ladies' talents it will only enhance an already charming tea experience for years to come. Perhaps they could paint it lavender.

Open Tuesday through Saturday, 10 a.m. to 4 p.m.

LOVEJOY'S AT PIER POINT

85625 Highway 101 S.
(P.O. Box 433)
Florence, OR 97439
Phone (541) 902-0502

Lovejoy's

Tea is linked so completely to Great Britain that it is often overlooked that Britons have the Dutch to thank for their introduction to the brew. You're unlikely to forget that bit of tea history at Lovejoy's where charming Dutch East Indies born Maryann shares the kitchen duties with her distinguished husband Martin Spicknell, formerly of London and Essex. That they serve it in one of our favorite Oregon Coast haunts makes this authentically European rooted tea experience one to savor.

Florence's location halfway along the glorious Oregon coast and hugging the river bank of the slow flowing Siuslaw is only part of its charm. Enlightened locals have restored the buildings that constitute Old Town Florence with more than the usual cursory nod to historic preservation and the result is more charm than 'tourist trap.' Local lore recalls the town being named after some ill-fated vessel, torn asunder on the perilous coastline whose masthead bearing the name "Florence" washed ashore after a storm. A beachcombing merchant hung it above his business portal, and when it came time to name the post office, locals adopted it as the town's name.

The largest oceanfront dunes in the world, over 12,000 years in the making, form the back porch to Florence, and nearby Honeyman Park with its thousands of rhododendrons is also memorable for its 150 foot dune that ends in Cleowax Lake, inviting generations of belly-floppers (ourselves included) to run, roll and tumble down its face at breakneck speed into the warm waters. During late May an annual Rhododendron Festival celebrates the local flora and fauna with events that range from a floral theme parade to a time-consuming slug race.

Continued on next page

TeaTime in the Northwest

By the charming Art Deco styled bridge that heralds the approach to Florence from the south is Pier Point where you will find the new Lovejoy's. Lovejoy's began modestly in a small storefront in Florence, but soon throngs of people were enjoying the traditional British fare and delightful afternoon teas and it quickly outgrew its location. Now with five chefs and more than 10,000 square feet of restaurant, English pub, and Victorian tea room, good tea is served at any time with numerous and tempting menu choices. The tea room offers the best view of Old Town Florence across the tide-pulled river and replicates the ambience of a true parlor with comfortable sofas, colorful area rugs, Victorian furnishings, framed art, fresh flowers, fine porcelain and antiques set in rose beige surroundings. The dashing fictional antique dealer for whom the business is named would relish the vintage touches.

There is a tremendous amount of well justified regional enthusiasm for Lovejoy's, and the Spicknells are equally enthusiastic about their adopted community (another Lovejoy's location graces San Francisco) to the point that monthly dinner dances and entertainment by Scottish and Irish musicians are on the future agenda. Currently refurbishing a vintage black Austin with its original right hand drive to transport visitors across the bridge to Old Town, an overnight at the adjacent Pier Point Inn and a refreshing tea at Lovejoy's will give you the perfect base to explore the glories of the central Oregon Coast.

A tea experience authentically rooted in the best Old World traditions of England and Holland awaits you at Lovejoy's and is rapidly becoming a revitalizing stop on the beautiful Oregon Coast.

Open for breakfast, lunch, and dinner, with tea service all day. Seasonal hours may vary, so it may be best to call ahead.

Up above the world you fly, like a teatray in the sky!
Lewis Carroll

STRATFORD HOUSE TEA PARLOUR

207 E. Main Street
Hillsboro, OR 97123
Phone (503) 648-7139

In 1849, when Hillsboro was still known by its earlier name Columbia, Abraham Sulger opened his general store here. Selling everything from gunpowder to fine china, the very first tea sets to be sold to the hardy pioneer residents graced the window of Abraham's store. It isn't hard to imagine the longing these symbols of gentility caused in the female residents, many of them had lost so much along the difficult Oregon Trail. Simply basking in the beauty of fine imported china in front of Mr. Sulger's window revived the memory of gentler, more refined times in the lives of these hardy pioneers and brought them joy.

Joy, once again in the guise of tea, resides today in the Stratford House Tea Parlour, a dignified 100 year old brick building on a corner of Main Street. Tea is served with a flourish on Tuesday, Wednesday, and Thursdays at 3:00 p.m. and at approximately 15 special tea events throughout the year. Owners Alice and Stephen Stratford present tea in the formal Victorian parlour atmosphere they have recreated behind the temptations of their upscale gift and antique shop. Opulent furnishings and vintage heirloom pieces grace the tea area, with a montage of glorious patterns and colors created by the soft parlor rugs underfoot. Three tiered serving trays laden with fresh scones with devonshire cream, seasonal fruits, imaginative tea sandwiches and rich desserts are heralded by the soft sound of a bell. Attention to detail is exceptional here, with fresh flowers and food garnishes verging on art.

The hardy pioneer spirit created Hillsboro. Help yourself to the gentler more refined aspects of life for which the early settlers longed, and if you choose to toast Abraham Sulger and his customers with a hot cup of tea, it would be especially appropriate.

Tea is served with advance reservation and deposit only every Tuesday, Wednesday, and Thursday at 3:00 p.m. Special Event Teas include Easter, Hat Day, Secretaries' Day, Mother's Day, Daddy & Me, Teddy Bear, White Linen, Grandparents' Day, Harvest Day, Mystery Tea, Thanksgiving, Dickens Candlelight Tea, Boxing Day Tea, and Low Fat Superbowl Tea.

THE TAO OF TEA

3430 S.E. Belmont
Portland, OR 97214
Phone (503) 736-0119

At the turn of the last century an anonymous tea lover wrote,

"And let us bless those sunny lands so far away across the seas
Whose hills and vales gave fertile birth
To that fair shrub of priceless worth
Which yields each son of Mother Earth
A fragrant cup of tea."

Those sunny lands have a special new forum in which they are celebrated daily in Portland. The flagship location of a planned network, the Tao of Tea opened in the regentrified Belmont neighborhood in the autumn of 1997, and a uniquely international and unusual experience awaits the tea lover here.

Home for this Asian tea adventure is a building the color of orange pekoe with teal trim and large cast bronze sculptures of hands beckoning you to slow down, relax, come in and maybe even learn something new about the world's oldest beverage. Tea chests have been transformed into sidewalk tables and the wind gently rustles the tall bamboo and vines in pots marking the entrance. Signs for the companion businesses that share this interesting building herald a theater, an animal rights agency, a child adoption service, two environmental advocacy attorneys, and an Aids Memorial Room.

Verinder Chawla, originally of India, and his tea knowledgeable staff are your hosts. Rustic furniture and open shelving set the tone of simplicity punctuated by attractive pottery and ceramics, designed by the Tao of Tea, which are also for sale here. A huge variety of teas from India, Japan, China, and Sri Lanka are offered as is a menu containing tasty and unusual soups and snacks in the traditions of those "sunny lands so far across the sea". Educational opportunities on the first year's agenda include evening tea tastings, a Japanese Tea Ceremony, and a roster of fascinating tea experts.

Open 11 a.m. to 11 p.m. except Thursday through Saturday when they are open until midnight.

TEA COTTAGE

**235 E. California St.
Jacksonville, OR 97530
Phone (541) 899-7777**

In the late 1800s the unpleasant howling emanating from the little white cottage in historic Jacksonville would have been the protests of the patrons of Dr. Will Jackson, the town dentist. Fortunately for us, dentistry has come a long way in the past 100 years since Dr. Jackson hung up his pliers. Also fortunately for us, the little white cottage in Jacksonville now houses The Tea Cottage.

Four generations of ladies from one family all work together joyfully at The Tea Cottage now. The dream of mother Susan Sullivan and daughter Lisa Shipley, the circle widened to include Susan's mother Jean and Lisa's daughter Steffanie when it opened in November of 1996. With tables set with fresh linens and vases of flowers, the Tea for Two Deluxe arrives on a tiered server and features a variety of tasty tea sandwiches, scones with jam and cream, and a rich dessert of the day.

Resplendent with Victorian era treasures, the tea room features a gift shop as it may have appeared when Jacksonville, now a National Historic Landmark village, was in the flush of gold fever. The building, in fact, was purchased by Dr. Will's wife Hattie for $600 in gold coin. Dr. Jackson's dedication to cavity prevention may have limited his enjoyment of the scones with jam and cream or the Marmalade Madness tea sandwich, but the sound of contented sighs from The Tea Cottage patrons and the tinkle of silver on porcelain is a vast improvement.

Tea and lunch are served 11 a.m. to 4 p.m. Tuesday through Saturday.

TEATIME IN THE NORTHWEST

TEA TIME ON HAWTHORNE

3439 S.E. Hawthorne
Portland, OR 97214
Phone (503) 231-7750

It's fun to think about. If you could invite some people, living or dead, for an afternoon tea, who would you invite? My list changes all the time, but the pool almost always includes Eleanor of Aquitaine, Barbara Kingsolver, Princess Diana, Gilda Radner, The Dali Llama, Sister Wendy, Mark Twain, Saint Dunstan, Deepak Chopra, great grandma Jesse Wells Gregory, Oprah Winfrey, Paul Wylie, Tom Hanks, Maya Angelou, and Elizabeth I. Ken's list has Winston Churchill chatting with John Kennedy (no cigars allowed, gentlemen) and Alexander the Great passing the sugar bowl to Henry V, Mary Queen of Scots nibbling daintily, his Aunt Margie would pour.

Because I don't want to have to worry about baking and straightening my house (and where would all those limos and chariots park anyway?) I'd have them all meet us at one of the newest and best tea rooms in Portland, Tea Time on Hawthorne. Owned and operated by the mother-daughter team, Judith and Sarah Bennett, that has made The British Tea Garden in downtown Portland an institution to tea lovers, Tea Time on Hawthorne opened in the summer of 1997 under the experienced management of Melanie Templeman, a fellow transplanted Brit.

The delightful, sparkly white two story building that looks like it could have been built when Churchill was a boy is actually brand new. A big round clock, neighborly white picket fence, outdoor sidewalk tables, mullioned windows, and potted plants add to the old time charm. Inside, pinks and greens of floral chintz and white lace, skirted tables and a comfy couch of the soothing English country decor provide a comfortably elegant space. Light and airy in feeling, this bright new venture has provided the much needed elbow room for the ladies to offer a full breakfast, (with the lean back bacon and bangers to remind you of those B&B mornings in England) and dinner menu (complete with Roast Beef and Yorkshire Pudding) in addition to their lunches and incredibly popular teas. A full spectrum of entertainment and theme teas are planned, ask during your visit about their upcoming event schedule.

If you hear a commotion and, "Off with her head!" from our table, it just means we ended up with both Elizabeth I and Mary, Queen of Scots at the same tea party. Oops!

Open daily, 9 a.m. - 6 p.m. Sunday through Wednesday, 9 a.m. to 9 p.m. Thursday, Friday, and Saturday.

TUDOR ROSE TEAROOM AND GIFT SHOP

480 Liberty St. S.E.
Salem, OR 97301
Phone (503) 588-2345

Salem is a town that respects neatness and order. Its tree-lined streets are home to gray squirrels that are polite enough to let traffic flow, one small paw gathered up by their chests in an inquiring pose, and then scamper across when the light changes. Manicured lawns and artfully arranged flower beds are the norm on Gaiety Hill, a cheerful sounding historic district of Salem where you will find Tudor Rose Tearoom and Gift Shop.

In 1996 longtime Salem residents, Bob and Terry Brooks, purchased Tudor Rose and brought to it their 15 years' experience as successful gift shop owners. Completely revamping the gift area they re-fixtured dramatically with antique wardrobes, secretaries, and parlor tables imbuing the area with a luxurious Victorian ambience. A broad range of teas, gifts, fine china teapots and teacups, books and an expanded section of British foods are now temptingly displayed in this comfortable, rich environment.

With a short pause to welcome their first child, baby Hailey into the business in 1997, Terry and Bob set about commencing what will be an ongoing regentrification of the large tea room. English rose wallpaper, live plants, and pink skirted tables with cream lace toppers combine to make the room alongside Pringle Creek as welcoming and warm as the service.

The Afternoon Tea, served on Wednesday and Saturday, keeps the menu flexible to allow for the freshest of local Willamette Valley ingredients to be used. It will always include two savories and four sweets with your tea, and there is a light lunch and homemade soup menu as well.

There have been a lot of visual changes at the Tudor Rose, but none quite as important as the attitude of the Brooks' tea room. They want to make absolutely sure it is a cheerful and friendly place where guests always feel welcome. "You hear a lot of laughter here," says Terry as she cuddles her baby daughter, "and since Hailey has been coming to work with us since she was three weeks old, it goes without saying that we are delighted to have children come in too!"

Open Monday through Saturday 10 a.m. to 5:30 p.m. Afternoon Tea is offered on Wednesday and Saturday from noon to 4:30 p.m. and reservations are recommended. Closed Sunday.

WILD ROSE TEA ROOM

**422 S. W. 6th St.
Redmond, OR 97756
Phone (541) 923-3385**

In the rarefied air of the sunny high desert of Central Oregon, wild roses bloom and flourish with their more rugged companions, juniper and sage brush. When Bessie opened her tea room in 1996 she chose the beautiful and enduring Wild Rose as her name, a name that evokes hardiness and beauty, strength and gentility, attributes of the Central Oregon region itself.

Inspired to tea, as many were, upon reading Emilie Barnes' delightful "If Teacups Could Talk", Bessie tapped into the skills she had already finely honed of baking, food service, and gracious hospitality. A welcoming storefront nestled down the hall between the Memory Shoppe and Past & Presents Antique Stores in downtown Redmond became the home to Wild Rose, heralded from the hallway by a whimsical replica of a proper English butler. The bright aquamarine blue walls, period antiques, vintage glass display cases, plate rail overflowing with interesting collectibles and lace covered tables invite you to be soothed in period comfort. In keeping with her philosophy that tea is a retreat from a busy world, Bessie provides the soft music and traditional tea goodies to ease you into that peaceful mode.

When your busy life feels prickly from everyday thorns, the solace you seek is at the Wild Rose Tea Room in beautiful, rugged Central Oregon.

Tea is served Tuesday through Saturday from 10 a.m. to 4:30 p.m., with reservations advised for groups of 6 or more. Special High Tea is served by reservation only Friday and Saturday with three seatings, 11:00 a.m., 1:00 p.m., and 3:00 p.m. Private parties and children's dress-up teas are available by special arrangement.

YVONNE'S ESPRESSO AND TEA HOUSE
at Yvonne's Kitchen Shoppe

1600 N. Riverside #1085
Rogue Valley Mall
Medford, OR 97501
Phone (541) 776-9845

Short on vision but long on wind, orator Daniel Webster is accused of ranting before Congress against the acquisition of Oregon, "What do we want with this vast, worthless area, this region of savages and wild beasts, of shifting sands and whirlpools of dust, cactus and prairie dogs?!"

For those whom the region's glorious beauty and abundance were not enough, the question got answered dramatically with the discovery of gold in the early 1850s Medford is built on the banks of Bear Creek, in a valley of mild climate and glorious blooming fruit trees that formed a major industry for those remaining after the gold rush.

Today home to many retirees, it has to be great news that tea is now being served in Medford at Yvonne's Espresso & Tea House in the Rogue Valley Mall. Yvonne's is no newcomer to the area, having filled the needs of shoppers looking for gourmet kitchen ware from the mall for ten years. Expansion completed in late 1997 allowed seating for ten for tea at small, lace covered tables with floral accents, tea lights, and floral cushioned chairs where freshly baked goods are served with tea by the pot or the cup. Another little haven has been created with seating for an additional eight at tables in the mall common area where you can watch the flow of shoppers.

French presses and Russian teapots share shelf space with all the accoutrements of tea, cups, mugs, infusers, gourmet gifts, and bulk teas and coffees in the retail kitchen shop.

It's a real pity that Daniel Webster couldn't have just slowed down a little and gotten his facts straight over a pot of good tea in this most pleasant Oregon town. Obviously he was spending way too much time back east with politicians.

Tea is gladly served during all retail hours, Monday through Saturday 10 a.m. to 9 p.m. and Sunday 11 a.m. to 6:00 p.m.

Tea Parties of Oregon

There is a growing business trend in the Pacific Northwest to the catered tea party. These can be brought to your home or business by the following providers, or in certain cases the provider opens her delightfully decorated home for your group. Naturally tea parties lend themselves to bridal showers, baby showers, birthdays and holiday celebrations like Mother's Day but many businesses are now happily turning their business meetings over to these ladies to announce promotions, show employee appreciation and graciously solidify espirit de corps.

Afternoon Tea by Stephanie

508 S.E. 9th Avenue
Canby, OR 97013
Phone (503) 266-7612

In 1592 the British essayist Sir John Harington mused "When I make a feast, I would my guests should praise it, not the cook." This mirrors Stephanie Allen's selfless philosophy of her tea catering business. "When I'm in the kitchen preparing all the tasty delights and I hear everyone's 'oohs and ahs,' I feel somehow I have enriched their lives by sharing an almost lost art of a relaxing hour or two of afternoon tea."

Two years ago this enterprising ex-travelling sales rep followed her passion, donned an impeccably white pinafore, and began providing tea parties in customers' homes and businesses. For a per guest rate which varies with your selections, Stephanie will provide the delightfully presented foods, send out invitations, select fresh flowers, set a tone with soothing music, dress the table, act as hostess, and even do the cleanup. Let Stephanie work with you to develop your own signature tea party, or choose one of her own acclaimed formats which include English Country Tea with tea sandwiches, scones with lemon curd, berry mousse, truffles and shortbread; Queen's Tea with fresh fruit, scones, mini quiches, tea sandwiches, tortes, tea cakes and petit four; Princess Tea with gentle etiquette lessons for young ladies featuring fruit tarts, finger sandwiches, tea cakes, charming heart-shaped petit four, cream puffs and brownie; Bride's Tea with a beautifully sculpted fondant cake, tea sandwiches, heart shaped scones, mini quiche, fruit tart, petit four and a wedding cake cookie; or the popular Nursery Tea for Mother-to-Be with tea sandwiches, fresh fruit compote, scones, nursery rhyme tea cookies, seasonal tart, petit four, and a rich chocolate truffle individually boxed with a gold ribbon.

All you have to do is relax and graciously accept the praise for your feast.

The Campbell House

**252 Pearl Street
Eugene, Oregon 97401
Phone (541) 343-1119**

You can almost picture the pioneers, exhausted from their westward trek through unrelenting deserts and the craggy Cascade Mountains driving their wagons into the rich, fertile Willamette Valley. With a sense that this was the place of their dreams, many settled in, building the agriculture and lumber industries in the process. When the railroad arrived, and the University of Oregon was established in the 1870s Eugene's bright future was solidified as a diversified center for agriculture, lumber, dairy, transportation, arts and academia. Twenty years later, pioneer John Cogswell built a lovely home for his daughter Idaho Frazer on the east side of prominent landmark Skinner's Butte.

The Campbell House, as Mrs. Frazer's Victorian dwelling is known today, is now home to charming tea parties during the two popular tea seasons of Mother's Day and Christmas. Fresh flowers grace the white damask covered tables set in the library and dining room, and several seatings for Mother's Day are set in the beautiful garden surrounding the house.

Primarily a popular city inn, special teas can be booked in the rich Victorian surroundings by special arrangements for groups. Call for details of special teas, or for reservations for Mother's Day and Christmas.

CREATIVE POSSIBILITEAS

14843 Bobs Avenue
Aurora, OR 97002
Phone (503) 678-1244

"We need to be gentler with ourselves, each other, the earth. Tea is about that. It speaks to a kinder purpose," says Jane Blackman celebrating her fifteen hundredth cup of tea poured since launching Creative PossibiliTEAS in late 1996. From tea for two to tea for two hundred, Jane's wildly successful tea catering business has served tea and tranquility in boardrooms and backyards, from tents or gourmet kitchens, under chandeliers or starlight to well derserved applause.

Jane ostensibly left the fast track over two years ago when a business trip brought her to the Pacific Northwest as a convention planner. Quitting her job and moving across country from Florida with her daughter Holly as a willing accomplice in the getaway, Jane hasn't had the time or the inclination to look back. The Creative PossibiliTEAS seem endless, as Jane followed her love of tea into a vocation. Spare time is filled with creating custom tea blends, testing tea party recipes, and preparing to launch a children's tea line called "Little BeLeafers".

Jane provides the table display, decor, napkins, china, flatware and serving pieces, fresh cut flowers and musical background to complement the theme you choose from her extensive and imaginative list or develop one of your own with her help. Set up, tea service, and cleanup are all provided. The attention to detail includes the perfect teapot for your theme, a vegetable shape for her Garden Tea, Noah's Ark for the Baby Shower Tea, and a kitty cat pot for the Toyland Children's Tea, just to name a few. Tea and art combine brilliantly when Jane presents her OriginaliTEA with a personal appearance by selected Northwest artists with displays of their talents.

Treats include ginger marmalade with kiwi slices, hazelnut scones with lavender cream and berries, and burnt sugar mini muffins with honey butter. Tea sandwiches are often festively tied with a bow, and Jane's Mandarin Clove or Pomegrante Syrups provide a delectable sweet touch to your French tea. With Jane Blackman's energy and talents at your tea gathering, you will revel in Creative PossibiliTEAS and enjoy grace and tranquility in the process.

CREATIVITEAS

211 Porter Street
Silverton, OR 97381
Phone (503) 873-8525

I once owned a washing machine that would get off balance during Spin Cycle and march drunkenly across the floor to the end of its hose where it would make horrendous racket until someone shifted the load. That washing machine was a perfect metaphor for my own crazy life at the time.

Virginia Weitzel genuinely cares about people's lives, and as a professional counsellor and lifelong tea lover she advocates taking some time from the "grab and go" world we all spin in and slowing down for tea. Several years ago Virginia began incorporating tea into her client's stress healing and depression reduction therapy with happy results. Now in her private home, in a private tea room in her cozy hometown of Silverton, Virginia presents tea by appointment only to from one to six people at a sitting, during either a one or two hour teatime.

Virginia presents the tea from various cultural and historic perspectives, using ceremony and ritual as a means of restoring communication skills and also promoting cultural awareness. Each tea is served in a costume for the theme. Among the most popular are Scottish Highland Tea, Irish Breakfast Tea, Tea with Queen Victoria, Afternoon in Vienna, or a simple Tea for Two, in which she invites you to "bring a friend and restore some intimacy." The menus and background music are chosen to complement your choice, and Virginia encourages dressing up or costuming to enrich the experience. She even provides some hats for you to have fun wearing during tea. Each guest receives a keepsake gift as a reminder of a slow paced afternoon, a culture explored, a relationship renewed.

Remember at the other side of that dial from the Spin Cycle setting is something called Gentle Wash. We all need it now and then.

Go on loving what is good, simple and ordinary.
R. M. Rilke

SHELTON-MCMURPHEY-JOHNSON HOUSE

303 Willamette Street
Eugene, OR 97401
Phone (541) 484-0808

By the economic standards of 1888, $8,000 was a tremendous amount of money to spend building a house, especially in light of the fact that lumber around the Eugene area was cheap and plentiful. As you can imagine, and see for yourself when you have tea here, that $8,000 built such a splendid house that it came to be called "the Castle on the Hill". Today the East Skinner Butte Historic Landmark Area encompasses the area that constituted fledgling Eugene and contains a marvelous collection of 1850-1925 architectural styles, including the Shelton-McMurphey-Johnson house, where you are invited for a pot of tea and a scone the first Sunday of every month and for elaborate High Teas in November and April.

Owned and lovingly preserved by the vision of the City of Eugene and capably directed by sociable Jan Alberg, the teas are served to growing numbers of tea and history buffs since beginning this past year. The High Tea is a highlight of the Eugene tea scene, the first Sunday in November and the third Sunday in April, when the charm of the late 1800s is recaptured with fine china, costumed servers, live music, and professional story tellers. Tour the grand old house and relive through many of the original furnishings and old photographs the lineage of this remarkable dwelling.

TEA AND ROSES

19300 Robin Circle - Suite 36
West Linn, OR 97068
Phone (503) 636-0483

> "...you may shatter the vase, if you will,
> But the scent of roses will hang round it still."
> Thomas Moore 1779-1852

Two years ago when Lynda Neidlinger locked the door for the last time on her Victorian tea room and gift boutique, Tea and Roses, in downtown Lake Oswego it had to be with a lump in her throat. The beautifully decorated shop, reminiscent of an English country manor, was one of the first upscale retail establishments to offer a monthly High Tea and it had been enthusiastically embraced by the locals. Specializing in Victorian accessories, linens, laces, and collectibles, the shop was the culmination of years of antique collecting and research. Life is what happens when you're expecting something else, the saying goes, and it is with real pleasure that we can welcome Lynda back into the domain of Northwest tea.

In the winter of 1997 Lynda opened her tea catering business under the same masthead as her successful retail operation. Tea and Roses now brings the elegance of tea to your location as well as planning several teas in historic bed and breakfast locations in the area. To get more information and to get on her mailing list for special events, drop a postcard to Lynda at the above address.

The vessel may change, but the aroma of tea and roses is timeless.

TEAS PLEASE!

9810 S.W. Dapplegrey Loop
Beaverton, OR 97008
(503) 524-4756 or (503) 245-7033

Tea caterers Patty Ennis and Annette Suchy understand that behind the philosophy of teatime is peace and tranquility. They also know that those two elements can be extremely elusive for the host or hostess with so many details of a tea party to consider and coordinate. So what could be nicer than turning the entire event over to professionals?

Annette and Patty bring to the tea table all their attention to the fine details: linens, flowers, antique English bone china, utensils, candles, as well as the labor of menu planning, shopping, food preparation, set up, serving, all the way through cleanup. The tea party will come to your home or office, indoors or outside. This is a flexible arrangement designed to suit your needs.

Several teas that Teas Please! suggest are the Business Tea as an alternative to the usual restaurant lunch to dazzle clients or celebrate a promotion in a relaxed atmosphere that highlights your good taste. Even consider the benefits of the 'Business Tea' once a month in appreciation of your own office or sales staff.

The 'Afternoon Tea' is a lovely way to celebrate a shower, a job promotion, or club meeting and features all the traditional fare created with the professional flair. Their 'Candlelight Tea' is a three course meal that just possibly could replace the cocktail party for the millennium. Brainstorm with these ladies to create the perfect tea party for your group of 8 or more . . . and then relax!

YOUR HOUSE OR MINE

117 S. College
Newberg, OR 97132
Phone (503) 538-7155
or (503) 281-0001

Your House or Mine

What do you get when you take two high energy ladies, an 1896 Queen Anne style house, more than 100 vintage hats, a sense of elegant fun, and good tea? The recipe for the successful tea party business - Your House or Mine!

Cathie Rawlings and Suzanne Gilliam have spent the last five years hosting English tea parties and are known as much for their impeccable style as their delectable tea treats. The tables and menus reflect the season, utilizing a dazzling array of lovely linens, bright flowers, and fine china. You just might find several of your very own treasures woven into the decor scheme of the table if the party is at your house, as these ladies have an appreciative eye for the unusual and a fresh approach to entertaining. The Victorians would have loved it.

The tea party can come to your house or office, or your band of 6 or more will be welcome in either Cathie or Suzanne's lovely homes. More than 100 vintage hats beckon you to discover the perfect 'chapeau' to add spice and drama to the party. (Who could resist playing dress-up just one more time?)

Fresh hot scones made at the party are offered with fresh fruits, a variety of tea sandwiches, vegetables and at least three sweets . . . one of which will always be chocolate. They will work with you to plan just the perfect menu for your tea event, and make it a truly fun, memorable time!

Gift certificates are available.

TEAROOMS OF WASHINGTON

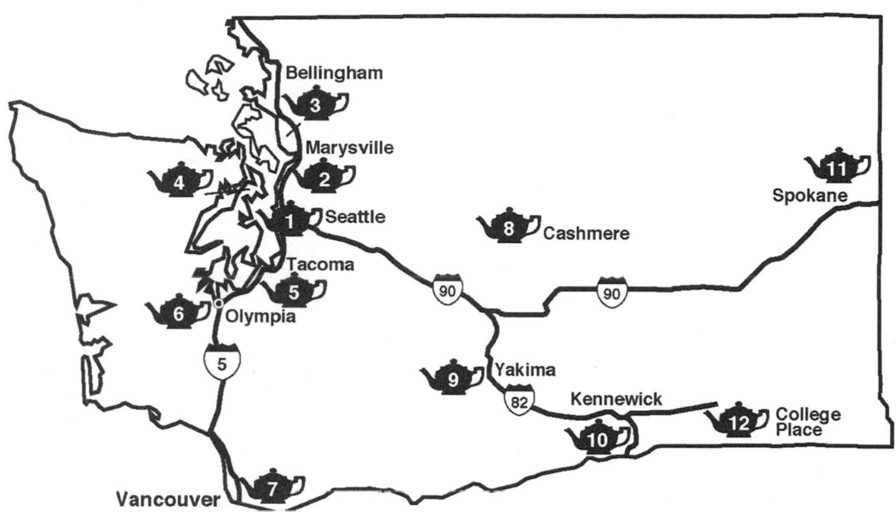

1. GREATER SEATTLE
Cheshire Grin
Chez Nous
The Crumpet Shop
The Garden Court
Green Gables
High Tea
Kado Teagarden
Pekoe
Perennial Tea Room
Queen Mary
The Scottish Tea Shop
Sheraton Club Lounge
Shoseian Teahouse
Sorrento Hotel
The Teacup
Teahouse Kuan Yin
The Wellington

1. SEATTLE EASTSIDE
British Marketplace
The British Pantry
Nordstrom
Whiffletree Tea Room
The Woodmark Hotel

2. NORTH OF SEATTLE
Attic Secrets
Kate's Tea Room
Piccadilly Circus
Tea, Thyme & Ivy
Village Tea Room
Windsor Garden

3. SKAGIT VALLEY AND NORTH
Abbey Garden
The Langley Tea Room
Tea & Other Comforts

4. KITSAP PENINSULA
Judith's Tea Rooms
Victorian Rose
Ye Olde Copper Kettle

5. Victorian Tea Potts

6. SOUTH PUGET SOUND
Golden Plum
Jean Pierre's
Tea & Crumpets
Wigley's

7. VANCOUVER, WA
Cheshire Cat
Pomeroy House

8. The Pewter Pot

9. Country Tea Garden

10. KENNEWICK
Country Register
Kennewick Herb Store and Tea Room

11. SPOKANE
The Arrangement
Home, Heart & Friends
Te'Antiques

12. Ivy Tea Room

ABBEY GARDEN TEA ROOM *in Old Fairhaven*

1308 - 11th St.
Bellingham, WA 98225
Phone (360) 752-1752

"Nowhere is the English genius of domesticity more notably evident than in the festival of afternoon tea."
George Gissing, (1857-1903)

We all have special places that nourish our spirit and renew peace within ourselves. For me, a small hidden cove, where agates lie at the base of a waterfall like unstrung gems is one of my sanctuaries. Part of its magical allure lies in it being accessible only during certain low tides on the southern Oregon coast. For Anne Graham Oliver, the gardens cloaking the Abbey House in her mother's ancestral town of Winchester, England, have always provided creative inspiration and refreshment for her. It was in that spirit that she decided to open a new tea room in Bellingham's Old Fairhaven historic district, and the choice of a name came easily.

Housed in the same building as her daughter, Chinook Graham's paint-your-own ceramic studio, both vintage and contemporary styles meld to create an atmosphere that is cozy and relaxed. Comfy over-stuffed chairs snuggle by a gas fireplace, and antique tables covered in soft green and blue chintz with lace toppers afford a view from the mezzanine to the scrubbed pine tables of the ceramic studio. Fine china, both old and new, as well as tea-theme gifts provide an elegant counterpoint to the old brick walls of the charming building.

Offering a wide range of quality tea, the menu offers light lunches and an Afternoon Cream Tea. With Italian dinnerware and tea sets waiting to be personally painted, it is Anne's fond hope that "painting and taking tea together will become a regular family event for locals and visitors." The recuperative blend of a delightful creative outlet and the refreshing aspects of an Afternoon Tea combine here. The refreshment of your spirit is the result, and you don't even need to wait for low tide.

Open Tuesday-Friday 10 a.m. to 8 p.m., Saturday 10 a.m. to 6 p.m., Sunday noon to 5 p.m., closed on Monday.

THE ARRANGEMENT GIFT SHOPPE & TEA ROOM

West 1101 Garland
Spokane, WA 99205
Phone (509) 327-8194

For eleven years thoughtful people have come to The Arrangement to buy that special gift for a loved one. While proprietor Leona Frick enjoyed knowing that the unique and carefully selected things she offered in her shop, would bring a smile to someone's face, she decided it was time to give a gift of her own. It wouldn't be the kind that left her shop wrapped and re-ribboned in a bag though, for what Leona had in mind was converting some valuable retail space into a delightful little tea room for her customers.

With the assistance of her lovely daughter, Jackie Torstenson (who spreads her time between the world of gifts and the gift of healing as a Registered Nurse) Leona converted a room of the 90 year old house with gingerbread trim into a soft peach colored haven for tea. Decorated with the flowered wreaths and swags for which The Arrangement is named, as well as vintage art and tea gifts. The rattan bench and bistro table of the room seat six for dessert tea, which is served from 11-3 Tuesday through Saturday. Treats to accompany the tea include delectable Champagne Cake, lemon and raspberry tarts, Mexican tea cakes, and delicious shortbread. When weather permits, a wrought iron table on the front porch is a charming spot for tea especially with the cheerful red geraniums and blue lobelia that grace the planter boxes.

Shoppers and browsers continue to come to The Arrangement for those special gifts as they always have, only now they also find the gift of a little peaceful break in their day with tea.

The gift shop is open Tuesday through Friday 10 a.m. to 5 p.m. and Saturday from 10 a.m. to 3 p.m. During January 15 through April 1 the shop os open Tuesday, Thursday, and Friday only, same hours. Tea is offered 11 a.m. to 3 p.m. any of those days.

ATTIC SECRETS

4229 - 76th St.
Marysville, WA 98270
Phone (360) 659-7305

"At last the secret is out, as it always must come in the end,
The delicious story is ripe to tell to the intimate friend."
W.H. Auden

Since 1995 the delicious secret of a sweet little tea room has passed by word of mouth endorsement from happy patrons to their intimate friends. One of the very first tea rooms in Snohomish County, the mother-daughter team of Chris Freeman and Jeni Anderson still run one of the best.

A visit to Attic Secrets is like an afternoon browsing through a favorite auntie's attic. A rich Victorian profusion of treasures, vintage jewelry, hats, garden accessories and tea gifts spilling from antique furniture and garden benches is unabashedly romantic, but that's only part of the charm. Two cozy rooms are dressed for tea. Light floods the front room, decorated in cheerful floral Waverly prints and Battenburg lace. In the Garden Room alcove, a painted garden mural and wicker or iron garden furnishings set a casually gracious tone for tea. All tables are set with bone china tea strainers, pristine white china, and fresh flowers.

The Queen's Tea, Victorian Tea and Garden Tea are presented on tiered servers to your table, probably by Jeni who also prepares most of the refreshments. The tea sandwiches vary with the freshest local ingredients, and the currant sour cream scone has a big fan club.

"The delicious story is ripe to tell," as the poet says, so do take a friend to share Attic Secrets soon.

The gift shop is open 9:30 a.m. to 5 p.m. Monday through Friday and Saturday 10 to 5 p.m. Tea is served 11 a.m. to 4 p.m. Monday through Saturday. Closed on Sunday.

BRITISH MARKETPLACE AND COPPER KETTLE TEA ROOM

24-26 "B" St. N.E.
Auburn, WA 98002
Phone (253) 833-2404

Two prickly but adorable English hedgehogs, Preston and Gromit, have found their way to our Camano Island home. Seemingly unfazed by their 500 mile journey in the back of our friend Gracie's Suburban, they have settled into hatbox sleeping nexts rousing themselves for treats like cottage cheese and boiled eggs but mostly sleeping, preparing to sleep and waking slowly from sleep. It seems like a nice life. When these nocturnal little beings don't want to be handled they roll into a ball and make vibrating, puffing, snuffling and snorting noises that seem battery operated. This spring we'll let them patrol our garden for their favorite yummy pests, and hopefully find a more suitable spot for their play boxes than our dining room.

While there may not be hedgehogs in the dining room of the Copper Kettle Tea Room, other equally authentic and certainly more hospitable English touches abound. Proprietor Tracy Rodway acquired the business this past year from family members Margery Hiscox and Clive Barker who are settling into blissful retirement in a garden cottage in the south of their native England.

The dark wood beams and horse harness brasses give a Tudor air to the cozy and bustling tea room that seats 22 on a side street in downtown Auburn. The menu offers Morning Tea from 10:30 to 11:30 a.m., a few delicious lunch specialties midday, and then Afternoon Teas from 2:00 to 4:30 p.m. consisting of assorted finger sandwiches, scones with real Devonshire cream, crumpets, fancy cakes, trifle or Pavlova and any number of delicious variations served on tiered silver trays. Deep rose pinks and burgundy table covers echo the floral themes of the china, and beaded Honiton lace covers the sugar bowls. The other part of the building is a British gift and food market.

I can appreciate the pace at which the hedgehog chooses to live his life, and a soothing tea at the Copper Kettle is conducive to that level of studied relaxation. However, I think I might draw the line at rolling up in a tight ball and making snorting noises, at least at teatime.

Open Tuesday through Saturday, 10:30 a.m. to 4:30 p.m.

THE BRITISH PANTRY

8125 - 161st Ave. N.E.
Redmond, WA 98052
Phone (425) 883-7511

I love to prowl foreign grocery stores when I travel. To read labels and speculate on the various uses of mixes and sauces and exotic sounding foodstuffs is one of my vacation joys. On my first trip to England I bought a can of "Mushy Peas" simply because I liked the name. For years that unopened can graced our office bookshelf as an object d'art. While I suspect there may be others like me, you never see "grocery store tours" listed in any travel guidebook. Fortunately, we do not have to travel far to indulge this avocation between vacation trips.

Nestled in a nondescript strip mall on a speed-bump-lined side street of Redmond lies a little bit of England. This unassuming location, heralded from the parking area by Union Jacks, is a favorite of relocated Britons seeking to recapture some of the flavors and aromas of home. Part grocery store, bakery, gift shop, and tea room, the British Pantry is much more than the sum of its parts.

The cozy tea room, which is always bustling, is entered through the well-stocked grocery and gift area. The on-site bakery produces a wonderful array of baked goods, from meat pies to fruit tarts and yeast breads. Ease your nostalgia with a vast array of English cheeses and beers, kippers, teas, biscuits, preserves, and authentically seasoned sausage and lean bacon. The gift area has a well sourced collection of teapots, tea cozies, books, David Tate miniature cottages, Christmas crackers, toys, English greeting cards and stationery. It's a delightful spot to explore before taking tea in the adjoining rooms. A comfortable lack of pretense is the hallmark of this tea room and the service is with warmth and good cheer. The food is fresh, authentic, and delicious. The decor with ladder-back chairs, fresh flowers, and floral curtains is homey and relaxed. The walls are home to a chronicle of British life in traditional framed prints - castles and thatched cottages, Queens and horses, Stonehenge and cathedrals, all blending with copper accent pieces to make a hospitable and jolly setting.

Excellent food in a comfortable, unassuming setting have made the British Pantry a popular spot for tea and browsing for the past 18 years, and will be well worth your effort to locate, as you will certainly want to go again and share your find with friends regularly.

The British Pantry is open everyday. Sunday through Tuesday from 10 a.m. to 5 p.m. and Wednesday through Saturday 10 a.m. to 9 p.m.

Use the phrase "As American as apple pie," around a Briton, and the less restrained ones (like Ken) are likely to sputter "What?! You think Americans invented apple pie?!" (Those with more highly evolved social graces will simply think it.) In deference to this dispute I suggest we change the term forever to "As American as a tea bag."

THE CHESHIRE CAT

2801 Fort Vancouver Way
Vancouver, WA 98661
Phone (360) 735-1141

A coffee-drinking friend of mine once picked up my flowered tea cozy, examined it quizzically and said, "I give up. What is it?" Thinking she was kidding I told her it was a poodle jacket. This seemed to satisfy her until she remembered we had a huge, lumbering malamute that would have required a much roomier cozy, and probably not floral chintz.

Avril Massey introduces legions of new tea drinkers to the trappings of tea everyday in the congeniality of her own little tea room, The Cheshire Cat. Opened in 1996, the authentically British enclave has become an institution to throngs of transplanted Britons. Any attempt to capture the spirit of all British women in a single page is, of course, doomed to failure from the outset. It seems to me, however, that Avril Massey embodies that particular spirit of resilience, good cheer, quick wit and strength that I ascribe to most British ladies. Living as a girl in wartime England, Avril "crossed the pond" in 1969, raised a family, supported the career of husband John, and worked in personnel management. When confronted with widowhood in 1993, Avril decided she needed "a new life" and moved from Seattle to Vancouver, where, encouraged by her daughter, she opened the cozy tea room and shop.

Spritely and funny, it is apparent that Avril is energized by playing hostess. When I mentioned to her that my husband was from Liverpool she chirped, "Now we must try to not hold that against him!" In addition to an excellent pot of tea the menu includes such traditional favorites as Shepherd's Pie, a variety of pot pies, and Cornish pasties. Tea sandwiches are on the daily menu, but with a reservation a special High Tea is offered that includes trifle. An astute businesswoman must assess her own strengths, "My scones were so heavy you could fire them like lead shot," she laughs and set about finding the very best made fresh locally and delivered daily.

Settle in for tea here and keep your ears tuned for all the wonderfully comfortable banter and gaiety that is created daily. Cast any preconceptions of teatime stuffiness aside. The Cheshire Cat in Vancouver is not that kind of tea experience.

Open Wednesday through Sunday 10 a.m. to 6 p.m.

CHESHIRE GRIN

313 East Pine
Seattle, WA 98122
Phone (206) 287-1762
e mail: stonesd@aol.com

Alice - "Would you tell me, please, which way I ought to walk from here?"
Cheshire Cat - "That depends a good deal on where you want to get to."
Alice - "...so long as I get somewhere."
Cheshire Cat - "Oh, you're sure to do that, if you only walk long enough."

There's a clear sense of direction at the Cheshire Grin, a trendy fashion and art boutique on Capitol Hill specializing in Northwest designers. Since 1996 Diane Stone has provided a forum for the rising stars of Northwest fashion to offer their designs to the public in the atmosphere of a cozy four table tearoom.

The designs of more than thirty local artisans of fashion, gifts, art, accessories are offered side by side with more than twenty bulk teas. A pot of tea will steep while you browse this youth-oriented marketplace, and a few cookies and light refreshments are also sold.

Spearheading the trend toward retailers offering tea on premises, a stop at the Cheshire Grin will leave a lingering smile on your face too.

Open daily, Monday through Saturday 11 a.m. to 7 p.m. and Sunday noon to 7 p.m.

CHEZ NOUS

723 Broadway East
Seattle, WA 98102
Phone (206) 324-3711

If it is true, as a contemporary humorist once surmised, that mankind is divisible into two great classes: hosts and guests, Jennifer Johnson must have been born knowing where she fit in. In fact, in the four years Jennifer has run a private dining room in her stately Capital Hill home, she has moved to the head of her class.

Drawing upon her British upbringing and extensive culinary experience, Jennifer began offering a traditional English Tea by reservation with one seating at 2:30 Tuesday through Saturday since April of 1997. Decorated in the graceful tradition of stately country manors in her native England, elegance and refinement are the hallmarks. Situated as it is in a private residence, the surroundings are comfortable and intimate. Mary Ann Lee entertains at a grand piano, as Jennifer attends to all the unique and lovely touches, fresh flowers, three tiered serving trays and food presented with grace, style and excellence. When the season allows, seating for tea is available in the courtyard.

As the large brass chandelier gently illuminates the floral chintz setting and the piano music soothes, be glad you were born into that class of mankind destined to be comfortable guests. The hostess in Jennifer Jones would have it no other way.

Tuesday through Saturday by reservation only, one seating at 2:30 p.m.

THE COUNTRY REGISTER TEA ROOM

8310 Gage Blvd.
Kennewick, WA 99336
Phone (509) 783-7553

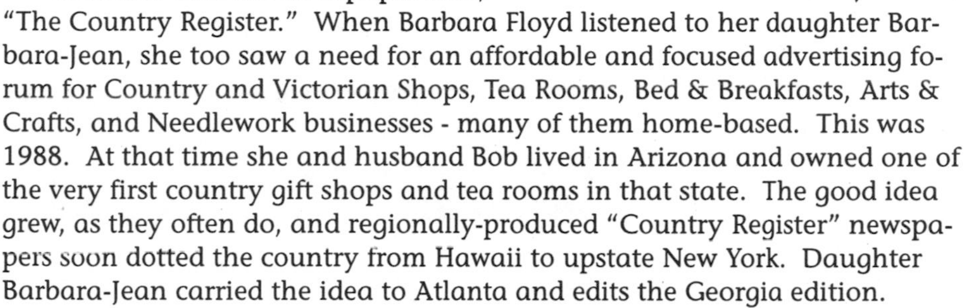

Nobody in the Floyd Family has never heard of an eight-hour work day.

It started with the newspaper idea, "The Country Register." When Barbara Floyd listened to her daughter Barbara-Jean, she too saw a need for an affordable and focused advertising forum for Country and Victorian Shops, Tea Rooms, Bed & Breakfasts, Arts & Crafts, and Needlework businesses - many of them home-based. This was 1988. At that time she and husband Bob lived in Arizona and owned one of the very first country gift shops and tea rooms in that state. The good idea grew, as they often do, and regionally-produced "Country Register" newspapers soon dotted the country from Hawaii to upstate New York. Daughter Barbara-Jean carried the idea to Atlanta and edits the Georgia edition.

Visits from the Arizona desert to the Tri-Cities area of Washington became frequent with other daughters Brenda and Bobbi Jo, and son Brook and his fiancee Beth all living in the region. So the Arizona gift shop and tea room was sold, and the Floyds all ended up living happily along the Columbia River together. The first Southern Washington edition of the paper came out shortly thereafter in 1993 and has now grown from the first 8 page black and white issue to a full color 20-page magazine. But wait, that's not the end of this success story.

Never ones to rest on their laurels, husband Bob had a brainstorm and encouraged Barbara, Bobbi Jo, Brook and Beth to fill the need in the Tri-Cities area for a good quality tea room. (Brook by now had married Beth.) So in 1994, when the big building on Gage Boulevard became available, the Floyds all opened "The Country Register Cafe & Tea Room".

Today teas are served by reservation Monday through Saturday in the country-style setting. The Cream Tea includes scones with lemon curd and various preserves with Devonshire Cream with your tea at a truly reasonable price, and their High Tea includes cucumber tea sandwiches and Brenda's famous lemon bars in addition. The roomy facility houses the Ivy Wedding Chapel where some truly unique weddings have been conducted, a banquet room, and a gift shop, and features a full service restaurant for lunches Monday through Saturday, and gourmet dinners Monday through Friday. The menu by-line sums up the family philosophy "With freshness and flavor as our motivation, let the food be our message."

For information on "The Country Register" newspaper subscriptions or advertising call (509) 783-1620. For tea reservations, call (509) 783-7553.

The Country Register Tea Room is open by reservation Monday through Saturday from 2 to 4 p.m.

THE COUNTRY TEA GARDEN

220 Johnson Road
Selah, WA 98942
Phone (509) 697-7944

After our first book came out we were grateful at book-signings to be notified of other locations for tea that we had overlooked. On more than one occasion we had a bookstore conversation that went like this, "You missed a great one, oh, what's it called? It's in the country, out near Yakima and they serve tea in a lovely garden. Oh, what's it called, why can't I come up with the name?" Well, in fact they did, they just didn't know it. Those lovely teas that are served in a garden in the countryside, we discovered, are at The Country Tea Garden.

Ever since the Chinese emperor Shen N'ung first discovered tea when the leaves drifted into his drinking water while gardening, tea and gardens have been inseparable. At The Country Tea Garden those same breezes stir the more than 200 rosebushes lovingly tended by owner Bev Gabbard as manager Nel Alden serves tea and a light menu to up to 75 garden lovers in five gazebos on the property. During the summer, tea sandwiches, scones with their own lemon curd and cream, salads and a varying dessert menu are offered on lace topped tables set amid the lush perennial gardens with three fish ponds and statuary.

In winter, the garden sleeps under a veil of lights and the warmth of the indoor tearoom with six tables beckons. Christmas is a special time here, with the tables covered in red skirts and lace toppers, poinsettias and lights. Renowned locally for an impressive array of angel and Santa motif gifts, the gift shop also carries everything a tea lover could crave. Mid-November to December 20 the menu reflects the turn of the season with heartier fare; and the air, although no longer filled with the rich musk of the roses, is redolent with the inviting aromas of homemade soups, hot breads, green salads, and desserts. No doubt the gardening emperor would be most comfortable at The Country Tea Garden. Bev Gabbard would have it no other way.

Open June-September: Tuesday through Friday, and the second Saturday of the month 10-4 pm. Closed in October, reopening mid-November to mid-December: Tuesday through Saturday 4-8 pm. Available for small weddings, receptions and group events. Call for information.

THE CRUMPET SHOP

1503 First Avenue
Seattle, WA 98101
Phone (206) 682-1598

In 1907 two brothers awash in riches from the Alaska gold fields improved upon a little farmer's market operating unofficially at the foot of Pike Street in Seattle. Building shops and laying out stall space in an organized manner, the Goodwin brothers created what is today the oldest continuously operating farmer's market in the United States, the Pike Place Market. The market provides a forum where farmers and craftspeople can sell their goods directly to the public. The food is always the freshest, and the presentation often artistic, even theatrical. Today the market is visited by 9 million shoppers a year, many of them tourists.

The market was founded on the belief that fresh is best, and that credo is adhered to with gusto at The Crumpet Shop. Simple fresh crumpets with a light and delicate texture give the shop its moniker, but the colorful wallboards at the order and go counter tell a story of crumpets turned into an artform. You can have your freshly toasted crumpet with Vermont maple butter, or hot pepper jelly and cream cheese, or egg and smoked salmon spread, or simply slathered with butter and your choice of a wide variety of fresh local preserves. Old fashioned "English sandwiches on Scottish groat bread" round out the simple menu, and once again the emphasis is on the freshness of Washington chicken, salmon and veggies. A large colorful cat on the wall proclaims "the tea is out of the bag," and the whole leaf teas are served in a bottomless mug.

Nancy, the owner, takes pride in a counter staff that is helpful and knowledgeable. This little place is always busy, but you are not rushed when ordering. Simple and refreshingly non-prissy, The Crumpet Shop provides a couple of tables street-side and a couple more inside along with a small window bar. Twelve whole leaf teas are on the menu, as well as freshly squeezed lemonade. Local and British preserves, tea pots, and private-label packaged teas are all for sale along a wall opposite the counter.

The Crumpet Shop is open 8:00 a.m. to 5:00 p.m. all week long, but the hours may vary a little in winter so it might be best to call. Closed major holidays.

THE GARDEN COURT

FOUR SEASONS OLYMPIC HOTEL
411 University St.
Seattle, WA 98101
Phone (206) 621-1700

The Garden Court at the Four Seasons Olympic Hotel

Local historian and journalist Nard Jones described early Seattle as "a sea of mud punctuated by stumpage," and early photographs don't do much to dispute his viewpoint. The Great Fire of 1889 erased, perhaps fortuitously, most early rudimentary attempts to imbue the structures of the city with anything approximating grace and beauty. It wasn't for another 35 years, when Seattleites appropriated $3 million, that this clean palette could be used to create their masterpiece Olympic Hotel, today the Four Seasons Olympic Hotel.

As you would expect, comfort and good taste abound. An enlightened renovation project in the 1980s has heightened the glamour and majesty of the setting, which in turn attracts glamorous and majestic people.

Almost from the beginning the hotel became the epicenter for Seattle tea culture. In the peaceful elegance of the high-ceilinged, naturally-lighted Garden Court, four or five generations have relaxed over afternoon tea. Unobtrusive, yet impeccably attentive service is the standard here. Excellent cream scones, tea sandwiches, petit fours, and tea breads served on fine china fulfill both your hunger pangs and your high expectations.

From Thanksgiving through New Years each year hundreds of teddy bears ring in the holiday season in the Yuletide Teddy Bear Suite open to the public. It's a delightful stop before or after tea.

Seattle has come a long way from "mud and stumpage," and nowhere is that evolution more evident than over a pot of tea in the Garden Court of the Four Seasons Olympic Hotel.

Tea is served in the Garden Court daily from 3:00 p.m. to 5:00 p.m, Sunday 3:30 p.m. to 5:00 p.m. Reservations are strongly recommended

GOLDEN PLUM

311 West Main
Elma, WA 98541
Phone (360) 482-3839

With the exception of a landslide victory of the deer over the rose bushes and the defeat of the nasturtiums by the slugs, it's been a good season for the Home Team. The hummingbirds outwitted the cats, the cats outmaneuvered the eagles, and the raccoons tied with the neighborhood dogs for domination in the garbage can event. Four swallows returned in March and twelve left in August gorged on a bumper crop of mosquitoes, and obviously pleased with the birdhouse condo Ken built for them (when he realized I was actually considering ordering one for $300 from the glossy pages of a catalog, but that's beside the point.) It's been a good year on our hill.

It's been a good year for the little town of Elma too. This is the year they saw long time resident Betty Smith expand her Golden Plum Gift Shop to twice its size and create the first tea room in town. Elma is a gracious little town, named for an early pioneer Miss Elma Austin, with streets lighted at night by old-fashioned gas lights and 40 colorful murals painted on buildings to celebrate the local history. With live theater and an annual Blackberry Festival that turns lips black from Olympia to Aberdeen, Elma has retained its small town charm.

Collectibles, antiques, and floral wreaths and swags, most made by Betty herself, decorate the delightful tea room at the Golden Plum. A stunning large mural of a Victorian lady and child in the front garden of a manor house decorates and dominates the softly painted wall, framed as though you are looking out French doors and fanlight to join her vignette. English floral fabric covers the seven tables and Victorian silk shaded floor lamps cheer the high ceilinged room with gentle light. Warm scones, crepes, pies and homemade soups and baked goods complement the teas offered, and High Tea and special theme teas are just being added to the schedule. Call Betty for particulars as her new tea room is evolving. It's been a good year.

Tea is served Tuesday through Saturday, 11:30 a.m. to 4 p.m. with the gift shop open Monday through Saturday, 10 a.m. to 5 p.m.

GREEN GABLES GUESTHOUSE

1503 Second Avenue West
Seattle, WA 98119
Phone (206) 282-6863
Toll Free (800) 400-1503

In 1851 one of Seattle's founding fathers, David Denny, gave a quick shove to Northwest tourism as he pushed the city to center stage declaring, "There is plenty of room for one thousand travelers - come at once."

Near the heart of the city is Green Gables Guesthouse. Of classic craftsman styling, the 1904 inn embodies the best of Seattle hospitality with seven tastefully appointed period rooms on Queen Anne Hill. Beautifully polished wood window frames reveal mature gardens beyond, and the air is redolent with warm scones and fresh fruit. Since 1991 afternoon tea has been available by reservation only from November through May.

The three course tea menu, worked out with you to make sure it's just as you wish, can include delectable Washington pears steamed in brandy, cashew chicken tea sandwiches, stuffed sauteed mushrooms, oven crepe with compote, open faced smoked salmon sandwich, lemon tarts, rice pudding, shortbread cookies, lemon souffle or iced pound cake. It begins with a black tea and ends with complete satisfaction and a lighter fruit tea for the dessert course.

David Denny may have thrown open the doors of Seattle to the thousand tourists he hoped for, but the Green Gables Guesthouse limits the size of their teas to fifteen maximum, four minimum in the interest of keeping the tea experience one of quality and intimacy. But do come at once!

Reservations only, November through May, rooms in the guesthouse are available year round.

On wings of hospitality, she flew to brew the tea.
Tom Hegg

HIGH TEA

4106 Brooklyn Ave. N.E. - #102B
Seattle, WA 98105
Phone (206) 634-0785

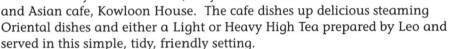

Leo Baquiran has melded his appreciation of fine tea and good food with a commitment to hard work. The result is High Tea, located on a sunny corner of a boxy commercial building in a quiet part of the University District in Seattle. Since August of 1994, Leo has devoted 14 hours a day to his business, a hybrid tea room and Asian cafe, Kowloon House. The cafe dishes up delicious steaming Oriental dishes and either a Light or Heavy High Tea prepared by Leo and served in this simple, tidy, friendly setting.

The Light High Tea includes a pot of tea, a variety of pastries prepared by Leo's friends and relatives in the bakery business, and fresh fruits. The Heavy Tea also includes a half sandwich on a light and tasty wheat bread. Looking for something completely different than your usual tea experience! You're likely to find it here. For instance, try Leo's absolutely delicious Spring rolls and Lumpia with your pot of Assam, or one of his value-priced daily specials. Hand-lettered signs taped to the wall herald tea choices ranging from Green Teas and Oolong to six Black Teas, six flavored Black Teas, and five Herbal infusions including New Zealand Sunny Slope. You can indulge your penchant for variety and true international flavor each time you visit.

Becoming a favorite midday haunt of local neighborhood business people and sleepy-eyed students with textbooks open on the table, Leo greets each customer, many of whom he knows now on a first name basis. There are 11 tables inside and in spring and summer you can choose to sit outside and savor your tea along with the local color from the sidewalk cafe. Intentionally limiting complexities to his cooking and his tea selections, the decor of High Tea is simple, clean and uncomplicated. A potted primrose adorns each scrubbed table, and tea is served from the simplest of pure white ceramic pots.

Leo's only regret is that with the long hours he has worked to make High Tea a success, he simply has not had the time to meet many people or to make many Northwest friends. But as he finishes that sentence two more ladies enter, local office workers and regular customers returning from a European vacation and greet him with a big hug. It would appear that with High Tea Leo has many friends and should be making more soon.

Open Monday through Friday 8 a.m. to 8 p.m. and Saturday 10 a.m. to 7 p.m., closed Sundays.

Home Heart & Friends

1221 W. Knox
Spokane, WA 99205
Phone (509) 328-9046

Ordinarily when someone tells me they are renovating and redecorating an old Victorian house for their retail business the pragmatist in me who has lived with building, remodeling and aspirations of getting around to decorating all her married life thinks, "That'll take a lot longer than they expect." Mentally I flip the pages of my imaginary calendar to add an extra six months to their Grand Opening. That was not the case when I first met Vicky Marburger. Vicky is a lady with such infectious joyous energy, that there could be no doubt that anything she set out to achieve would be accomplished, perfectly, beautifully and ahead of schedule with everyone still smiling. Maybe even without dust and paint splatters.

While the true heart of the aptly named new venture is a delightful upscale Victorian gift shop and custom framing business, Home Heart & Friends is exemplary of the latest Northwest trend in specialty retail toward offering tea to guests in an elegant relaxed setting. Vicky has dedicated several small comfortable tables throughout the charming two story business, and during warm months on her gingerbread-trimmed front porch, where you are invited to relax in true Victorian opulence and enjoy a cup of good tea.

Opened in the autumn of 1997 to Victorian enthusiasts, many in authentic costume, this new enterprise embodies the spirit of the era in a most charming way.

Open Monday through Saturday, 10 a.m. to 5:30 p.m.

IVY TEA ROOM
at BJ's Corner Cottage

30 S.W. 12th
College Place, WA 99324
Phone (509) 525-4752

My mother doesn't have a snobby bone in her body, and still considers "Taster's Choice" a gourmet beverage. Don't get me wrong, she likes a good cup of tea or coffee when it's made for her, but if it's hot and brownish it's probably good enough. Ivy Tea Room proprietor Pat Chaisser's mother, on the other hand, passed on the genetic encoding for a natural born tea lover. With English heritage, and childhood tea parties with bone china, Pat grew up with a lovingly steeped 'cuppa.'

Today nine tables are dressed for tea in a quiet corner of her Victorian style gift shop, located in a storefront in a commercial area near the college. Rose patterned walls and soft pink lighting create the gentility of Victorian times. Tea is delivered, snuggled in its floral tea cozy, along with a timer so you can steep it just right for you. Pat's emphasis is on low fat and mostly vegetarian tea treats. The fresh scones are served on heart shaped china to the crochet covered tables, and the teacups are vintage mismatched patterns. A little fireplace and bubbling fountain lend a peaceful parlor atmosphere. While drop by's are welcome, Pat requires a day's notice for her four course, 1-2 hour teas which include fresh fruit plate, salad, a variety of open-faced tea sandwiches and a dessert finale. The tea room is also available for private parties of up to 30 guests and children are welcome.

Open Sunday noon to 5 p.m., Monday and Wednesday 9:30 a.m. to 5:30 p.m., Tuesday and Thursday 9:30 a.m. to 7:00 p.m., Friday 9:30 a.m. to 4 p.m., drop-ins are welcome, but for the four-course tea, please give a day's advance notice.

Each cup of tea represents an imaginary voyage.
Catherine Deuzel

JEAN-PIERRE'S GARDEN ROOM

316 Schmidt Place
Tumwater, WA 98501
Phone (360) 754-3702

In 1845 Tumwater was founded as the first American settlement north of the Columbia River. Leading the party of pioneers from the "Show Me" State of Missouri into the Northwest woods was Michael T. Simmons, who built, among other accomplishments, a grist mill and a lovely house. After more mundane incarnations as home to the Tumwater Policy Department, today civility has been restored to that lovely Victorian by Jean-Pierre's Garden Room, serving tea in the finest European tradition.

French-born Jean-Pierre and his American wife Kerri use family heirloom china to create a special ambience as you take tea at a table by the fireplace, in an armchair, or at a table in their renovated Victorian home. During summer months a dozen tables dot the gardens. Now entering its second year, High Tea is served with a day's advance notice and includes traditional finger sandwiches, pasties, scones with fruit-enhanced butters, and fresh seasonal fruits.

A raconteur in the finest tradition, Jean-Pierre will gladly share interesting tea lore, his philosophy being that "tea is a good taste to be shared with good friends". Kerri will be pleased to gently guide the children in your party in tea etiquette. The next time someone says "Show Me" a good tea in Tumwater, make reservations for tea in an historic setting with distinctly European savoir faire.

Tea is served with 24 hour advance reservations from 11:30 a.m. to 2:30 p.m., Monday through Friday. Catering services are also available.

Lady Nancy Astor was an American woman, the first woman ever to be elected to the British Parliament. Her countless disputes with Winston Churchill on the floor of the House of Commons culminated in a memorable exchange in which Lady Astor sputtered that if she were his wife she'd poison his tea. Unbowed, Churchill replied, "My dear Nancy, if I were your husband I'd drink it."

JUDITH'S TEA ROOMS

and Rose Cafe
18820 Front St.
Poulsbo, WA 98370
Phone (360) 697-3449

Stress levels seem to run high at espresso stands, and I think it's more than the caffeine content causing that nervous fidgeting in espresso cart lines. I think it's because there is a whole coffee-culture language foreign to most people. Ordering a coffee has become something of an art, "Gimme a skinny double tall, no whip!" they shriek shamelessly over the roar of a passing bus at the corner stand. "I'll have a grande half-half wet cappuccino!" This language separates those in the coffee aficionado loop, so to speak, from those of us who just want a cup of it occasionally. It's a harsh language too. A sign at a coffee cart I stopped at on a business trip in Oregon recently threatened me with "A Slap Alongside the Head" for $2.00, (which to my relief turned out simply to be an extra shot of high-octane espresso in their java drink du jour.) It's certainly no wonder in these fast-paced times that tea is growing in popularity. Tea is simple, it's civilized, it's peaceful, it's romantic, and with any luck at all we will never, ever be subjected to a drive-through tearoom.

Judith Goodrich respects civility and romance. In the introduction to her popular new book, Favorite Recipes from Judith's, she recalls, "As a young girl reading romantic English novels, tearooms and teatimes were always mentioned as part of a very civilized ritual. I dearly love tradition, afternoon teas, fine china, and fresh flowers."

You will find all of those essential teatime elements at Judith's Tearooms and Rose Cafe On Front Street next to the old Olympic Inn in Poulsbo. Consistently honored as one of the Northwest Best Places, Judith's Tearooms evolved from a formal tearoom to a relaxing European style, open air cafe serving lunch and afternoon tea seven days a week.

The only possible stress you could encounter here is in narrowing your selection of totally delicious choices from Judith's extensive menu.

Judith's Tea Rooms is open daily from 11 a.m. to 5 p.m.

Loose tea will keep more than a year in an unopened, airtight container kept out of the direct sun. Teabags last for only about six months.

KADO TEAGARDEN

**at the Seattle Asian Art Museum
Volunteer Park
1400 East Prospect
Seattle, WA 98102
Phone (206) 344-5265
Toll Free (888) 242-1660**

There is a timeless Asian proverb, "Teachers open the door, but you must enter by yourself." Flanked as it is by two reclining camel sculptures, the doors of the Seattle Asian Art Musuem and Kado Teagarden are not only easy to find but provide access to a world of riches in both art and tea.

While admission to the museum is not required for tea here, it certainly would be a shame to miss this Seattle treasure in Capitol Hill's Volunteer Park.

Teas have been selectively blended, many as Kado's original blends, to enhance your cultural discovery. With the avowed philosophy that "The nuances of each country, each culture, are unveiled in a cup of tea," more than 50 teas are available from around the world. The tea menu is rounded out with lively or soothing floral and herbal tisanes. Tea service includes your choice of tea "properly brewed in an individual ceramic teapot presented on a tea tray with a tea cozy." Scones, cookies and treats are welcome companions in any culture, and the appropriate teacup for your choice of tea is an especially nice touch.

The setting for tea is serene and uplifting with a bubbling rock fountain and soft Asian music enhancing, never intruding upon, your teatime. In the words of Kado's own welcoming statement, "As your hosts, we are here to provide you a calming, restorative experience; an oasis of reflection and peace. And we are here to encourage and assist your exploration of tea; to answer your questions about tea, and its culture and manufacture around the world. To Peace in Your Cup."

Open Thursday, 11 a.m. to 5:30 p.m. Friday, Saturday and Sunday, 11 a.m. to 4:30 p.m. Call for current schedule of tea tastings and demonstrations.

KATE'S TEA ROOM & CURIOS

121 N. Lewis
Monroe, WA 98272
Phone (360) 794-5199

I used to think that you reached middle-age when your age was a higher number than your bra size. (I realized this system was flawed because it only works for women and cross-dressing men.) Later, when that number arrived too quickly, I reevaluated my system and decided I would recognize middle age when I started buying shoes with complete disregard for style or fashion. When the purchase criteria was comfort and sensibility only, sometime in the distant future, then I would have reached middle age.

My sturdy laced-up oxfords (with wiggle room for toes) make a happy scrunching sound on the crushed hazelnut pathway to Kate's Tea Room and Curios. Welcomed at the door by owner Kathy and manager Tammy Lundquist, it is apparent from the start that your teatime here will be simple, genuine and homey. Decorated with sturdy antiques and vintage finds, Kate's main tea room is bright, comfortable and unpretentious. Costumes and hats are a lure to the children's tea room, and this day finds several groups of young mothers engrossed in revitalizing conversation as their children quietly participate in a tea party of their own making, complete with hats and giggles.

The tea list is extensive and well thought out, with an emphasis on the superior quality blends of local tea importer Blue Willow Teas. The menu offers guests a delightful traditional Garden Tea, a lighter Afternoon Delight Tea, a simple Tea Sandwich Plate garnished with fresh fruit or a Teddy Bear Tea for the children. Fresh sandwiches, salads, and homemade soups round out the comfort food menu.

Everyone deserves a bit of comfort in their day. It may be something as simple as stretchy waistbands and comfortable shoes, or it can be a relaxing tea at Kate's in the old part of Monroe, perhaps both. Either way, welcome to middle age!

Open Monday through Saturday, 10 a.m. to 5 p.m., call to confirm seasonal hours and a proposed Sunday Brunch schedule under consideration as we go to press.

KENNEWICK HERB STORE & TEA ROOM

211 W. Kennewick Avenue
Kennewick, WA 99336
Phone (509) 582-7464

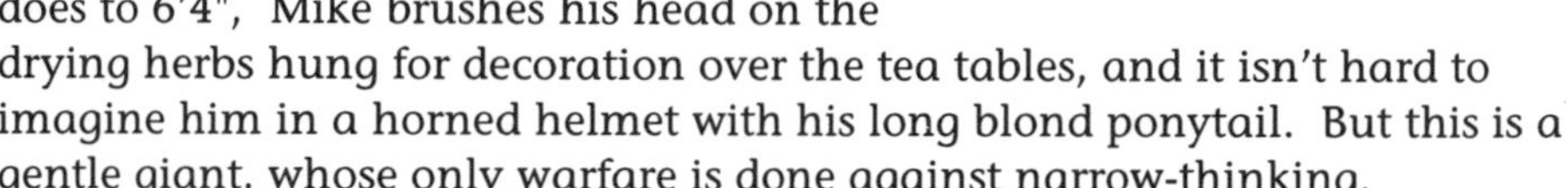

A local poet once described Kennewick Herb Store & Tea Room co-owner Mike Priddy as a "Haight-Ashbury Viking." Rising as he does to 6'4", Mike brushes his head on the drying herbs hung for decoration over the tea tables, and it isn't hard to imagine him in a horned helmet with his long blond ponytail. But this is a gentle giant, whose only warfare is done against narrow-thinking.

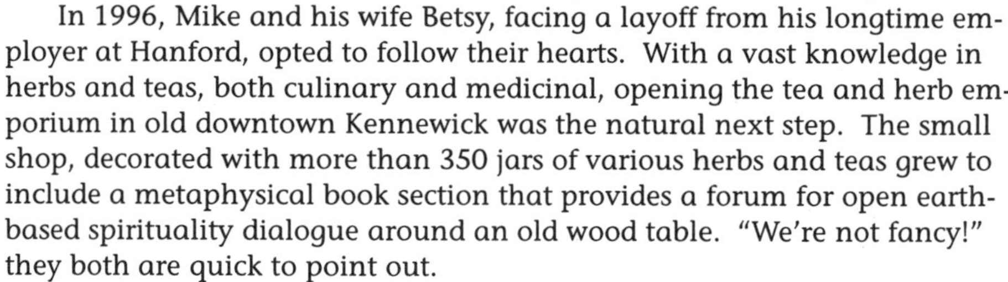

In 1996, Mike and his wife Betsy, facing a layoff from his longtime employer at Hanford, opted to follow their hearts. With a vast knowledge in herbs and teas, both culinary and medicinal, opening the tea and herb emporium in old downtown Kennewick was the natural next step. The small shop, decorated with more than 350 jars of various herbs and teas grew to include a metaphysical book section that provides a forum for open earth-based spirituality dialogue around an old wood table. "We're not fancy!" they both are quick to point out.

In the front of the shop are five glass topped tables where a pot of tea can be enjoyed. A few muffins and cookies are also available. "Tea is a chance to be kind to yourself," Betsy muses, "and that can only lead to a gentler life."

Open Monday through Saturday, 10:00 a.m. to 5:30 p.m. Call for the schedule of symposiums offered on diverse herbal and metaphysical subjects.

LANGLEY TEA ROOM

221 - Second Street #15B
Langley, WA 98260
Phone (360) 221-6292

Aunt Marwayne and Ken's mum Emily Lewis at the Langley Tea Room

When Captain Vancouver explored the shoreline of the Pacific Northwest more than 200 years ago, a glimpse of nostalgia accompanies his journal entry. "A picture so pleasing could not fail to call to our remembrance certain delightful and beloved situations in Old England," he rhapsodized. After two years of rugged coastal exploration who can blame the young captain for leaning on the deck rail of the Discovery, gazing wistfully at the view and longing for a good cup of tea?

Today in the charming village of Langley on Whidbey Island, Pat Powell has created a delightful tea room Captain Vancouver (and the more refined of his crew members) would have enjoyed. Decorated in vibrant English country cottage style with floral chintz covered tables and cut-work toppers, books, fine art, murals by her talented artist husband, and abundant fresh flowers, the Langley Tea Room was created to simultaneously soothe and invigorate. Exactly like a good cup of tea. In the outside seating area, the lovely garden courtyard of cobbled brick echoes the relaxing sound of a bubbling fountain.

The menu includes an assortment of fresh and tasty tea sandwiches, salad, and dessert. The preserves are from Whidbey Island's famous fresh loganberries, and the fresh gingerbread is layered with rich whipped cream and jam. Crumpet varieties include egg and chive, veggie patty with lemon mayo and marinated locally grown tomatoes, garden cucumber with herbed cream cheese, or the simplicity of honey butter and marmalade.

Travel to Whidbey is scenic from both directions, either through LaConner to dramatic Deception Pass and down the island, or on board a Washington State ferry from Mukilteo. When you find yourself leaning on the deck railing, enjoying Captain Vancouver's view, and wistfully longing for good tea, you now know where to go.

Tea is served 11 a.m. to 5 p.m. everyday except Wednesday. It would be wise to confirm this the day you plan to go, since Langley is a flexible environment for creative businesses.

NORDSTROM GARDEN TERRACE

100 Bellevue Square
Bellevue, WA 98004
Phone (425) 455-5800

I have a confession that may shock you. I am not a good shopper. It simply is not a sport I enjoy. That's why for years when I need something I have just warmed up the old brown Nordstrom charge card and put myself in their well manicured hands. That the words 'Nordstrom' and 'excellent customer service' have become synonymous should surprise none of us Pacific Northwest folks, but what may surprise you is that these same standards of excellence are now being applied to Afternoon Tea in many of their larger stores.

At The Garden Terrace in the Bellevue Square Nordstrom this soothing break awaits daily between 3:00 and 5:00 p.m. with a special setting on Friday and Saturday with the bistro tables transformed with fine china, cloth napkins and flowers or greenery. Assorted finger sandwiches, dainty petit fours served on a pretty platter and a pot of tea are just the perfect way to take a gracious break from browsing and shopping, and of course the service is, well, 'Nordstrom'.

Tea is offered daily from 3:00 to 5:00 p.m.

Russians drink their tea from glasses with lots of lemon, sugar, or sweet jam stirred in.

PEKOE, A GLOBAL TEAHOUSE
at World Spice Merchants

1509 Western Avenue
Seattle, WA 98101
Phone (206) 682-7274
email: hill@worldspice.com
website: http://www.worldspice.com

Asking Tony Hill to name his favorite tea is like asking a father which child he loves best. It really isn't fair. Here is a tea lover with a palate so sophisticated to flavor nuances that "Guess the Tea" is a favorite fame played all day long in his exciting new spice and tea emporium perched at the top of the Pike Street Hillclimb in the shadow of the Public Market.

With comfortable plush couch and armchairs, tea chests, world maps, and a century-old leather topped English table that's seen a bit of tea in its day, the shop is furnished in global eclectic style in a color range from pekoe to jasmine. Reminiscent of a well-traveled friend's comfy living room, you are invited to sample any of the 100+ pure estate teas on hand. Baked goods and light tasty treats are available under the direction of Tony's beautiful girlfriend Dianne.

Even more exciting may be to have your very own signature tea blend created just for you. Custom tea blending is a specialty of the house at Pekoe, A Global Teahouse, and is a fascinating, educational experience. What could make a better gift than a gift certificate to a tea lover for the creation of their own tea blend? A schedule of monthly seminars on a variety of tea and spicy topics can be acquired during your visit or through the website.

Incidentally, on this day at least, Tony's favorite tea was a rich, malty Assam from the Manjushree Estate. (Assam is the blend base for many Irish Breakfast Teas.) Tony's own business philosophy, "Authentic flavors from everywhere," also sums up the ever-changing and unlimited world of tea.

Open 10 a.m. to 7 p.m. except Sunday noon to 6 p.m. with extended summer hours available with a phone call.

Moderation is the very essence of tea. Tea does not lend itself to extravagance.
Francis Ross Carpenter

THE PERENNIAL TEA ROOM

1910 Post Alley
Seattle, WA 98101
Phone (206) 448-4054
Toll Free (888) 448-4054

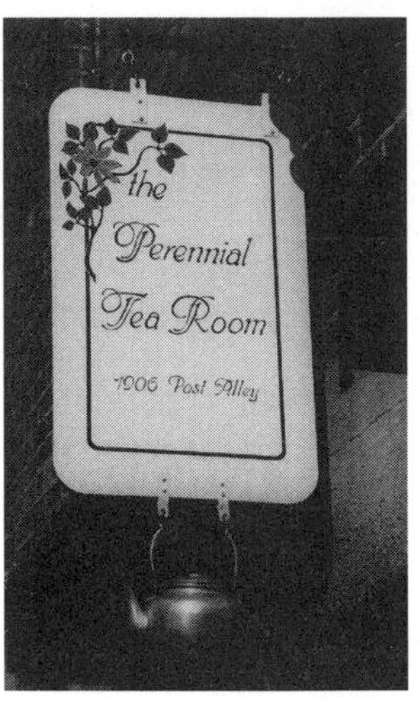

There's a teapot at the Perennial Tea Room that just sends me into a fit of giggles. By Oregon artist John Groth, the teapot is an anything but vicious looking gray wolf that comes with a mock sheepskin tea cozy. He is eyeing his shelf-mates with more than passing interest, a creamer and sugar bowl in the shape of grazing sheep. The pot is titled "A Wolf in Sheep's Clothing," and is only one of about 250 pots that festoon the shelves of this tea emporium. Serious Yixing or crazy wolves, sturdy Brown Betty to delicate bone china, The Perennial Tea Room is the spot to find the absolutely perfect pot from all over the world.

Julee Rosanoff and Sue Zuege

The quest for the perfect pot has been the ongoing passion of Julee Rosanoff and Sue Zuege since 1990 when these two friends left the field of social work for the social fun of tea. Heralded from the narrow Post Alley promenade by the traditional suspended tea kettle marking the entry, this historic building is in a pedestrian friendly area of benches and flowering pots.

"Tea is for fun!" Sue and Julee's business mantra sums up their tea philosophy. "There is no right or wrong way to enjoy tea," Sue declares, "It's just important that you enjoy the drinking of tea, that you enjoy your teapot, that you enjoy preparing the tea. Whatever we can do here toward that end, is what makes it fun for us."

With more than 70 loose teas in sniff jars, sample pots always hot, tea advice if you ask for it, every possible accoutrement known to the tea-drinking world, hard to find packaged teas, and a friendly and knowledgeable staff; it's clear Julee and Sue are doing a great deal toward sharing that sense of fun and exploration. Two small tables in the window offer a nice respite in this unpretentious environment, where you can have a cup or a pot of tea and one of four different shortbreads. Hot tea and warm hospitality await your visit to the Perennial Tea Room, where Julee and Sue are making tea fun for countless Northwesterners one cup or one crazy wolf pot at a time.

Open everyday 10 a.m. to 5:30 p.m. except Sunday 11 a.m. to 5 p.m. Mail order too!

THE PEWTER POT

124-1/2 Cottage Avenue
Cashmere, WA 98815
Phone (509) 782-2036

In 1903 the first wagon load of juicy apples rattled out of Cashmere to eager markets, and passed some equally anticipated cargo arriving in town from the opposite direction. Heralded by an advertisement in the Fruit Valley Journal for Ira Freer's local store, gentility had at last come to Cashmere: "Just arrived from the east...Tea Sets, of latest, up-to-date designs."

Cashmere began as a settlement called Old Mission, in deference to the hand-hewn log mission established in 1863 by Jesuit priests along a small creek near the Wenatchee River. Early chroniclers described the area as dry and barren, but the pioneers who settled here, hardy types like Prussian immigrant Alexander B. Brender, shared a vision of the green and fertile valleys of their homelands. By the 1880s, irrigation systems were in place that had transformed Old Mission into a cool and inviting oasis where fruits, vegetables, and families thrived. A well-travelled circuit court judge, comparing the area's grandeur to the exotic Vale of Kashmir in northwestern India, proposed the new name, which was officially adopted in 1904.

Today Cashmere is home to 2,700 residents, many of them active in the bountiful fruit industry for their livelihood. Liberty Orchards, producers of world famous Aplets & Cotlets since 1918, calls Cashmere home. Founded by Armenian immigrants using an ancient recipe for the fresh fruit and nut confection from their homeland, the internationally known company still welcomes visitors with the enthusiasm of a home town enterprise. Call (509) 782-4088 for tour schedule.

In 1980 Kristi Biornstad opened the Pewter Pot Restaurant on Cottage Street. Cozy and inviting, the burgundy skirted tables embellished with ecru lace and fresh flowers earned it the distinction, at least with the good-humored men of the town, as being the "sissy restaurant." Kristi's local advertising played on that theme, asking "Are you man enough to eat here?" Many of them are regulars there now.

An excellent quarterly newsletter of local events, recipes, and remarkable insights is available by adding your name and address to Kristi's mailing list. Drop in for tea, or drop her a note. Special tea theme events abound and vary with the season.

It has been 94 years since the first tea sets arrived in Cashmere, rattling in on the back of a wagon, and many of them may even be chipped or broken now; but the civility and elegance that rode in with them is alive and thriving at The Pewter Pot.

Open Tuesday through Saturday, 11 a.m. to 2:30 p.m. for lunch. Seating for Afternoon Tea is 2 p.m. to 3 p.m. Reservations are appreciated.

Yet let's be merry; we'll have tea and toast;
Custards for supper, and an endless host
Of syllabubs and jellies and mince pies,
And other such ladylike luxuries.

Percy Bysshe Shelley

PICCADILLY CIRCUS

1104 First Street
Snohomish, WA 98290
Phone (360) 568-8212

"No little lily-handed baronet he,
a great broad-shoulder'd genial Englishman..."
Alfred, Lord Tennyson

There would be no way that the great bard Tennyson could have known he was describing Geoff Wall, owner with his lovely American-born wife Marion of the wonderful new Piccadilly Circus in old town Snohomish, but describe him he did. Apart from a few achy middle-aged joints from sports injuries, Geoff looks like he should be leading his beloved Manchester United Football (soccer, to folks like me) team onto the field, and you'd want to clear a path for him. Instead, the couple has created a little bit of Geoff's homeland in quaint downtown Snohomish with some marvelous twists.

The front door to Piccadilly Circus delivers you into a perfectly recreated British corner store, replete with foodstuffs and teas to make an Anglophile or transplanted Brit stop in their tracks and sigh. A large gift and collectible area of the softest Scottish woolens, glistening Tutbury crystal, horse brasses, Irish linens, fine bone china, framed art, teapots and tempting tea accessories are just a few of the wonders to be found in the high-ceilinged and high quality gift section. The Walls make frequent buying excursions to the U.K. to keep this gift section fresh and Marion's talent for eye-catching display is apparent in this turn of the century storefront.

The aroma of freshly baked scones and simmering meat pies beckons from behind an English country cottage door in the back of the gift shop. Passing through that door, like finding yourself in an unexpected garden, one enters the enchantment of rolling Yorkshire Dales which have been lovingly painted onto the walls of the indoor Tea Garden. Green flower-filled fields and hedgerows, gentle farm animals, lie painted beneath a domed sky-blue ceiling with gentle wisps of clouds. It's always springtime on these Yorkshire Dales. As Geoff dims the lights, one by one the stars appear on the ceiling dome. This is the magical setting for your afternoon tea or hearty lunch from Piccadilly Circus' extensive and authentic British menu.

As Geoff and Marion's advertising flyer ponders, "Why go to London when Jolly Old England is right here in Snohomish?" Why indeed, when you can enjoy the food, tea, gifts and ambience of your genial hosts Geoff and Marion Wall in charming Snohomish?

Open seven days a week, 11 a.m. to 5 p.m.. Reservations for the Tea Garden are advised. Ask about their plans to be open periodically for dinner too.

POMEROY HOUSE – THE CARRIAGE HOUSE TEA ROOM

20902 N.E. Lucia Falls Road
Yacolt, WA 98675
360-686-3537
e mail:
pomeroy@pacifier.com

The blossoms are bright on the fruit trees of the old orchards we pass on the country road enroute to Pomeroy House. For the last three miles the asphalt road has hugged the bank of the Lewis River cascading through a lush narrow valley, and we are reminded of Wales. With the car window down we eavesdrop on the domestic disputes of nesting robins while carousing crows belt out a song to which only they can appreciate the melody. All the sounds of the countryside of this southwestern Washington valley seem amplified in this bucolic setting. It seems timeless here, probably part of the original appeal it held for Mr. E.C. Pomeroy, the son of English immigrants, when he brought his wife and five children to make the valley their home in 1910.

The Pomeroy House is the oldest house in the Lucia Falls area, crafted into a formidable two story, six bedroom dwelling from logs felled by Mr. Pomeroy and his son Tom right on the property. Still owned by the same family and recognized by the National Register of Historic Places, the estate is now a nonprofit Living History Farm. Included on the grounds are an extensive British theme gift shop and tea room. Lil Freese is the granddaughter of the pioneer Pomeroys. In bringing her personal dedication, gracious hospitality, and sense of order to the daily operation she must indeed personify the strongest traits of that hard-working family.

The Pomeroy Living History Farm is a functioning museum that captures the essence of 1920s Pacific Northwest rural life. Under the guidance of educator Bob Brink, visiting student groups are invited to share in a typical day on the farm. From grinding corn and using a scrub board for laundry, to sawing logs and pressing cider from the orchard, the farm is a learning experience that instills appreciation of all the back-breaking, hand-powered effort that preceded electricity and talking farm animal movies. School groups are invited to make arrangements by calling 360-686-3537.

The farm is open to the public the first full weekend of the month, June through October, Saturdays 11 a.m. to 4 p.m., and Sundays 1 p.m. to 4 p.m. You are invited for tea in the Carriage House year-round Wednesday through Saturday 11:30 a.m. to 3 p.m. and the temptations of an upscale British gift shop beckon Monday through Saturday, 10 a.m. to 5 p.m., Sunday 1 p.m. to 5 p.m. The calendar of special events is literally brimming with activities to interest everyone: a huge annual spring Herb Festival; craft workshops that include candle-dipping, spinning, weaving, quilting; an old-fashioned Fourth of July celebration and "baseball game in the back 40" (bring your mitt); barn theater puppet shows and dramatic presentations; educational forestry walks; horse logging demonstrations; a functioning blacksmith shop; horse-drawn hayrides; wiener roasts and cider pressing. To get on the mailing list for their delightful "Down on the Farm" quarterly newsletter, drop a request for it in the mail, or get on the mailing list when you come for tea. (As a nonprofit group staffed with many volunteers, a donation would no doubt be appreciated if you are able.)

Meanwhile in the tea room on the second floor of the Carriage House, teas are served Wednesday through Saturday 11:30 a.m. to 3 p.m. to a growing clientele appreciative of all the attention to detail with which Lil and her staff imbue the occasion. The food is excellent and the menu takes full advantage and appreciation of fresh farm-grown produce and herbs. There is an extensive tea list. The Easter, Mother's Day, and Alice in Wonderland Teas are becoming extremely popular and those should be booked in advance as they are held in the festively decorated old Pomeroy House, where space is more limited than the Carriage House Tea Room. Once a month a special theme tea is presented in the Pomeroy House. Your newsletter will hold the valuable information on these fun events.

The quote under the banner of the quarterly newsletter seems especially appropriate, "When you appreciate and preserve the ordinary as well as the exceptional, you fill in the full spectrum of History." At the Pomeroy House, the ordinary is indeed celebrated in a very special way.

You are invited for tea in the Carriage House year-round Wednesday through Saturday 11:30 a.m. to 3 p.m. and with special teas throughout the year. The temptations of the upscale British gift shop beckon Monday through Saturday 10 a.m. to 5 p.m., Sunday 1 p.m. to 5 p.m. The farm is open to the public the first full weekend of the months June through October, Saturdays 11 a.m. to 4 p.m. and Sundays 1 p.m. to 4 p.m.

QUEEN MARY

2912 N.E. 55th
Seattle, WA 98105
Phone (206) 527-2770

Mary C. Greengo's eye for detail and penchant for perfection caused one loving, and no doubt envious, friend to roll her eyes and query "Who do you think you are? Queen Mary?!" The moniker was too perfect to pass up, and in 1988, Mary opened her intimate little storefront restaurant under that regal banner.

Situated in a charming single story brick building with climbing ivy and coach lights, the curb appeal of the flower boxes and bright banners have beckoned many a new customer to her door. The attentive service, exceptional presentation, and pleasing quality of the teas have always brought them back. National publicity in glossy lifestyle magazines like Victoria contributed to this urban legend. Since opening, Queen Mary has become the acknowledged grande dame of cozy Afternoon Teas in Seattle.

Laura Ashley chintz, English lace, rich wood paneling and comfortable vintage wicker chairs combine to create an ambiance that is romantic and comfortable. Fresh flowers gently perfume the air, and the emphasis on freshness carries through to the produce and preserves. The Formal Afternoon Tea is lavish, beginning with a fresh fruit sorbet. Included on the three-tiered serving tray are finger sandwiches of Chicken-Almond, Cucumber, and Tomato-Basil; an array of freshly baked miniature currant scone, crumpet with fresh whipped butter and preserves, cookies, lemon curd tart (from an old family recipe), assorted fresh fruit and Chocolate-Raspberry Teacake. Choose from 20 varieties of teas. Queen Mary has a small gift and teapot section with elegant offerings as you might expect.

Celebrate attention to detail as an artform. Queen Mary - long may she reign!

Afternoon tea is served 2 p.m. to 5 p.m. daily, with reservations taken for parties of 6 or more. The restaurant is open Sunday through Wednesday 9 a.m. to 5 p.m., Thursday 9 a.m. to 9 p.m., and Friday and Saturday 9 a.m. to 10 p.m. offering an extensive menu with many family recipes and British flavor.

THE SCOTTISH TEA SHOP

1121 - 34th Avenue
Seattle, WA 98122
Phone (206) 324-6034

> "Farewell to the Highlands, farewell to the North,
> The birthplace of valour, the country of worth."
>
> Robert Burns

The plaintive sound of bagpipes drifted through the crisp night air in the Madrona neighborhood of Seattle, as plaid-kilted pipers ushered in the New Year 1998. It was also a celebration of the realization of Jackie Dunbar's dream, the grand opening of The Scottish Tea Shop. No need to say "farewell to the Highlands" with the arrival of this unique tea and specialty Scottish gift shop, home to all that is created in Scotland.

When Jackie and her Dunblane, Scotland-born husband found the Arts and Crafts style house near Union and 34th, its styling was reminiscent of their favorite Glasgow tearoom "Toshie's", the Blue Willow Tea Room designed by famous stylist Win McIntosh. They gutted and restored the dwelling right down to its 1902 hardwood floors, stocked the gift shop with a wide variety of Scottish goods, jewelry, foods, newspapers, books, and CDs, and then created what Jackie calls "a simple neighborhood tea room."

Five green tables in the restored dining room with a bay window offer a place to relax, read, talk a little Scottish history (the proprietor's passion is to create a cultural center in this business for all with an interest in Scotland, and particularly the Scot-Irish immigration of the 1700s). Tea is delivered to your table in a pot, and a few light pastries, oat cakes, shortbreads and sandwiches are available. While Jackie is quick to point out "It's not a fancy tea room," she does use real china. Tea treats are listed on a blackboard.

With three buying trips to Scotland every year, the shop will be constantly changing and evolving. Travelling art and special events will be on the agenda, so ask about them during your visit. And do plan to "Take a cup o' kindness yet" at this shop rooted in the Highlands.

Open Tuesday through Saturday 10 a.m. to 5 p.m. Buying trips in February, May and October may cause schedule changes so call if you plan a visit during those months.

SHERATON SEATTLE
Club Lounge

1400 Sixth Avenue
Seattle, WA 98101
Phone (206) 621-9000

On a June afternoon in 1889, an apprentice cabinet maker, distracted perhaps by the novelty of a cloudless day in Seattle, allowed a pot of glue to bubble over. In panic he poured water on the blazing goo, which proved not to be a good idea. Still, the fire might have been contained to Mr. McGough's cabinet shop if the fire chief hadn't been in San Francisco attending a fire-fighting seminar, or if the mayor and the acting fire chief hadn't spent time bickering, or if the tide had been in so the steamer pump could have gotten some water from Elliot Bay. Circumstances, in other words, conspired against containment. With water pressure low and panic high, the bucket brigade was soon out-matched by the rapidly spreading inferno. Historians would later call this Seattle's Great Fire of 1889, and in its wake 32 city blocks lay smoldering.

Today the formidable Sheraton Hotel looks out over the grandly rebuilt blocks to Elliott Bay, and the latest bit of excitement in the city relates to tea being served in the Club Lounge. Afternoon Tea is served from the lofty 32nd floor perch daily. Steeped in the comfort of leather chairs, fresh flowers, and ecru and floral print linens, the service includes assorted finger sandwiches, light and delicious petite scones made on site with Northwest fruits and nuts, cream and preserves and tea cookies, all served on a three tiered server. Windows afford a view of the city while your French press steeps at your table, and inside the view includes handsome works of regional artists such as Dale Chihuly's glass creations.

For tea in a lofty urban setting, the Sheraton has risen to the occasion. Maybe you'll be lucky enough to have one of those cloudless days too.

Tea is served daily from 2:00 to 4:00 p.m. Drop-ins welcomed.

SHOSEIAN TEAHOUSE

at the Seattle Japanese Garden, Washington Park Arboretum
1501 Lake Washington Blvd. East

Mailing address:
Urasenke Foundation
1910 - 37th Place East
Seattle, WA 98112
(206) 324-1483

In 1959 the people of Tokyo gave Seattle a treasure. A teahouse, exquisitely handcrafted in Japan, was carefully reassembled on a site selected in the Japanese Garden. Later, when our community was devastated by the loss of this haven to a fire in 1973, the Arboretum Foundation, with the assistance and guidance of the Urasenke Foundation of Kyoto, stepped in and built it again.

Chado (the Way of Tea) has been codified and carefully nurtured for 400 years by fifteen generations of descendants of Sen Rikyu, founder of the Urasenke tradition of tea. The past two generations have lifted the silk veil surrounding this living tradition of the Japanese Tea Ceremony and brought it to benefit the entire world, setting up branch schools in Europe, Australia, Asia and North and South America. One part of Chado is known as Chanoyu, literally translated, it simply means "hot water for tea." Translated spiritually, it is a ritual of transformation derived from Zen Buddhism and considered by scholars to be "one of the strongest and most pervasive cultural influences of the past five hundred years in Japan," influencing art, social matters, philosophy and hand crafts. Participating in chanoyu requires detaching oneself from all worldly matters and focusing completely on harmony, respect, purity and tranquility in a highly symbolic and ritualized setting. Suggesting the atmosphere of a secluded mountain retreat, the tranquil teahouse is central to activities and on-going education by the Urasenke's Seattle branch. Membership is $40 for individuals, $60 for families. Benefits include invitations to seasonal tea gatherings honoring nature such as Moon Viewing and Cherry Blossom Viewing.

The general public is invited to tea presentations April through October, the third Saturday of each of those months at 1:30 p.m.; free with admission to the Garden. General admission is $2.50 for adults and $1.50 for students and seniors. The Japanese Garden is open every day, March through November, 10 a.m. til dusk.

SORRENTO HOTEL

The Fireside Room
900 Madison Street
Seattle, WA 98104
Phone (206) 622-6400

Four or five generations ago, cable cars wobbled up steep Madison Street enroute to the forested shoreline of Lake Washington on the far side of First Hill. One of the first stops it creaked to was the Sorrento Hotel. Here elegant ladies in long dresses and gentlemen in hats would disembark and drift through the iron-gated courtyard to spend an afternoon by a cozy fire having leisurely tea with friends. In 1908, when the Sorrento was built, it rapidly became the most prestigious destination for Seattle's lavish events or intimate wedding nights.

The cable cars are gone now, early victims of debatable progress in the transportation system. The stately mansions of the neighborhood, winter residences for many of Seattle's early upper crust and nouveau-riche gold prospectors, have gradually been replaced by a battalion of physicians' offices, clinics, and full care multi-story hospitals, earning the area the medicinal nickname "Pill Hill." But time has been kind to the Sorrento. Inspired by structures of the Italian Renaissance, the warmth and character of this hotel have aged and mellowed like a late-harvest Tuscan wine.

The warmth is not limited to the old world facade. What really sets the Sorrento apart from many other fine Seattle hotels today is the attentive and personal service you receive here. The servers are so genuinely engaging and concerned for your comfort that it's possible to forget that you're not visiting a wealthy friend's private home. Elegant without being ostentatious, the Sorrento achieves that easy balance between relaxing comfort and traditional formality.

Especially nice on a blustery winter day in Seattle, teatime here by the fire will be a pleasant tradition for you to begin, but arriving at the cobbled courtyard by cable car is no longer an option.

Tea is served daily from 3:00 to 5:00 p.m. in the mahogany panelled Fireside Room in the lobby.

TEA & CRUMPETS

109 S. 2nd St.
Shelton, WA 98584
Phone (360) 427-1681

Connie Holman loves tea and hospitality. The daughter of a lifetime by choice waitress and the granddaughter of a restaurant owner, her mother would sometimes find her sleeping under the tables. Now committed to the Pacific Northwest, Connie doesn't have time to sleep under the tables, owning the most popular lunch and tea spot in timber-fueled Shelton since 1995. As a tribute to her hospitality skills, the business is expanding in the spring of 1998 to encompass the timber baron's bank building next door in order to accommodate the crowds. She will be offering a dinner menu for the first time under the upscale name Chez Constance and can seat 100 for all meals, including tea.

The timber baron's turn of the century bank building boasts the original white marble floors with tall oak wainscoting and rich colors converging on the 16-foot ceiling painted a deep midnight blue. Tea is presented at the white-clothed tables with flowers on tiered caddies. Various mis-matched vintage bone china reflect the candle light with your selection from the menu section titled "Tea and Other Diversions," and what pleasant diversions they are. Antiques collected over 35 years, and punctuated with fresh flowers, tempting gifts and art, enhance the period decor. From the large windows you can see a little piece of timber history, the locomotive and caboose occupying the last little bit of logging railroad right-of-way that Shelton grew up around. Its noise and smoke have given way to the tinkle of bone china teacups and the sighs of contented diners. Now that's progress.

Open daily, 11 a.m. to 10 p.m. with tea served from 2 to 4 p.m.

It is a funny thing about life – if you refuse to accept anything but the best, very often you get it.
Somerset Maugham

Tea & Other Comforts

9730 State Route 532 - Suite F
Stanwood, WA 98292
Phone (360) 629-2668

Stanwood is, in the English sense of the word, our personal market town. It's the closest hardware store and bakery, fruit stand and library, to our rural Camano Island home. After-dinner-party conversation eventually turns to "What would make living on Camano Island perfect?" And for those who thought it wasn't perfect already, only two answers would consistently emerge – a movie theater and a tea room in Stanwood. Driving through Stanwood in the crisp autumn of 1996 we were cheered to see a small, hand-lettered butcher paper banner taped to the window of a vacant coffee shop in a commercial complex that simply said "Tea Room Coming."

When the permanent sign was erected and it said "Tea & Other Comforts" my heart rejoiced with the knowledge that whoever selected this wonderful name truly understood the very nature of tea. Mother and daughter team Dawn Coons and Kerri Kirk have proven that six days a week since their December 1996 opening to growing numbers of tea drinkers in this delightfully decorated Victorian tea room. Lace curtains, floral fabrics, and vintage wallpaper combine with locally crafted quilts and framed art to give a soft, imperturbable comfort to the establishment. Weekly regulars now play bridge and catch up on each other's lives or simply read a book or write a letter over a pot of excellent Blue Willow tea.

Charmingly mismatched china is the perfect counterpoint to four different tea services: Elevenses, Cream Tea, Garden Tea, or the filling and truly outstanding Victorian Tea. Also offered is their Teddy Bear Tea (with sweet teddy bear-shaped sandwiches and chocolate banana) to delight children. The presentation is authentically Victorian with three-tiered trays and floral garnishes. Kerri, the most visible partner, also offers a daily salad trio, homemade soup, and specialty croissant sandwiches .

Highly anticipated and adeptly executed special events are carried out throughout the year. In autumn the tea room hosts a very special "Best Friends Tea," and other times of the year the agenda will feature tea leaf readings, barbershop quartets and other special comforts to accompany your tea. Several evenings during the year, a full-meal High Tea is presented to appreciative crowds.

Now, if we only had a movie theater.

Open Monday through Friday, 10 a.m. to 6 p.m. and Saturday, 10 a.m. to 5 p.m.

TEA, THYME & IVY
at Country Village

23710-1/2 Bothell-Everett Highway
Bothell, WA 98021
Phone (425) 482-1668

Day begins when the rooster proclaims it at the Country Village on the Bothell-Everett Highway. Driving into the parking area lined by boardwalks I find myself humming "ducks and geese and chicks better scurry", and as the bumper carefully parts the poultry I picture myself in a surrey with fringe on top instead of a Subaru sedan. It's easy to be transported to a different era at this captivating little collection of specialty and antique stores nestled as it is off the pastoral-feeling Bothell-Everett Highway.

Old time boardwalks connect many of the little awning-fronted shops and curving pathways meander past ponds and benches. A haven for suburban wildlife as much as for unique gifts, the Country Village has long been a destination for shoppers looking for a departure from the standard mall experience. A redwing blackbird whistles from a cattail as a mother hen leads her little brood of chicks toward the comfort of shade. An amusing vending machine dispenses bird goodies. The creature comforts of the shopper are not overlooked either, with umbrellas all over the area for convenience in case of rain, and a delightful new little tea room for all weather.

Tea Thyme & Ivy is the result of tea lover and comfortable hostess Debbie Paulson's vision for a bright little tea shop that would be every bit as unpretentious, carefree and homey as Country Village. Debbie made the transition from full time mom and casual teaware collector to entrepreneur tea lady in the summer of 1997 with a few gallons of light paint, sandpaper, stencils, talent and support from her husband and four teen and young adult offspring. Daughter Laura, a rising young Northwest figure skating talent, can be found working beside Debbie on many weekends. Delightful tea gifts ranging from whimsical teapot garden art to elegant porcelain and dainty decorated sugar cubes form eye-catching displays.

Three tables in a bright garden room provide a delightful spot to collect your thoughts, write a letter, read a book or connect with a friend in an unhurried setting over a cup of tea. Scones with Devonshire Cream and seasonal sweet treats are available. In the spring and summer an outdoor table in a charming little fenced garden allow you share a crumb or two with the songbirds. Casual, comfortable, and charming, Tea Thyme & Ivy provides the perfect pick-me-up for an afternoon exploring Country Village.

Open seven days a week, 10 a.m. to 6 p.m. except Sunday, 11 a.m. to 5 p.m.

TEA-AN'TIQUES

618 N. Monroe
Spokane, WA 99201
Phone (509) 324-8472

My grandmother Ideala, known to all as "Granny," lived to be 98-years-old, and died this year. She planted a garden and stacked her own firewood every year of her adult life until she turned 90 and simply couldn't do it anymore. I remember the delicious raspberry jam she would make from berry plants she had nurtured, but it wasn't until I became an adult and began tending my own garden that I truly appreciated the effort of love this jam was. Its taste has become sweeter in my memory. Occasionally some well-intentioned but needlessly concerned family member would say to her as she hunkered down to pull a weed, "Why do you go through all this trouble, Granny?" She'd just lean on her hoe and smile a big smile and the answer was always the same, "If I don't do it, who will?!"

That same spirit of joy in hard work is alive and well in Tea An'Tiques in Spokane. Owner Jackie Hayes, who opened the business in 1994, is the reservationist, baker, cook, waitress, dishwasher, cashier and bookkeeper. The job titles just go on and on as does Jackie's enthusiasm for her tea room. By combining her extensive knowledge of antiques with her love of tea parties, she has succeeded in creating the perfect amalgam of setting and style for a delightfully relaxed afternoon tea.

Located in Spokane's earliest commercial district, now experiencing a regentrification as antique row, everything at Tea An'tiques is for sale. If you like the teacup you just sipped from, it can go home with you. Jackie has scoured the gift and antique markets around the country to keep a fresh supply of interesting and fun old treasures flowing through her business.

Tea is served 11:00 a.m. to 4:00 p.m. Tuesday through Saturday. Jackie will be pleased to provide tea for private parties of 8 or more people on Sundays or Mondays as well with advance reservations and deposit. Children's tea parties are invited to play dress-up with gloves and hats for sale in the shop. It's sure to be a party they remember. Jackie offers a variety of options for tea, including a Full Fare Tea with sandwiches, whipped cream scones, and desserts. You can simply have tea with a variety of scones or her delicious tea and banana bread spread with a thick layer of cream cheese, chutney, curry and almonds. The fresh homemade soup of the day, made by Jackie herself of course, can come with a scone too. Somehow I think she must get asked that question my grandmother used to get asked, and I'll bet her answer would be just the same, "If I don't do it, who will?!"

Tea-An'Tiques is open 11:00 a.m. to 4:00 p.m. Tuesday through Saturday.

THE TEACUP

2207 Queen Anne Avenue North
Seattle, WA 98109
Phone (206) 283-5931
Fax (206) 284-6754

Queen Anne Hill holds court 450 feet over Seattle and from Kerry Park you can look the Space Needle straight in the eye. On this lofty perch Seattle's founding fathers built grand homes in the Queen Anne style of architecture for their families in the mid-1800's. While Seattle at that time was boisterous and rough-hewn, Queen Anne City, as it came to be called, was refined and peaceful. And in this rarified air a comfortable community could take tea in their parlors and look down upon Seattle, literally and figuratively.

Today that comfortable sense of community remains and the Queen Anne neighborhood of Seattle is home to many bistros, ethnic restaurants, salons, custom clothing, and gourmet specialty shops compressed into a seven block retail area that invites relaxed exploration. And thanks to Brian Keating's vision you can still take tea on Queen Anne Hill seven days a week at The Teacup, "Tea Lover's Paradise". Brian Keating is well known nationally as an expert on tea and tea business trends.

The Teacup is primarily a tea retailer, with over 125 varieties of bulk teas dispensed by a knowledgeable staff in a bright urbane setting. You are invited to have a pot or cup of tea and a scone or sweet baked goodie at a standing bar and four simple wood tables with teapot centerpieces inside, or when Northwest weather permits, at two sidewalk tables. It makes a nice break from neighborhood wandering. The Teacup has one entire wall devoted to every variety of teapot and other tea hardware known to mankind. If you can't find the absolute perfect teapot here for everyone, you're not even trying.

A quarterly newsletter called The Teacup Exchange is a wealth of general tea information and history as well as a catalog of the vast array of bulk teas available for sale by mailorder from The Teacup, truly "Tea Lover's Paradise" on Queen Anne Hill.

Open Monday through Saturday 9:00 a.m. to 6:00 p.m., Sunday 10 a.m. to 5 p.m.

Tea is second only to water as the beverage
most consumed by the world.

TEAHOUSE KUAN YIN

1911 N. 45th St.
Seattle, WA 98103
Phone (206) 632-2055

Kuan Yin is the Buddhist goddess of mercy. In many classic images she is portrayed lounging on a rock, a look of wisdom and compassion on her face, a lotus blossom extended in her right hand. The lotus blossom, like a good pot of tea, symbolizes solace and comfort. A different Kuan Yin, in 6th century B.C. China, was a disciple of the old tea philosopher Lao Tse. It was this Kuan Yin who instituted the ritual mark of hospitality that survives to this day of offering a bowl of tea to a travel-weary guest. At Teahouse Kuan Yin, the owner Miranda Pirzada dispenses the comfort and the tea in a unique multi-ethnic atmosphere that just may be evidence of her own wisdom and travels.

Rich patterns in Indian and Balinese fabrics and tapestries, Afghan carpets, and Chinese art mingle into a delightful visual blend that serves notice that you are about to enjoy a truly international tea experience here in the eclectic neighborhood of Wallingford. The calming effect of fish lazily exploring the environs of their large aquarium and peace-inducing music further guarantee that you will slow your pace here. Linger and enjoy, because Kuan Yin does not serve tea to go. Indeed, here you are encouraged to embrace the essence of taking tea, which requires that one slow down, reflect, and relax.

Five or six choices of fruit or nut-laden scones are offered as well as Green Tea Ice Cream. Rice paper wrapped spring rolls bulge with a surprising blend of crunchy jicama, scallions, cucumber, lettuce, pineapple and mint served with a spicy Indonesian peanut dipping sauce, and are a rare treat. Choose from almost 40 teas and tisanes from literally every corner of the globe, Kuan Yin's own imports and blends. You can almost hear the bells of the caravan. Teahouse Kuan Yin even offers a Kashmir version of chai, and an authentic whisked Mattcha. Even further evidence of the international bazaar atmosphere is the tea-related gift assortment that includes timeless Yixing clay pots and cups.

Open everyday, long hours to serve travel-weary and others.

VICTORIAN ROSE TEA ROOM

1130 Bethel Avenue
Port Orchard, WA 98366
Phone (360) 876-5695

Somehow my childhood zoomed by before I got around to whining to my parents about wanting a doll house. I doubt they would have trusted me to handle the upkeep of a small residence with frilly curtains. I have never been able to keep lace on anything. While my playmate, Suzy Granger, played gently with pristine girl dolls in pink flowered dresses, I had "Rusty" who came with a day-into-evening ensemble of denim overalls and a plaid shirt. He had chewed off fingers and the misfortune of losing his head (literally) on a regular basis. A kerchief tied like Roy Rogers' held his head on. If I had a doll house for Rusty it probably should have been a mobile home, not even a double wide. So you see, I simply can't help my adult fascination for pretty doll houses with lace curtains.

The building that is home to Victorian Rose Tea Room in Port Orchard looks like a great big doll house with its charming gables and big round turret painted a soft dusty rose hue. Appropriately it is also home to Springhouse Dolls and Gifts.

Old fashioned charm permeates the tea service at Victorian Rose Tea Room. Servers in traditional black and white present an elegant five course High Tea once a month, the fourth Saturday of the moth at 3:00 p.m. by reservation only. With a party of 15, this special tea can be arranged on any day of your choosing, with or without a lovely take home gift of a floral tea cup for your guests. Fresh vegetable plate, cheeses, sweet scones hot from the oven, flavored butters and whipped cream, tea sandwiches, mini quiche and an assortment of desserts are all garnished with fresh flowers and fruit. Afternoon Cream Tea with hot scones, flavored butters and preserves and a dessert is available daily 2:30 to 4:30 p.m. Their lemon meringue pie is the stuff of legends, made fresh by owner Sandy O'Donnell's mother. Children's parties

Come oh come ye tea-thirsty restless ones . . .
the kettle boils, bubbles and sings musically.
Rabindranath Tagore

are made all the more special with tea theme party favors. Special theme teas throughout the year sell out early, so do inquire on your visit. Weather permitting the outdoor patio is a pleasant spot for tea, or if you have a group you can reserve the turret.

After tea you will enjoy a stroll through the doll gallery, where hundreds of beautiful dolls, many of them collectible, every single one of them with their heads on, dwell in lace-filled luxury.

Country breakfasts are served daily 9-11 a.m. Lunch soups, salads, and sandwiches are served 11a.m. to 2:30 p.m. Cream Tea and other desserts are offered 2:30 to 4:30 p.m. High Tea is the fourth Saturday of every month at 3:00 p.m. with prepaid reservations required. High Tea can be served to your group of 15 or more any time with advance reservations. Call for a Special Occasion Planner flyer.

When the tea is brought at five o'clock,
And all the neat curtains are drawn with care,
The little black cat with bright green eyes
Is suddenly purring there.

Harold Monro
Milk for the Cat

VICTORIAN TEA POTTS
at the Pacific Run Antique Mall

10228 Pacific Avenue
Tacoma, WA 98444
Phone (253) 537-5371

The idea for the very first tea shop in England was cooked up by a bakery worker who put a few tables in some unused space, put the kettle on, and the rest is tea history.

After 27 years as a professional baker, you'd think Mrs. Potts might want to dust off the flour and take a little break from food preparation. Instead, she and other supportive family members have opened a little haven for tea in the back of the Pacific Run Antique Mall. With seating for 36 guests at mock lace-topped tables with centerpieces, tea is served with advance reservations only in their little soup and sandwich establishment. Tiered servers hold an assortment of tea sandwiches, fresh fruit, scones with cream, and a sweet dessert that varies. Currently offering tea by the pot from teabags, the plan is to branch out a little on the tea limb and offer loose teas soon.

The scenery changes all the time because everything is for sale including the teapots, framed art and china.

Some of the best ideas get cooked up by bakers, petit fours for example, and the idea to provide a comfortable and casual spot for a break from antique browsing may just be another.

Open 10 a.m. to 6 p.m. daily. Reservations required for Afternoon Tea.

When you have flowers, books and tea,
you are never alone.
Alexandra Stoddard

VILLAGE TEA ROOM

7526 Olympic View Drive - Suite A
Edmonds, WA 98026
Phone (425) 778-8872

Emerging from the manicured suburbs north of Edmonds, many drivers are surprised to discover the pleasing neighborhood shopping area known as Perrinville. Constructed to resemble a country Victorian retail center, Perrinville Village has provided a compatible environment for the unique country craft and antiques businesses that flourish here.

Nestled in a cozy back room of Village Crafts and Collectables, Terry and Dave Slater have created The Village Tea Room. Inspired by fine turn-of-the-century country hotel dining rooms, their tea room is enhanced by abundant antiques, lace and linens, flowers and period art. A tall evergreen tree is festooned with colorful antique teacups as ornaments in a delightful year-round display. Lining a replica wood fireplace mantle, and on every peg of a clothes tree close by, are some of the dozens and dozens of vintage hats collected for you to wear for own tea party here. A photo album on a table near the door shows giggling little girls in flowered hats sipping tea. Regal Edmonds matrons crook their pinkies and look sufficiently prim under various outrageous bonnets. Contemporary gentlemen in battered top hats strike an elegant posture for the camera, and you are left to wonder, what is it about hats that turn us into someone else? It's a fun, relaxed, yet elegant, setting for your tea which includes assorted sandwiches, delicious sweet cream scones with your choice of topping, Scottish shortbread, assorted tea breads, muffins, cookies and pastries that vary weekly. And, of course, your choice of a delicious pot of tea.

Open for teas and good fun Tuesday through Saturday noon to 4:00 p.m. by reservations only. It's a great place for parties and for introducing children to the delights of tea. Be sure to call ahead to book space.

Ecstacy is a glass full of tea
and a piece of sugar in the mouth.
Alexander Pushkin

THE WELLINGTON

Tea Time at
The Wellington

4869 Rainier Avenue South
Seattle, WA 98118
Phone (206) 722-8571

"Polish it until you can see your smile in it, Sweetie!" Gwyn Baker fondly recalls her grandmother Betty urging her as a little girl during preparations for teas on the porch during hot North Carolina summers. Time hasn't dimmed the memory of the meticulous preparation, but it has sweetened the recollection of warm times shared in the closeness of family and friends over those teas.

In 1993 Gwyn Baker opened her own tea room on a maple lined street of Seattle. Housed in a dignified brick building built in 1910 as a pharmacy and soda fountain, a tall clock on the block reminds Gwyn that life moves quickly, and we could all benefit from slowing down and connecting with friends and family with a gracious Afternoon Tea.

A recent renovation has imbued this popular spot with an elegance and charm befitting its well known hospitality. Gold fleur-de-lis on rich burgundy fabric cushion the chairs and cover the over-stuffed couch by the gilt enhanced fireplace. White skirted tables, tealights with elegant gold beaded shades, and soft floor lighting impart the essence of a manor house. Luxurious damask chenille drapes the window and provides a softened lighting.

The menu has new elegant touches as well, with such delicacies as salmon cream cheese pate garnished with red caviar. Gwyn's High Tea is served on three tiered trays by servers in formal black and white, a lighter tea is served plated to your table.

Once again Gwyn, who won the National Association of Mayor's Small Business of the Year award, has managed to create an ambience that is a fusion of formal elegance and the warmth of southern hospitality. Grandmother Betty would have been proud.

Tea, lunch, and dinner are served Wednesday through Friday noon to 9 p.m., Saturday 9 a.m. to 5 p.m. and Sunday by reservation. Closed Monday and Tuesday.

WHIFFLETREE TEA ROOM

14-102nd Ave. N.E.
Bellevue, WA 98004
Phone (425) 451-0062

In 1945 a band of volunteer firemen pitched in and built a firehouse for "Old Bellevue" that today is home to the charming Whiffletree Tea Room. Apparently more adept at fire-fighting than carpentry, "The crooked walls and high ceilings remind us," says Sherrill Shamitoff, co-owner with her mother Pat Ellis, "that we have created a bright and charming atmosphere in two fire engine bays."

South facing windows with lace curtains drench the nine table tea room in brightness even on a gray day. The tables are set with linens and lace, and antiques, collectibles, and tea time treasures and gift items are a feast for the eyes. Sherrill and Pat offer a full lunch menu with a daily soup or salad special, and a variety of yummy desserts that change daily. While take-out is available for folks on the run, going to a fire maybe, tea and treat time is anytime so do plan to stay. Near the big Downtown Park, there is a small town feel to Old Bellevue that deserves discovery. One quirky thing, the street address dates to a time when the door faced a different way. The front door of the Whiffletree actually faces N.E. 1st Place which will help you find it.

The fire of hospitality burns brightly at the old firehouse, and Sherrill and Pat have painted their door a cheery "fire engine red" to help you find your way.

Open Tuesday through Saturday 10:00 a.m. to 4:00 p.m. with once a month theme teas. Call for a schedule of events.

WIGLEY'S

310 N. Tower Avenue
Centralia, WA 98531
Phone (360) 736-4808

When President Clinton visited Centralia last year the local high school band didn't have time to learn "Hail to the Chief" so they played the next best thing, "Hit Me With Your Best Shot" by pop diva Pat Benetar. He loved the music (after all he has taken a smack or two during his term and plays a wailing sax) and the homestyle welcome, but what he really needed was some 'comfort food' for his entourage, 375 meals to be exact. Who did they call? Nancy Wigley of Wigley's Fine Food.

She recalls, "My first reaction was to scream for (my husband) Russell - and then just to scream, period." But Nancy is a trouper, with a black belt in croissants. All went smoothly, of course, and the fresh cobbler, made from fresh blackberries picked at Nancy and Russell's own Country Classics Farm, was such a hit that we have it on good authority that President Clinton was at least tempted to lick his plate, (and the other 374 probably.)

After 10 years baking and selling their goods at the Olympia Farmers Market, the Wigley's opened a deli-cafe to showcase their culinary talents, found some delicious teas to offer, and the rest is history. Located within walking distance of the train station, shoppers headed for the Factory Outlets by train make it a regular stop.

Tea service is available any time, and the deluxe tea consists of a variety of tea sandwiches, sliced fruit bread, fresh fruit, dessert, and one of their own handmade chocolates with a pot of tea. Reservations are appreciated for large groups, but not required. Private parties can be held at Wigley's after hours, and we all know that the size of the catered affair or the star quality of the guest list doesn't intimidate her at all.

Open Monday through Saturday 7:30 a.m. to 5 p.m., Sunday 9:30 a.m. to 4:30 p.m.

WINDSOR GARDEN TEA ROOM

110 Fourth Avenue North
Edmonds, WA 98020
Phone (425) 712-1387

It has long been noted that tea has a healing aspect to it, so it seems especially appropriate that the Windsor Garden Tea Room has nestled into a charming old doctor's office in Edmonds. Heralded by the MD symbol in mosaic on the entryway, there is no mistaking that this 1936 brick building was destined to be a house of healing in one form or another.

Joy Pohl and I laugh that we may be the only tea business owners in the country who grew up with parents who still consider Taster's Choice a gourmet beverage. Joy bought the popular tea room from its original owner Libby Hustler (who moved into tea distribution for Kinnell's Scottish Teas) in 1997. While Kinnell's is still the tea of choice here, Joy has infused the business with her own sense of style and Victorian charm.

The cozy five room tea house is dressed in soft mauves and pinks, with rose wallpaper and wainscotting, rich fabric draped walls, lace curtains and fresh flowers on each table. English bone china, charmingly mismatched, grace a linen covered table with tiered serving caddy and elegant touches like floral garnishes. A glass door opens onto a little garden. A cozy gift alcove features a wide variety of books, cards and gifts as well as estate sale china.

When you walk out of the Windsor Garden Tea Room after a lovely afternoon tea into the fresh sea breeze blowing up from the Edmonds ferry dock, you just might notice like the good doctor's patients years ago, that you feel a whole lot better than when you went in.

Open for tea Monday through Saturday, 11 a.m. to 5 p.m.

THE WOODMARK HOTEL

1200 Carillon Point
Kirkland, WA 98033
Phone (425) 822-3700
(425) 803-5595

Kirkland's hillside was once clothed by ancient widespread forests. City dwellers from Seattle would make the weekend crossing by steamboat in the early 1900s to the verdant Kirkland shoreline for communion with nature and lake-shore relaxation. Today a fast-paced, four-lane floating bridge unites Kirkland and Seattle blurring the distinction between city and retreat, and yet Kirkland retains the casual appeal of a lake-side village with a lavish dose of urban elegance and worldliness. Nowhere is that combination more evident than at the Woodmark Hotel on Carillon Point.

The Woodmark Hotel holds the distinction of being the only hotel located on the lengthy and convoluted shoreline of metropolitan Lake Washington. Intimate, by hotel standards, with 100 beautifully-appointed guest rooms, it is at the same time imposing due to its location. The four-story Woodmark presides with an air of businesslike authority over the 30-acre lake front that includes marina, pier, gardens, waterfront promenade and salmon stream. Wherever the eye turns it catches the glint of water.

Afternoon Tea is served daily on fine Lenox China in a comfortable, book-lined nook known as The Library Room. As their tea menu indicates, "Afternoon Tea at The Woodmark Hotel offers a continuation of the European custom of taking mid-afternoon respites between rounds of shopping, business appointments or simply to treat yourself to a small whim." The service is impeccable and thoughtful, and the setting is elegant and restful.

In addition to six tea blends and herbal tissanes from local blenders Barnes & Watson Fine Teas to ponder, you can also make your tea a truly festive occasion by adding a glass of sparkling wine, Champagne, or sherry. Three different tea menus are offered, a Full Tea with savories, sweets, and scone; Savories and Tea with a fruit scone without the sweets; and Sweets and Tea which is exactly as rich and yummy as it sounds. For children under the age of 12, a special afternoon tea is prepared that includes childhood favorites P.B. & J. and Egg Salad.

The Woodmark's quiet charm and attention to creature comforts make their teatime a special treat. Once again, as in years past, Kirkland offers a soothing retreat for the jangled sensibilities of urban dwellers.

Tea is served daily between 2:00 and 4:00 p.m., reservations are appreciated.

YE OLDE COPPER KETTLE

18881 "B-1" Front St.
Poulsbo, WA 98370
Phone (360) 697-2999

As recently as the 1920s Norwegian was the language of choice in Poulsbo, but by 1992 you could be just as likely to overhear, "Cuppa tea, luv?" as an "Uff-da" at the opening of Ye Olde Copper Kettle. With the arrival of transplanted Brits Tina and John, a cozy little English eatery in the heart of old Poulsbo has been lovingly recreated. And with their success, the international cuisine horizon of Poulsbo has expanded beyond lutefisk to include the freshly made Shepherd's Pies, Cornish Pasties, and Victoria Sandwich Cakes of the British Isles.

With cheerful pinks and abundant copper kettle accents, framed British prints of castles and manor houses, there can be not mistaking that a good cup of tea can be found here. Using fresh local produce and smoked salmon, a variety of finger sandwiches, freshly baked scones, Devonshire cream and preserves are served for tea. This delightful English fare can be augmented with any number of delectable sweet treats on the imaginative menu.

Open Tuesday through Thursday, 10:30 a.m. to 3:30 p.m., a little bit later on Friday and Saturday, Sunday, 11 a.m. to 3:00 p.m. Catering and private tea parties on site are available. Reservations advised for parties of four or more.

TEA PARTIES OF WASHINGTON

COUNTRY COTTAGE TEA PARTIES

12645 N.E. 68th Place
Kirkland, WA 98033
Phone (425) 827-3366

Peter Pan: "Do you want an adventure now...or would you like to have your tea first?"
Wendy: "Tea first, quickly!"

When Pam Fox's granddaughter came to live with them two years ago, her husband Greg created the playhouse of every little girl's dreams. Behind the pink Dutch door was floral wallpaper, rose carpeting, handpainted and wicker furniture. It had both heat and lights for year-round use and looking out the windows over the window boxes planted with colorful blooms you could see the gazebo and waterfall ponds of Pam's backyard. The first birthday that Rachel spent with her youthful grandparents, Pam created a teaparty so special that it launched her new business.

Today Pam and Greg open their property to teaparties by reservation only. While she gladly puts on teas for adults, children's tea parties are still her specialty with whimsically shaped tea sandwiches, chocolate dipped strawberries, pretty cookies, and warm orange marmalade scones. In good weather, the party-goers play croquet on the grass near the Battenberg lace covered tables, have a high spirited game of musical chairs, and create a special craft project. Fresh flowers and a sweet wrapped gift for each guest make the tables memorable. In colder times, the party moves indoors and old fashioned parlor games, played at many a Victorian child's party, create timeless fun.

A tea party with all the enchantment of a little girl's playhouse awaits the clients of Pam Fox. Book one today for a child you know or the child in you.

THE FOTHERINGHAM HOUSE BED & BREAKFAST

2128 West 2nd Avenue
Spokane, WA 99204
Phone (509) 838-1891
e-mail: www.ior.com/fotheringham

When asked what led her and husband Graham, two retired State employees, to take on the project of renovating an 1891 Queen Anne Victorian and run a Bed & Breakfast, there was no pause at all before Jackie Johnson blurted out, "Impulse!"

The Fotheringham House was built by the first mayor of Spokane, David B. Fotheringham in the late Queen Anne style. While most of the window glass (including the dramatic curved glass in the foyer), carved fireplace with its unusual tile faces, and intricate ball and spindle fretwork are all original to the dwelling, it's the touches, all in keeping with the historic perspective of the house the Grahams have added that make it truly remarkable. Once again following impulse, Jackie has completely transformed the yard into a Victorian cutting garden rich with those hallmarks of period gardens- hostas, ferns, fountains, benches and curving veranda. The six color "painted lady" paint scheme on the outside and the rag-rolled walls and vintage wallpaper, stained glass and restored tin ceilings earned them the coveted Eastern Washington Historic Preservation Award. This same celebration of history extends to the furnishings and fixtures which include a luxurious four poster feather bed, clawfoot tubs, carved wood, and Graham's family heirloom, a player piano.

The player piano entertains as a soft accompaniment to tea for your group of 12 to 28 people at the Fotheringham House. Served at tables set with lace tablecloths, flowers from the garden, and fine porcelain, the antique samovar holds the delicious Kinnell's Scottish Tea that is served with a hot savory, 3 tea sandwiches (one is always traditional cucumber), fruit or nut breads, fresh scones with Jackie's fresh lemon curd and Devonshire cream, and three desserts (one is always chocolate by popular demand.) A travelling minister's pump organ from 1889 is available for musically-inclined guests to play. In keeping with the history of this lovely home, a program celebrating the Age of Elegance is always a part of the tea. These highly anticipated programs range from a tour of this Master Gardener's Victorian garden, to programs on antique clothing, antique doll collecting, local Spokane and Browne's Addition neighborhood history, tea etiquette...always interesting and steeped in a historical perspective.

While it's true Jackie, the ebullient innkeeper, is a lady who works on impulse, she absolutely requires three weeks advance notice for your group of 12-28 to enjoy a couple of hours immersed in the rich history and luxury of the Age of Elegance.

HIGH TEA

5622 South Glendora Drive
Spokane, WA 99202
Phone (509) 448-9567

It was Thoreau who wrote, "To affect the quality of the day,
that is the highest of arts."

It was Jan Brandvold of Spokane who decided to use her love of tea as the means to improve the quality of not only her own day but those she meets during it. In late 1997 Jan Brandvold acted upon an idea that she had been germinating for several years. She concluded that many more people would find comfort and joy in an afternoon tea if the mystery was removed from it. She also noticed that many of her friends who professed to love the idea of an afternoon tea stopped short of actually hosting one because they lacked the necessary knowledge and paraphernalia, such as teapots, strainers, high quality teas, and pretty cups and saucers.

Today High Tea travels to the home of the hostess, whose mission it is to simply assemble some friends and provide some tasty treats to nibble on while Jan tells the story of tea. From her attractive display, Jan will offer tea tasting, discuss tea history, answer etiquette questions, and discuss the tea traditions of the British culture, and explain the procedures and customs. Her display consists of all the components of a proper tea, as well as a variety of tea themed gifts with a wide range of pricepoints, and guests can order the teas and accessories from her samples on display at the party.

Party by party, Jan is bringing the understanding of the restorative properties of a joyful afternoon tea to the Spokane area, and no doubt affecting in a truly positive manner the quality of many lives there.

SOUTH SEATTLE COMMUNITY COLLEGE

Rainier Dining Room
6000 - 16th Ave. S.W.
Seattle, WA 98106-1499
Phone (206) 764-7952 or (206) 764-5300
Website: http://seaccd.sccd.ctc.edu/-sshosp/cap/html/default2.htm

In 1860, the Earl of Lytton in England proclaimed (probably while his stomach was growling) "We may live without friends, we may live without books, but civilized man cannot live without cooks."

Thanks to the prestigious Culinary Arts program of the Food Sciences Department of South Seattle Community College, we may never be forced to test the epicurean Earl's theory. For the past few years this center of learning has been producing world-class cooks in growing numbers, and offering popular High Teas under the tutelage of Chef Stephen Sparks.

Offered twice a day on five Wednesdays during spring-summer school quarters, the High Teas have become so popular that advance tickets, limited to 45 guests each sitting, sell out quickly. The four-course meal, featuring premium teas graciously donated by Murchie's of Canada, provide a public forum for the creativitiy of these talented chefs-in-training. The imaginative four-course menu may include rose petal jam for your assorted scones and muffins, a soup course, ribbon sandwiches, shrimp and dill finger sandwiches, potted pork with toast points, tarts, petit fours and fruits presented with style and great care in the Rainier Dining Room.

To arrange for a schedule of the teas for spring and summer, call or write for a copy of the food Food Science newsletter "Bill of Fare" or check the college website listed above.

STORYBOOK TEA PARTIES

2239 S.W. 309th St.
Federal Way, WA 98023
Phone (253) 838-6504 or (425) 927-8703

"When I was young we always had mornings like this."
Toad of Toad Hall

The enchantment of a fairytale dwells in the hearts of sisters Kathleen Bourne and Sherril Filson. Known to their partygoers as Miss Kathleen and Miss Sherril of Storybook Tea Parties, they share their special magic at children's (ages 4 through 12) birthday parties in the Northwest.

Arriving at the party location for the guest of honor bearing a gold trunk full of silky, lacey storybook dress-up clothes for the girls (pirate garb for the lads) and a large treasure chest of sparkly jewelry they transform not only the setting for the party, but also the guests themselves. Once the table and the guests are decked out in their finery, the giggly group holds a fashion show.

The silky fabrics swish softly as the girls twirl and posture to show their fairy tale ensembles, accessorized with feather boas, mock furs, gloves, and flowered hats, or in the case of the guest of honor, a silver crown. Each gown is given a fairytale name and the transformation is complete. Imaginative old-fashioned games like 'toss the teabag in the pot' and nursery rhyme games are played.

Tea is served at a lace covered table from a three tiered silver stand, one tier holding pink tea sandwiches, rosebud topped chocolate tea cakes, and a lovely floral birthday cake graces the top tier. Fresh fruits of the season and Tinkerbell Tea or juice are served. Cinderella's slipper full of candies shares the table with a silver clamshell sugar bowl as light classical music, cloth napkins, and placecards set the table's elegant yet festive tone.

Later, the girls' storybook clothes are replaced with sparkling metalic halos and magic wands for them to keep, and as the guest of honors' special adult oversees the gift opening, Miss Kathleen and Miss Sherrill disappear like fairy dust (after magically cleaning the kitchen they've used to prepare the party.) The party lasts an hour and a half. The memories last a lifetime.

SURROGATE HOSTESS

1907 East Aloha
Seattle, WA 98122
Phone (206) 324-1945

"We'll call it Capitol Hill," declared Seattle pioneer founder Arthur Denny, revealing his fondest hope for Seattle to be named territory capitol, and envisioning a gleaming capitol building towering over Seattle. The political nod went to Olympia, of course, but the Seattle hill kept its name.

In the late nineteenth and early twentieth century Capitol Hill was the popular choice for residences of the Seattle elite, and many of those original structures remain today.

The building that is home to Surrogate Hostess was built during this period and served as a library and a barber shop in early incarnations. In 1994, a tearoom in the country French style was added to what has been a popular eatery for years. Available now for parties as small as 6 and as large as 40, the creamy plastered walls and black and white floors form the simple backdrop for a decor enhanced by travelling art exhibits, hanging baskets and gleaming copper kettles. Afternoon teas here can include imaginative finger sandwiches such as cucumber with mint butter, smoked salmon mousse and mushroom-walnut pate. A mini brie en brioche, fruit trifle and zesty orange scone round out a memorable menu.

Your Surrogate Hostess will also cater tea parties in other locations of your choice, so discuss your tea aspirations with them. Poor Arthur Denny could have drowned his sorrows over losing the capitol bid in a good pot of tea here. It's just as well, it's a lot friendlier environment without the politics.

Advance arrangements are necessary for teaparties, please call to schedule.

TEA FOR ME, PLEASE

1362 Jadwin
Richland, WA 99352
Phone (509) 943-0932
or (509) 943-3803

As Canadian author Margaret Atwood once joked, "For years I wanted to be older, and now I am!" Dressing up in my grandmother Lulu Kathryn Zimmerman-Skeels' dresses with a fox fur (I grew up to be an anti-fur activist so I'll apologize to the fox now) I remember pretending to be a teacher (although come to think of it, not many of them wore fur while writing on the blackboard), a shopkeeper (green leaves from the privet hedge were large denomination bills), and sometimes Royalty (which couldn't have been fun for my Commoner companions so I'll apologize to them here too.) Pretentious manners and a haughty demeanor distinguished these pitiful Bette Davis impersonations, but what fun it was, vamping with clothes and accents, the mantle of age weighing as heavily as Grandma Lulu's ample beaded bodices.

Shay Gloyn opened her business Tea for Me, Please over two years ago as part of Mrs. Gulliver's Miniatures and antique shop. Monday through Saturday by special arrangement beforehand, Shay provides grown up clothes and new personas to each guest. The girl becomes that special lady for the entire party and must remember to address her companions with their newly designated adult names. With a pretend shopping excursion throughout the store the girls' imaginations unfold, and when Mrs. Gulliver in the front of the store is introduced, it is with oh-so proper manners. A special story about a tea party and a gentle reminder of good manners precedes the highlight of the afternoon, a ladylike tea.

Indulge a special girl you know with this gentle adventure into good manners and good fun. Before you know it, she'll be all grown up.

TEA PARTIES BY PATRICIA MINISH

1006 - 14th St.
Port Townsend, WA 98368
Phone (360) 385-0159

Patricia Minish creates memories in her charming home in Victorian Port Townsend. A children's art teacher and lavish scrap book creator, her business and her passion have been in capturing and recording life's special moments. Lately, however, Patricia's art has grown to include creating cherished memories with delightful tea parties by advance reservation.

Her Fairy Princess Party for little girls, for example, includes an imaginatively original story she weaves about a fairy who has lost her wings. There on the wall is a beautiful poster of the hapless fairy, and a game begins of 'Pin the Wings on the Fairy'. The fairy's reward? Magic fairy dust, of course, which when sprinkled in Patricia's garden insures that wishes are granted.

With lovely linens, laces, and fine china, Patricia can expand upon any theme you can imagine (or allow her to create one for you.) Parties of four or more, any ages, any occasion, or maybe no occasion at all, are welcomed into her home. Pictures and memory album pages can be made available of your magical teatime.

Port Townsend is authentically Victorian, so do plan to spend some time exploring this, one of my personal favorite Northwest towns. One of my favorite gift shops, April Fool and Penny Too, makes its home here on charming Water Street and should not be missed, as well as a driving tour of the wonderful old homes of the era.

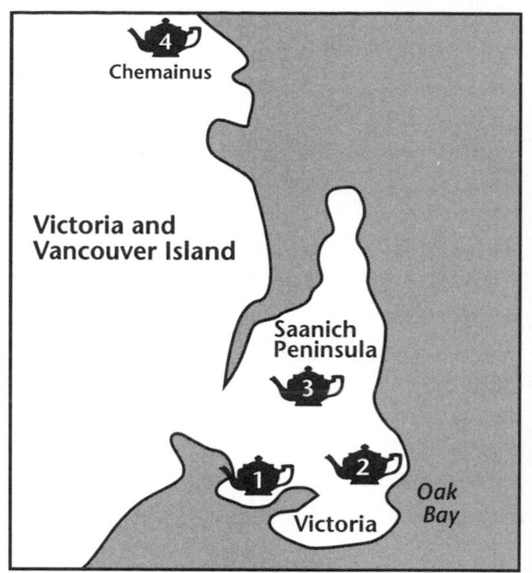

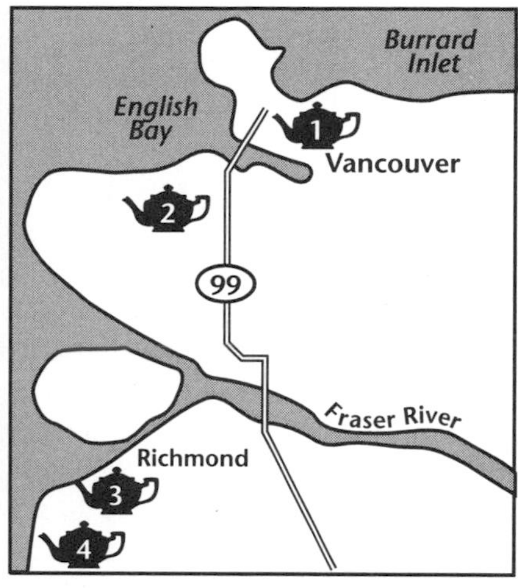

TEAROOMS OF BRITISH COLUMBIA

Vancouver Island

1. Near Downtown Victoria
   - The Empress Hotel
   - Gatsby Mansion
   - James Bay Tea Room
   - Murchie's
   - Olde England Inn
   - Point Ellice House
2. Oak Bay
   - Blethering Place
   - Oak Bay Beach Hotel
   - Oak Bay Tea Room
   - Windsor House
3. Saanich Peninsula
   - Adrienne's Tea Room
   - Butchart Gardens
   - The Gazebo
   - Four Mile House
4. Chemainus, Nanaimo
   - Calico Cat Tea Room
   - Harp & Heather

Mainland, Vancouver

1. Near Downtown Vancouver
   - Bon Ton Bakery
   - Hotel Vancouver
   - Murchie's
   - Sutton Place Hotel
   - Plaza Escada
   - Sylvia Hotel
   - Tearoom T
   - Wedgewood Hotel
2. Secret Garden Tea Co.
3. Steveston, Richmond
   - British Home
   - Cottage Tea Room
4. White Rock
   - Clancy's Tea Cosy
   - Pollyanna's Tea Shoppe

North of Vancouver
- Britannia House
- Chateau Whistler
- Grassroots Tea House

East of Vancouver
- Clayburn Village Store

ADRIENNE'S TEA GARDEN

at Mattick's Farm
5325 Cordova Bay Road
Victoria, B.C.
Phone (250) 658-1535

Farmer Bill Mattick's portrait in oils hangs in the entry to Mattick's Farm. In it Bill smiles proudly around a slim cigar, glowing with paternal pride at the two enormous cauliflowers he cradles with his one good hand and the hook that replaces the missing one. In his wool buffalo plaid shirt he looks folksy and colorful, probably brimming with advice on fertilizer and good common sense. Obviously he is a man with stories to tell and earthy wisdom to impart.

Today Mattick's Farm is a local landmark on the well-travelled scenic route from the Swartz Bay ferry terminal heading to Victoria. As folksy and colorful as Bill himself, Mattick's Farm houses a garden center and nursery, gift shop, florist, craft store, and Adrienne's Tea Garden. Farmer Bill has been gone for years, but his vision of abundance on this plot of land surpasses cauliflowers, and is his legacy to the merchants thriving here. What could be better on a weekend morning in spring than to stroll a nursery rife with perennials and then revel in the baked goods of a delightful country tea room?

Adrienne's Tea Garden owner Fay Hextall provides a comfortable, uncomplicated setting perfect for relaxing over tea. Here you can choose Fay's "High Tea" of finger sandwiches, assorted dainties, delicious raisin scone with Devonshire cream and homemade preserves, ice cream or fruit cup. If that sounds a little too abundant, you can opt for any of a vast array of fresh baked goods with your tea, such as sticky buns, cheese scones, apple or cherry turnovers, butter tarts, streudel, Nanaimo bars, Eccles cakes, bagels, brownies, apple crisp, apple almond cake spiked with rum and cream or one of seven different varieties of muffins. There are sausages in puff pastry, salmon in puff pastry, and ten different rich dairy fresh ice creams. Did we mention carrot cake and cheesecake? All are created on site with a nod to Farmer Bill's penchant for abundance with the freshest local ingredients.

Since Farmer Bill spent the greater part of his life supplying fresh produce and flowers to Vancouver Islanders, it seems especially appropriate that country crafts, flowers, gifts, and bakers grow on his property today. Open for breakfast, lunch, and Afternoon Tea.

Hours: 9:00 a.m. to 5:00 p.m. with Afternoon Tea available from 11:30 a.m.

THE BLETHERING PLACE

2250 Oak Bay Avenue
Victoria, B.C.
Phone (250) 598-1413

To describe The Blethering Place in purely physical terms seems somehow to miss the point We could describe it as enduringly charming, because it certainly is, being the oldest building in Victorian Oak Bay Village. We could tell you about the care and eccentric sense of humor that has gone into the collection of old toys, books and prints that cover the bookshelves and panelled walls of this former grocery and post office building. It all coalesces to create an inviting air of authenticity to the British hospitality here. We could describe the personal, friendly service and relaxed informality that allows hours to slip away uncounted in good company. While all this would be true, it still wouldn't capture the heart and soul of this place, for that lies in the story of owner Ken Agate, and that story is best told by his clientele.

In 1981 Ken Agate arrived in British Columbia from his home in New Zealand and set about creating a comfortable haven for locals. With many of the same Oak Bay Villagers still visiting daily, The Blethering Place is a meeting ground where good company and good tea often brew together. Ken now lives above the shop with a menagerie of collectible teddy bears that perch along the window ledges spying down on the Oak Bay street scene. On the day we visited, we were treated to introductions to many of the teatime regulars, all willing to share a funny or touching story.

At one table were two wonderfully colorful retirees, Freda and Valentine, from the profession of social work. Their vivid purple blouses and flowered hats mirroring the gaiety and enthusiasm with which these two embrace life, and their affection for owner Agate is heartfelt and reciprocal. They are quick to point out that Ken Agate never allows a Christmas Day to pass without offering a dinner with all the trimmings to any and all who come by. On many summer weekend evenings, you learn, the entertainment in the tea house will be a rousing and nostalgic songfest of music from the 40s hammered out on the old upright piano in the corner and an invitation for all to share the microphone with their own personal memories of their youth at the end of World War II.

The enchanting young woman in the broad-brimmed hat with a rose in the hatband sits sipping tea with her long flowing skirt billowing in the breeze of the open door. With a little wave to the other tables in passing she is off again to narrate the next double decker bus tour of the area on the Oak Bay Explorer. Only then do you learn she was at one time in the not so distant past, homeless with no job skills and little hope when hired by the Blethering Place. The work skills she sharpened in this supportive environment enabled her to grow into the wonderful public contact job in which she now thrives.

The Blethering Place offers a complete menu for breakfast, lunch and dinner in addition to Afternoon Tea. Here, as in the decor and service, much emphasis is placed on British foods - Guinness Ale basted chicken, Shepherd's Pie, Fawlty Towers Loin of Pork (with Basil sauce), Yorkshire Pudding - it's a fun eclectic mix as you would expect.

When the original quarters became a bit cramped for all the locals and tourists, Agate organized a work party after the close of business and arming all with sledge hammers, proceeded to enlarge the Blethering Place by knocking through a wall. It seems every table has a story to tell or a memory to share, with the common theme that this is indeed a magical spot.

'Blethering' is Scottish for 'senseless talking', but the pleasant interlude that awaits you here makes a great deal of sense to me.

Hours at Blethering Place for Afternoon Tea are 11 a.m. to 6:30 p.m.

Polly, put the kettle on, we'll all have tea.
Charles Dickens
Barnaby Ridge

BON TON PASTRY & CONFECTIONERY

874 Granville
Vancouver, B.C.
Phone (604) 681-3058

Tradition often improves with age. The Bon Ton is primarily a fine bakery and confectionery in the truest European tradition. About sixty years ago Italian-born Mr. Notte with his French-born bride opened the business, and the spatula has been passed to younger generations of Nottes to continue their standards of excellence. Continue it they have, and the art of baking has scaled new heights under their tutelage.

Entering Bon Ton you are flanked by glass display cases forming a corridor of compelling calories. Rich pastries, layer cakes, Florentines, meringue tarts, eclairs, marzipan, fruit tortes, truffles . . . the menu reads like a litany of guilty pleasures, and what a sinful treat they are. The walls are adorned, not with departed Notte family members, but with framed photos of cakes that have come and gone. Gone but not forgotten, no doubt. The ceilings are high, the decor simple so not to conflict with the elaborate pastries perhaps, and the mood European.

If you came to Bon Ton expecting a wide variety of teas, you would be disappointed. Your disappointment should be short-lived, however, just like your diet, once you perk yourself up with any of the myriad of delectable treats. In an area formed by simple garden lattice walls you will find 18 wrought iron bistro tables in a Meditteranean theme decor. Servers will leave before you a simple glass-domed tray containing at least 12 different creamy treats. How many are left when you are done with your pot of tea may be another issue entirely.

It doesn't take a fortune-teller to let you know you could easily pile on the calories here, but they do have a resident fortune teller (tea leaves or tarot cards) you can engage for a fee.

Bon Ton is open Tuesday through Saturday, 9:30 a.m. to 6:00 p.m. with tea served until 4:30 p.m. each day.

Canadians drink more than three times as much tea per person as Americans.

BRITANNIA HOUSE

Highway 99
Britannia Beach, B.C.
Phone (604) 896-2335

When Howard and Eileen Kelly aren't entertaining guests at their popular restaurant and tea room located between Vancouver and Whistler, they're on board their 36' charter boat running four to seven day tours up the Sunshine Coast of Vancouver Island to such wonders as Princess Louisa Sound. The beauties of British Columbia and the joy of working with the one you love are not lost on the Kellys.

The 1905 Heritage House, which is owned by the mining museum, is home to Britannia House. Located in one of the most beautiful areas of North America, the sweeping view from Britannia House encompasses Howe Sound, snowy mountain peaks and evergreen cloaked hills.

Afternoon Tea is served in a buttercream colored room heated by a cozy, crackling wood-burning stove. Tables are set with floral skirts and Battenberg lace toppers. Gentle classical music plays while a bone china three tiered tray is delivered to your table containing an assortment of finger sandwiches, a variety of sweets, and Devonshire Cream with the home baked scones that have won Eileen the nickname "Queen of Scones." As a real tribute to her tea and scones, Eileen received a letter from a couple from England who had visited for tea and wanted to thank her for the "most delicious scones" they had tasted on their entire trip.

A patio, surrounded by trees and rocky bluffs, is the ideal spot for tea in warm months. Britannia House is an ideal break on the often busy road to Whistler, and Eileen says more than one harried traveller has called their tea room "an oasis".

Open Thursday through Monday, 9 a.m. to 5 p.m. with full menu service, tea is served from 2 to 5 p.m., and elegant breakfasts all day. Reservations recommended on weekends.

BRITISH HOME

3986 Moncton at #1 Road
Steveston Village
Richmond, B.C.
Phone (604) 274-2261

On a warm morning in July of 1889, the 200-foot clipper ship, Titania, pushed off from the sleepy fishing village of Steveston under full sail. With a rich history in the tea trade, the vessel was now riding the winds of its rebirth as a freighter for another precious cargo - Fraser River salmon bound for the dinner tables of England.

This aging dowager's cargo was so well received in England that increased demand for salmon resulted in a dozen canneries opening in rapid succession. A "boomtown" atmosphere engulfed this once quiet tip of Lulu Island in southern British Columbia, and weekends would find the village swelling to 10,000 rough and tumble inhabitants. Enterprises that feed on a quick flush of money soon followed; gambling halls, saloons, and houses of ill-repute thrived along these shores of the Fraser River. Every Saturday night the Salvation Army band would parade along Moncton Street, admonishing with a flourish of a tambourine and a spirited bugle that fishermen and cannery workers' souls could be saved if they would just go home for the evening. Whether the advice was heeded is not chronicled.

Today the six-square-block area that constitutes the hub of Historic Steveston Village's commercial district is still bustling as it experiences its own rebirth as a "boomtown" in a new venue. Today's crowds are a better-mannered group presumably, happily partaking in the new enterprises that have cropped up to meet their needs. Gift shops, nautical bookstores, antique stores, seafood vendors, museum, T-shirt kiosks, Canadian crafts, street musicians, and more than three dozen restaurants and sidewalk cafes offer something for everyone by this busy harbor. One of the more unique businesses, delighting local expatriates and tourists alike, is British Home.

British Home authentically replicates every detail of the friendly corner store found all over Britain. Its cheerful proprietors, Mary and Ray Carter, stock a complete array of British groceries and meats, and offer some cooked food from recipes of their homeland in a variety of meat pies, sausage rolls, pasties, haggis, and black pudding that you request at the counter. Four tables by the window, covered in blue smocked gingham with captain's chairs, allow a break for good, strong tea under the regal countenance of framed members of the Royal Family. This engaging couple dispenses tea with affable good humor, and genuine friendliness in a comfortable setting. The bonneted ghosts of Salvation Army paraders must be smiling on this proper British business. Certainly they drank a lot of tea in their day.

British Home is open Tuesday through Saturday, 11:00 a.m. to 6:00 p.m. and Sunday from 1:00 p.m. to 5:00 p.m.

THE BUTCHART GARDENS

800 Benvenuto Avenue
Brentwood Bay, B.C.

Tea reservations (250) 652-8222
Garden information (250) 652-4422
Recorded information (250) 652-5256

There is a playful irony in the fact that the Butcharts earned their fortune with a product that is lifeless, gray, flat and boring. Those are certainly not descriptive of any aspect of their life when their cement business was thriving in the early 1900s, nor their masterpiece garden legacy today.

On the 130-acre site of an abandoned quarry on the shores of a picturesque inlet 13 miles north of Victoria on Vancouver Island, the Butcharts built their home, "Benvenuto," the Italian word for "welcome". To grace the naturally verdant setting, Mrs. Butchart ventured to plant her first rose bush and some sweet peas. From this simple act of horticultural, a dormant love of gardening sprouted, and over the next few years of nurturing Mrs. Butchart grew one of the most splendid gardens in North America, a garden masterpiece of world renown.

From the beginning, an almost constant flow of gardening enthusiasts were welcomed to the estate. With gracious hospitality the Butcharts saw to it that tea was always offered. In 1915 alone, it is reported that tea was served to 18,000, and it was not uncommon for strangers strolling the grounds to be invited to the family table for dinner and pleasant conversation.

Today, not only is Jenny Foster Butchart's glorious garden thriving, but that same spirit of gracious hospitality is as well. Afternoon Tea, in the Dining Room is lavish. It begins with fresh fruit cups with citrus yogurt cream, followed by a selection of delicate tea sandwiches that may include watercress and ginger cream cheese, smoked salmon mousse roll, egg salad with fresh spinach, Roma tomato and pesto, and edible flowers with lemon cream cheese. A plate of sweets that may include apple strudel, banana date loaf, chocolate brandy Napoleon slice, and a double chocolate dipped strawberry, as well as their delectably-light, candied ginger scone with whipped vanilla Devon cream. Manager Richard Schmidt sees to it that a large tea selection is offered. The presentation is at once formal and attentive, and the surroundings are impeccable with masses of beautiful fresh flowers gracing the antique-laden room.

Allow plenty of time to explore these glorious gardens. Internationally acclaimed, there is something special and unique about them at every season

The Butchart Residence - Summer. *Courtesy of the Butchart Gardens Ltd.*

of the year. During summer evenings, thousands of gently colored lights create a mystical setting for outdoor musical performances and sing-alongs.

Fireworks with musical accompaniment rival the brilliance of the blooms on some summer nights. In winter a special magic prevails with strolling carollers singing traditional tunes on crisp December days. Comfortable benches invite peaceful contemplation of the changing beauty of the gardens at all times of the year.

The estate was aptly named, Benvenuto. As in the days when Jenny Butchart approached guests in her garden to come in for tea, the tea room is offered as a service for today's garden visitors. As such, you will need to pay the reasonable admission price to enter the grounds where the tea room is located. Once there, you will, like countless international visitors for the past 92 years, feel very welcome in this glorious setting, a tribute to all that is good about warm hospitality and superior horticulture.

Tea is served seasonally 1 p.m. to 4 p.m. Please call (604) 652-8222 for reservations. Admission fee for garden is required for access to the tea room.

Like plants, most men have hidden properties
that chance alone reveals.

La Rochefoucauld
Maxims

CALICO CAT TEA HOUSE

1081 Haliburton Street
Nanaimo, BC V9R6N6
Phone (250) 754-3865

A calico cat sits sunning herself by the flower pots on the porch of the charming little bungalow. Heather Frank laughs when asked if this is the namesake kitty for her Calico Cat Tea House, "No, actually she just shows up everyday to be fussed over by customers. I don't know who owns her."

But the ownership of the historical 1910 railway cottage is apparent by all the renovations currently underway to expand the operation in March 1998 to include a Bed and Breakfast in this lovely Sunshine Coast community, where palm trees actually flourish. Husband Doug wields the hammer, and Heather handles the kitchen of this popular 24 seat eatery. With service to soon expand to seven days a week, it's more than a full-time job, and a labor of love.

Heather's affection for the cozy tea house began as a hired tea leaf reader. When it went on the market in 1995, she and Doug didn't hesitate. Now dressed in soft greens and burgundy, the dining area features the original fireplace and vintage stained glass, with tables set in burgundy linens with floral toppers. Tea on the patio is nice in spring and summer. Fresh, light cream scones, asparagus and cream cheese roll-ups, finger sandwiches and sweet treats made on site are served to your table on tiered servers.

With advance arrangements and a modest fee, Heather offers to spy into your future with a tea leaf reading. I'm not an expert, but I think I see a delightful Afternoon Tea in a cozy tea house in lovely Nanaimo in your future. Save a treat for the porch kitty.

Open 7 days a week with full menu, 8:30 a.m. to 4:30 p.m., with tea served anytime after 2:00. Dinners are served twice a week, Wednesday and Thursday.

Tea! Thou soft, sober, sage and venerable liquid . . .
Colley Cibber

CHATEAU WHISTLER

4599 Chateau Blvd.
Whistler, BC V0N1B4
Phone (604) 938-8000

Years ago I was invited to join a group of acquaintances in a condo at Sun Valley for a weekend of skiing. Quickly realizing my novice snowplow technique would never be able to keep up with them, (their shiny matching airline Ski Team jackets being my first clue), I struck out on my own. Unfortunately it was down the wrong side of the mountain, where I boarded the wrong bus, in search of a rented condo of which the only thing I could tell my helpful driver was that it was brown. It was a long day.

That never could have happened at Chateau Whistler. No, my skiing hasn't improved that much, but Chateau Whistler is hard to miss. Located at the base of Blackcomb Mountain about 60 miles north of Vancouver, the imposing chateau styled luxury hotel stretches its ten-plus stories into the clear mountain air. This extraordinary resort was voted the #1 ski destination by all three major ski publications, and since its birth in 1977 has attracted year round visitors for golfing, hiking, and now Afternoon Tea.

Tea is offered in the countrified elegance of The Wildflower Restaurant with its cheerful decor, or The Mallard Lounge with over-stuffed couches, rock fireplace and views of the tallest vertical drop in North America. Delicate finger sandwiches are served with fresh local berries, sweet tarts, and light scones with cream in these magnificent surroundings, where nothing, absolutely nothing could be described as just plain brown.

Tea is served everyday from 2 p.m. to 4:30 p.m. Reservations are recommended, but not required.

CLANCY'S TEA COSY

Pacific View
15223 Pacific Avenue
White Rock, BC V4B1P8
Phone (604) 541-9010

"May the roads rise with you and the winds be always at your back," begins a lovely Irish blessing, and as we climb the hill toward Clancy's Tea Cosy a fresh salt breeze blows gently off Boundary Bay behind us.

Family and tea are pleasantly intertwined in proprietor Dina Clancy's life. Her affection for tea time began as a child in the company of her Irish grandmother. Later her enthusiasm for tea time as a vocation was supported so completely by her father and mother, Patrick and Willy, that in 1994 they created the business with Dina; Patrick making the renowned fresh soup du jour, and Willy serving as an ebullient and gracious hostess. Dina personally prepares the fancy sandwiches and pastries served in Clancy's Tea Cosy, and her scones are so good her father refers to her as the "Wizard of Scones".

The cheerful tea room embraces you with rich deep colors, with hunter green wainscoting and floral border. Victorian garden art, a well-worn fiddle, wreaths and vintage plates form a delightful montage on the walls. Off the tea room is a little gift alcove full of temptations for tea and craft lovers. The tables, covered in white Battenberg lace are set with charmingly mismatched china, and a simple goblet of fresh flowers. Afternoon Tea is presented stylishly on a three tiered tray attractively embellished, and includes tea sandwiches of local salmon, cucumber and cream cheese, and egg. A light luncheon menu includes Patrick's homemade soups and fresh salads.

Clancy's Tea Cosy truly is an Irish blessing of its own special kind.

Open Tuesday through Sunday, 11 a.m. to 5:30 p.m.

CLAYBURN VILLAGE STORE & TEA SHOP

34810 Clayburn Road
Clayburn, B.C. V2S7Y9
Phone (604) 853-4020

I have a theory that it's tea drinkers who allow you to merge into rush hour traffic and then top it off with a smile and little wave. This doesn't necessarily mean that coffee drinkers are discourteous drivers, they might just be busy, reloading their weapons or something. Perhaps a government grant will fund this study someday.

Clayburn doesn't have to worry about rush hours. Located on peaceful Clayburn Road north of Abbottsford, Clayburn is a lovingly preserved company town. During the late 19th and early 20th century clay was extracted from nearby Sumas Mountain and fired into bricks in the village kilns giving the community its name and providing the townspeople with a proud livelihood. It was the brick industry in Clayburn that provided the building blocks for early Vancouver and Victoria.

If Clayburn has more than its share of tea drinkers, that's probably due to the Clayburn Village Store. Built in 1912, today the establishment offers gourmet and imported foods, old fashioned candies, and Devonshire cream teas, all in a turn of the century setting. The dignified brick building, its countenance softened by some climbing vines, features wood plank flooring and vintage display cases. Proprietor Trish Haber annually sources out new recipes from England such as Sticky Toffee Pudding, Gingerbread Cake with Cream and Maple Sauce, and a variety of cobblers using locally grown fresh fruits. English currant scones and Devonshire Cream are always available and always good.

The next time you are locked in bumper to bumper traffic, dream about your next visit to the peaceful village of Clayburn. Oh, and while you're sitting there, let me merge into traffic in front of you. I'll wave back.

Open Tuesday through Saturday, 9:00 a.m. to 5:30 p.m., Sunday noon to 5:00 p.m. Closes annually the last three weeks of January and the first three weeks of September.

COTTAGE TEA ROOM

100 - 12220 Second Avenue
Steveston Village
Richmond, B.C.
Phone (604) 241-1853

Cottage Tea Room

The south arm of the Fraser River forms a well-used harbor at historic Steveston Village. Seals spy back at tourists from the water and tourists spy at fishing boats docked at Fisherman's Wharf to off-load their catch. Sea gulls circle overhead hoping for dinner and making greedy noises. There is something to do in Steveston at every season of the year, with much of it revolving around this maritime activity. You can book a river tour at the dock, and in April and May special sea lion tours will give you a close look at these huge sea mammals. In the winter, the sound of the fog horn replaces the rousing street music of summer and forms a slightly melancholy counterpoint to browsing the quaint shops that cluster close to the docks.

One block north of all these nautical pursuits you can escape to Cottage Tea Room, an excellent break for a castaway from the dock-side scene. Well-lit and peaceful, this cozy little tea room is a tribute to the owner's fond childhood memories of Lake District tea rooms in England. A collection of crisp linen tea towels from many English towns and villages form a colorful montage on one wall and a massive antique hutch commands another. The tablecloths reflect the owner Margaret's love of nature in sepia-toned, lace-trimmed bird and flower themes. During good weather the outdoor courtyard holds two umbrella tables covered in bright tropical floral cloths.

The English Tea Set includes a chocolate, cookies, assorted finger sandwiches, a freshly made scone with Devon Cream and jam with your tea for a very reasonable price. The menu also extends to homemade soup, sandwiches, pies and pastries. Margaret has a wide variety of teas to complement the food, and invests a great deal of thought to the comfort of her guests. The service is with grace and attentiveness. Thus renewed, one can then really enjoy a dock-side stroll and gift shop crawl in this quaint and little known corner of British Columbia.

Cottage Tea Room is open daily from 10 a.m. to 5 p.m. in summer. Please call ahead for hours during winter months.

THE EMPRESS HOTEL

721 Government Street
Victoria, B.C.
Phone (250) 384-8111

In the beginning there was The Empress, and it was good.

For more than 80 years this bastion of old world dignity has kept a detached and imposing vigil over the heads of camera packing tourists and aspiring bagpipers on Victoria's Inner Harbour. Grand in the European chateau tradition, it is the quintessential teatime destination for those seeking an authentic Afternoon Tea served elegantly in luxuriant surroundings.

The oldest of Victoria's afternoon teas is served in the Tea Lobby year-round with additional sittings in the Palm Court and Bengal Lounge during the summer season. Reservations should be made in advance, and attention should be given to "appropriate attire" to save embarrassment since T-shirts, shorts, jeans, and sweatsuits will have you turned away at the door.

Tea is served from sterling tea pieces and bone china. No detail is too small for the Empress to have perfected it. Decidedly formal yet comfortable in its setting, the tea includes fresh seasonal fruits, toasted honey crumpets, raisin scones with Jersey cream and fresh strawberry preserves, assorted tea sandwiches verging on art, pastries and the Empress Blend Tea. Ample enough to replace a meal or to carry you through to a fashionably late dinner, this is one of the pricier teas in the Northwest, but tea at the Empress will continue to be an event you will remember.

Summer sittings in the Tea Lobby are 12:30 p.m., 2:00, 3:30, and 5 p.m. with extra sittings added during the peak summer months. The Palm Court opens June 25 and has sittings at 1 p.m., 2:30 and 4 p.m. Winter sittings are 2:00 and 3:30 p.m.

. . . and so the act of drinking tea must be attended by beauty.
Francis Ross Carpenter

FOUR MILE HOUSE

199 Old Island Highway
Victoria, BC V9B1G1
Phone (250) 479-2514

In 1849 Peter Calvert left his beloved Scotland to start a new life in Canada. At that time the Hudson Bay Company provided free passage around the Horn in return for a contract requiring work for five years in their employ. During the long voyage he fell in love with another passenger also bound for a new life, Miss Elizabeth Montgomery. After they married they worked hard and saved enough to buy six acres on a hill outside of Victoria where they built a cottage that grew along with their family.

Cognizant of the tough four mile uphill struggle the horse-drawn coaches had on the road passing their home, Peter and Elizabeth opened a road-house. The horses could rest and the passengers could quench their thirst and leave refreshed for the rest of their trip. Local lore recalls a time that the Calverts had a parrot that lived for years in a tree outside their door. The parrot would whistle at the horses and call out "Whoa!" as they struggled with the incline. The horses would stop and turn in.

Extensive renovation has preserved the building and restored the dignity this fourth oldest structure in Victoria's history richly deserves. For the past twenty years, tea has been offered to the road-weary. Served in Old World charm on tables set with linens and fresh flowers in the old beamed dining room, it includes a selection of sandwiches, cream & raisin scones served with jam, butter and whipped cream, a fresh lemon tart, pound cake and fruit and variations thereof.

The entrepreneurial parrot and the Calvert family have been gone a long time now, but the spirit of their hospitality remains.

Open seven days a week, tea is served from 2-5 p.m., reservations are advised, especially during the summer months.

GATSBY MANSION BED & BREAKFAST

309 Belleville Street
Victoria, BC V8V1W3
Phone (250) 388-9191

William Pendray made a promise to his new bride, Amelia. When they made their fortune, he would build her a home to rival the elaborate Queen Anne "painted ladies" she had admired on their honeymoon in San Francisco in 1877. True to his word, hard work at his soap and paint business allowed the construction of a mansion overlooking the Inner Harbor of Victoria at the turn of the century.

Layers of sweet molasses protected the Italian stained glass during shipment, and German fresco painters were commissioned to decorate the ceiling. Mr. Pendray's passion for topiary provided fanciful shapes on the yews, cedar and holly bushes. A huge teddy bear shaped shrub held hidden Easter eggs for his enchanted children.

Tea is served in all parts of the lovingly restored mansion resplendent with period antiques, original hardwood and old world charm. Its convenient location — within walking distance to the heart of town with views of the harbor — make it a favorite of visitors. The dining room seats 65, and tea sandwiches, fruit cup, and assorted tea sweets are served plated at the location of your choice in the ground floor rooms. The tone is casually elegant and comfortable.

A glimpse into the glory of an era is yours as a guest for tea at the Gatsby Mansion, formerly the Captain's Palace Inn. Now managed by the Huntington Manor Ramada for owner Mrs. Wilson, this charming Bed & Breakfast was renamed to recapture the high-spirited elegance of the 1920s.

Tea is offered daily from 2 p.m. to 4 p.m. with hospitable flexibility for other times, reservations advisable.

GAZEBO TEA GARDEN

5460 Old West Saanich Road
Victoria, B.C.
Phone (250) 479-7787

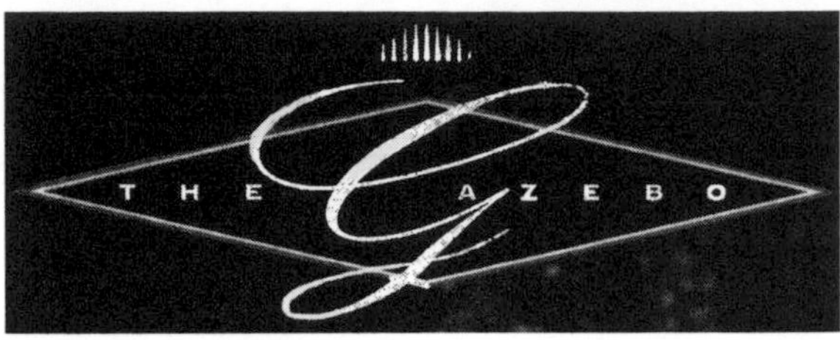

Halfway between Victoria and Butchart Gardens, on a meandering rural Vancouver Island lane, is Gazebo Tea Garden. Cushioned from the road by tall trees and shady landscaping, the Gazebo Tea Garden is something of a landmark, established more than 19 years ago. Recently acquired by Michael and Treva Wallber, who bring to it more than 30 years combined experience in creating truly special and dramatic events, the Gazebo is a peaceful pastoral setting for afternoon tea or casual country meals under a natural canopy of old trees and climbing vines.

In its newest incarnation, the Gazebo is now available for weddings, showers, corporate meetings and tour groups. Seating is provided at outdoor bistro tables in a spacious fountain courtyard, or on their large deck where you can watch the backyard songbirds. The blend of bubbling water and bird song is one of our favorite sounds and is guaranteed, like tea, to rejuvenate your spirit. In the evening, thousands of twinkly lights adorn the trees and add romance to the candle-lit setting.

This is a business that is evolving creatively under the new proprietors, so share your ideas for a special tea or event with Treva. Then relax and know that all elements of your event are in extremely talented hands.

Gazebo Tea Garden is open for tea daily 11 a.m. to 4 p.m. from Easter to October 1, then 11 a.m. to 4 p.m. Wednesday through Sunday through the winter. Call for details.

There is a great deal of poetry and fine sentiment
in a chest of tea.

Ralph Waldo Emerson

GRASSROOTS TEA HOUSE
at Riverside Park

262 Lorne Street
Kamloops, B.C. V2C6B7
Phone (250) 374-9890

It wasn't long ago that Thom Bell evolved from a professional philosophy of "We always get our man" as a Mountie for over 20 years to that of a tea house proprietor of "We always heat the pot." Gracious and lively, Thom and his wife Louise turned down a transfer by the R.C.M.P. that would have taken them out of the dramatic beauty of Kamloops. Instead they opted for a life in the hospitality business, as owners of the popular landmark Grassroots Tea House.

With a backdrop of the Canadian Rockies and the vigorous Thompson River passing by, the 40 year old stone front cottage (currently undergoing some renovation) is situated in pretty Riverside Park. Located just a scone's throw from the Rocky Mountain Rail Tour train stop, the setting for tea is one of casual elegance. Lace curtains, gleaming candlelight wall sconces reflecting off the hardwood floors, vintage mismatched china, and linen covered tables form a delightful decor for up to 50 diners. Open for lunch, tea and dinner on a seasonal basis, March 1 through September 30, tea is served ala carte. Finger sandwiches, tea biscuits, muffin and cheese accompany your pot of tea, which can also be served on the patio.

Dinner here is, says Thom, "Just like going to Mom's", with one main course served family style. Thom and Louise's roots are sunk deeply into Kamloops, which should please legions of tea lovers visiting The Grassroots Tea House.

Open March 1 through September 30, tea is served from 2 p.m. to 4 p.m. Lunch is served at 11:30 and one seating for family style supper is 6:00 p.m. Tuesday through Saturday. Look for their new website on the internet soon. Reservations are requested, and highly advised.

HARP & HEATHER

9749 Willow Street
Chemainus, B.C.
Phone (250) 246-2434

Chemainus is a little town that reinvented itself and lays rightful claim to the moniker "The little town that did."

Located on the eastern shoreline of Vancouver Island, about an hour north of Victoria with a view to Salt Spring Island, Chemainus is one of the island's oldest European settlements. In 1862 this farming community embraced the fledgling lumber industry by establishing a small water-powered sawmill in its midst, and for the next 120 years the production of high quality lumber defined Chemainus as a timber town. In 1983 the mill sputtered to a close after the single longest period of continuous lumber production in western North America, leaving this community of 4,000 shaken economically and rethinking its identity.

Local businesspeople stepped forward with a vision for Chemainus. Their plan, backed by British Columbia government financial help, would turn Chemainus into Canada's largest permanent outdoor art gallery. Talented muralists from around the globe travelled to Chemainus to capture the historical essence of the place and to translate it into colorful, giant illustrations painted onto walls and buildings all over the little town. With 32 murals and six sculptures now completed and many more planned, the spotlight of worldwide media attention has resulted in a strong new renewable resource industry for Chemainus, tourism. With more than 300,000 appreciative visitors a year drinking in the visual history of this place, the indomitable spirit of Chemainus has taken wing. Gift shops, inns, restaurants, antique galleries, theater, and one notable tea room, Harp & Heather, dispense good old fashioned hospitality.

Harp & Heather is located in an old building that, like the town, has gone through several incarnations. Built as the town library, it later opened its doors as the town's bank, and then a land management office. Charming in detail and rich in history, the Afternoon Tea at Harp & Heather reflects their Old World origins and are called the Welsh and Celtic Teas. It's a perfect place to relax from strolling the outdoor mural art and marvelling in the spirit of renewal of this charming little town. Call for details of special tea events.

Harp & Heather is usually open daily, 10:00 a.m. to 5:30 p.m., but best to call ahead.

HOTEL VANCOUVER
Griffins Restaurant

900 West Georgia Street
Vancouver, BC
Phone (604) 684-3131

The verdigris copper roof of the venerable Hotel Vancouver no longer dominates the skyline as it did in 1939 when the Canadian Pacific Railroad barons built it, but the allure certainly remains.

After extensive remodeling the Hotel Vancouver is again offering Afternoon Tea in a stylishly upbeat environment with some unexpected twists. With a color palette to enervate every bit as much as the tea, the sunny bistro environment provides a lively, refreshing setting. An assortment of imaginative tea sandwiches, pastry choices, Devonshire cream, fresh fruits and preserves are served from black wrought iron three tiered trays with colorful plates and teacups sporting a whimsical checkered pattern.

A great environment to chase away a gray day (or a gray mindset) awaits you now at the newly refurbished Hotel Vancouver.

Tea is served daily from 2:30 to 4:30 p.m. with drop-ins welcomed.

JAMES BAY TEA ROOM

332 Menzies Street
Victoria. B.C. V8V2G9
Phone (250) 382-8282

Early on sleepy Sunday mornings in summer, the peace of the Inner Harbour of Victoria is roused by a goofy little water ballet performed by the seven diminutive harbor ferries. To strains of The Blue Danube waltz over a loudspeaker, the seven little passenger boats chug around the harbor forming a chorus line from which they peel off to carve watery figure eights, starbursts, and fleur de lis formations, weaving in and out of each other's wakes with the precision of water bound Blue Angels. It's delightfully quirky to see these little water craft, which resemble Popeye's choice of cartoon transportation, performing intricate dockside maneuvers with a serious looking captain at the wheel and often a seagull riding along on the roof. It's part of the charm of the Inner Harbour and the silliness of the performance is what captivates and makes even the sleepy Sunday morning crowd begin the day with a smile.

The day begins early at James Bay Tea Room too, in the shadow of the dignified Parliament Buildings, a short walk from the harbor. Sunday through Saturday the hours are 7:00 a.m. until 9:00 p.m. with Afternoon Tea served anytime.

Touted as "An English Atmosphere in Victoria", this busy eatery operates from a charming old two story white clapboard house with cheerful striped awnings and hanging flower baskets, formerly a corner market in the early 1900's. Inside the English country decor manifests itself in frilly curtains, chintz, copper tea kettles, and stained glass lamps lighting the dignified half-smiles of the jeweled and medalled Royal Family portaits lining the walls. Comfortable and unpretentious, like the English country cooking that owners Bernd and Yvonne Woerpel champion, James Bay Tea Room has earned an excellent local reputation in its first ten years as the crowds will attest. Reservations are recommended, especially in summer. Sunday High Tea includes a rich English Trifle with the daily tea fare of sandwiches, tarts, cream scones and preserves.

It may be an English custom, but the James Bay Tea Room has perfected the ritual of Afternoon Tea, that most civilized of repasts. It is the perfect way to keep that silly ferry boat water ballet smile on your face through a pleasant Victoria afternoon.

Open 7 a.m. to 9 p.m. daily except Sunday 8 a.m. to 9 p.m. with tea offered all day everyday.

MURCHIE'S

Vancouver
970 Robson St.
City Square (12th & Cambie)
1030 West Georgia Street
Park Royal Mall (North)

Richmond
Richmond Centre (next to White Spot)

Burnaby
5000 Kingsway

White Rock
1959 - 152nd Street

Victoria
1110 Government Street

Mail Order: (800) 663-0400

Murchie's is a tea retailer with a fine 100+ year tradition in the field. John Murchie, the founding father, was a tea blender and entrepreneur who delivered tea in his horse-drawn carriage. Scones are available to accompany the myriad blends.

Tea and Khaki for the British Raj in India

I think it was Napoleon who coined the phrase "An army marches on its stomach" and for the British army you'd better make sure that there's a cup of strong sweet tea to go with the food. It's even been said that we've put wars on hold while we "brewed up" our tea.

But in India in the 19th century one inspired army officer found another use for tea besides drinking it. Realizing that the traditional red tunics were too heavy and warm in the Indian summers most of the men wore white duck jackets and trousers. However both the red and the white tunics made excellent targets for the eagle-eyed, enemy riflemen. So the officer had his men brew up vats of tea and use it to dye their uniforms to a dull brown or tan, almost matching the dusty brown landscape. This became known as karkee and later officially as khaki drab. "Khak" being the Hindustani word for dust.

OAK BAY BEACH HOTEL

1175 Beach Drive
Victoria, B.C.
Phone (250) 598-4556

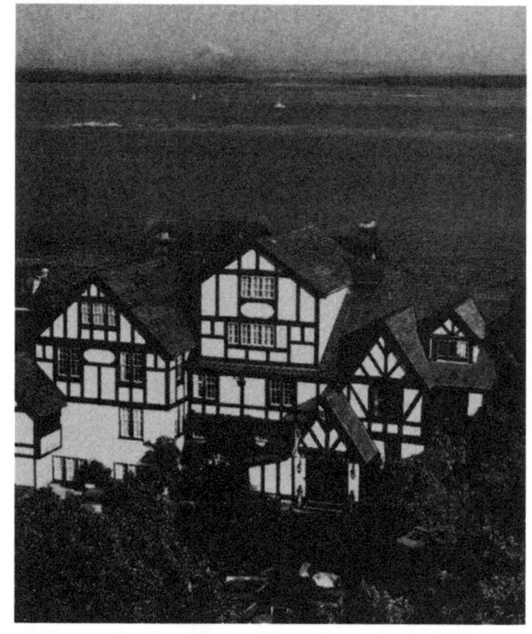

I am married to an optimist who will pull me onto a bus and then find out where it's heading. With the same anticipation that Captain Vancouver must have felt turning the bow of his ship "Discovery" into the uncharted harbors of the island that bears his name, my husband is always certain there is some destination worthy of exploration on any city's community transit bus he picks at random. We have done this all over the world. Sometimes he's right. That was how we ventured out of downtown Victoria one beautiful summer day and found ourselves in the enchanting little community of Oak Bay.

Oak Bay hugs the shoreline of Haro Strait, the passage that separates Vancouver Island from the San Juan Islands of the U.S. fifteen miles to the east. Mount Baker forms a majestic backdrop to this maritime scene, and the fortunate visitor with sharp eyes may see the distinctive dorsal fins of resident orcas cruising the chilly waters. It is this breathtaking view that the 70-year-old Oak Bay Beach Hotel proudly overlooks, a dignified dowager separated from the natural shoreline by well-manicured grounds and pristine flower beds. The Oak Bay Beach Hotel has the old world charm of an English country gentleman's estate. The half-timbered Tudor styling seems in perfect harmony with their reputation for "Olde English comforts and fine service."

Inside, the serenity of dark wood mouldings and traditional appointments imbue the dining room with a stately and tranquil air. Afternoon Tea is held here in the casually elegant dining room, Bentley's on the Bay, from 2:30 to 5:00 p.m. daily. Manager Suzanne Dobie provides an open menu offering crumpets or scones with Devon cream, petite sandwiches, assorted pastries made by Chef Graham Plews, or a rich Sherry-laced trifle. A sampling of all of these treats is offered in the Traditional High Tea in case you cannot decide, or want a little heartier meal. In addition to excellent tea, a wide range of Sherry and Port are available.

No dress code is enforced here, but good taste abounds. The service is affable and efficient, and the staff will share some delightful ideas of what not to miss on your visit to Victoria. They can even arrange a whale-watching expedition for you on the hotel's own yacht or area tours in the summer on the Oak Bay Explorer, a double-decker sight-seeing bus. It's a wonderful neighborhood for a stroll along the waterfront or through quaint specialty shops as well.

The Oak Bay Beach Hotel dining Room, Bentley's on the Bay is open for tea from 2:30 to 5:00 p.m. daily.

OAK BAY TEA ROOM

2241 Oak Bay Avenue
Victoria, B.C.
Phone (250) 370-1005

What we genuinely like about the tea experience in the Pacific Northwest is its diversity, and no where is that more readily apparent than with the two popular tea establishments that share a block of Oak Bay Avenue. Both have found their own tea niche and their own clientele. Both have a very clear sense of their own identity.

The cachet of a high style European tea awaits you at the Oak Bay Tea Room, heralded from the Avenue by a deep green awning. The presentation at your table by formal servers in the requisite black and white, is stylish and elegant. Careful attention to details of decor and presentation are enhanced by soothing classical music and a hushed, upscale bistro ambience. Hues of sage green and soft rose, fine linens and rich fabrics are as soothing to the spirit as a pot of fine tea, which you will also find here.

The Pacific Northwest celebrates its diversity in many ways. Now that diversity happily extends to Afternoon Tea in a popular block of charming Oak Bay.

Open seven days a week, 8:00 a.m. until 8:00 p.m. Reservations are recommended.

OLDE ENGLAND INN

429 Lampson Street
Victoria, B.C.
Phone (250) 388-4353

There is an interesting Yorkshire connection with a certain house in Victoria.

In 1910 a Yorkshire born investor, Thomas Slater, brought craftsmen over from England and Scotland to build his dream home, Rosmead. Built on a bluff overlooking the Strait of Juan de Fuca, and shielded from the road by tall Douglas firs, Rosmead was a rich example of half-timbered styling on a 5-acre estate. It changed hands several times over the next 20 years, and then in 1946 another Yorkshire couple, Sam and Rosina Lane, flew over from England intent on locating a mansion they could transform into an inn. They rediscovered Rosmead.

"From the start," Mrs. Lane explained, "our idea was to create a real English village of the Elizabethan period and we have now completed a number of replicas of famous places which are being added to the hotel."

They began with the birthplace of William Shakespeare and Anne Hathaway's Cottage. With a determination to maintain historical accuracy that included three years of exhaustive research, the Lanes tested the limits of endurance with the thatching of the roof of Anne Hathaway's Cottage. Through mildew and mice infestation they were able to nurse their thirteen acres of wheat to health and then flew an English thatcher in for the project.

Acquisition of a remarkable collection of period antiques occupied the free time of the Lane family, and many are displayed in the richly panelled Baronial Hall. A 300-year-old table once owned by the Bronte sisters may hold your tea service. Today Rosmead is known as Olde England Inn. It was named after Olde England Hotel on the shores of Lake Windemere in the English Lake District, and in the same spirit of hospitality, it offers unique rooms resplendent with antique furniture and period atmosphere. In the

Kings Rooms, for example, you will sleep in canopied royal beds where European crowned heads once rested (or tossed and turned depending on the state of the monarchy.)

Old Country Teas are offered Monday through Saturday, noon to 4:30 p.m. and on Sundays from 2 p.m. A full service restaurant offers meals served by a liveried staff of Elizabethan garbed "serviteurs and scullions." The Christmas feast here is legendary and an English Bobbie is on hand to direct traffic during the summer season and add to the English atmosphere.

What is the Yorkshire connection now? The menu indicates that the house Yorkshire pudding is from a 150-year-old recipe. Lose yourself in history and relax over tea exactly as they did in olde England.

Hours for tea are Monday through Saturday, noon to 4:30 p.m., and Sunday, 2:00 to 4:30 p.m.

Stands the church clock at ten to three?
And is there honey still for tea?

Rupert Brooke
The Old Vicarage

Point Ellice House

2616 Pleasant Street
Victoria, B.C.
Phone (250) 385-1518

When the cry of "Gold!" echoed along the canyons of the Fraser River in 1858, Victoria was transformed almost overnight from a quiet outpost for the Hudson Bay Company to the major outfitting headquarters for the goldfields. The price of building lots in Victoria rose from $5 to $500 as more than 20,000 fortune hunters camped around the town. Thousands more arrived from Europe flushed with the prospects of easy wealth. One of these emigrants was Peter O'Reilly.

The Honourable Peter O'Reilly was born in England, but was raised and educated in Ireland where he rose through the ranks of the Irish Constabulary. In 1859 he rushed to British Columbia to seek his fortune and was appointed Gold Commissioner. While his life from then on was devoted to the causes of public service he was also active as a private investor in land and mining ventures, and became well entrenched in the social life of Victoria's upper middle class.

During the latter half of the nineteenth century the waterfront areas that became fashionable places to live were known as Victoria Arm and Selkirk Water. Large homes were built by prominent families on both sides of this harbor. Late in 1866 Peter O'Reilly and his pregnant wife Caroline purchased Point Ellice in order that their daughter Kathleen could be born there on the eve of the New Year 1867. Kathleen's life and the story of Point Ellice House become so intricately interwoven, that it would be impossible to separate the two. There are many to this day that feel Kathleen's spiritual presence is still attached to Point Ellice House, her home for all 78 years of her life.

Kathleen enjoyed all the privileges of upper middle class British Columbia. The lovely Italianate home and waterfront gardens were the site of much of the province's social life, and numerous opportunities arose for the petite and pretty Kathleen to select a suitor. But since the selection of a lifetime mate would entail leaving her beloved Point Ellice home, Kathleen stalled and delayed the courting process until all such opportunities had passed. Decades ticked away and hearts were broken and mended, still Kathleen O'Reilly dwelled where her heart remained, among the gardens on the shores of Victoria Arm.

Today B.C. Heritage Attractions manages the property and conducts Afternoon Teas on the croquet lawn May 13 through September 8. A tape-recorded self-tour of the house and garden is the perfect introduction to tea.

All the furniture, art, wallpaper, china, clothing, ornaments, and even receipts are still as they were when Kathleen lived here. (See if you aren't aware of her presence as you pass the padded door that separates the servants' quarters from the main house and then again in the dining room.) The tea on the lawn includes fresh fruit, finger sandwiches, cream scones, fruit tart, short bread and lemon poppyseed cake. Evening and special events can be arranged, and a Fairy Tea in the garden for children is one of the popular seasonal activities.

As it was in the late 1800s, Point Ellice House has once again become a magnet for pleasant social activity and teas. Kathleen O'Reilly must be smiling again.

Tea at Point Ellice House is served outdoors on the croquet lawn May 13 through September 8, noon to 4:00 p.m.

With tea amuses the evening,
With tea solaces the midnight,
With tea welcomes the morning.
Samuel Johnson

POLLYANNA'S TEA SHOPPE

15228 Russell Avenue
White Rock, BC V4B2P6
Phone (604) 536-4322

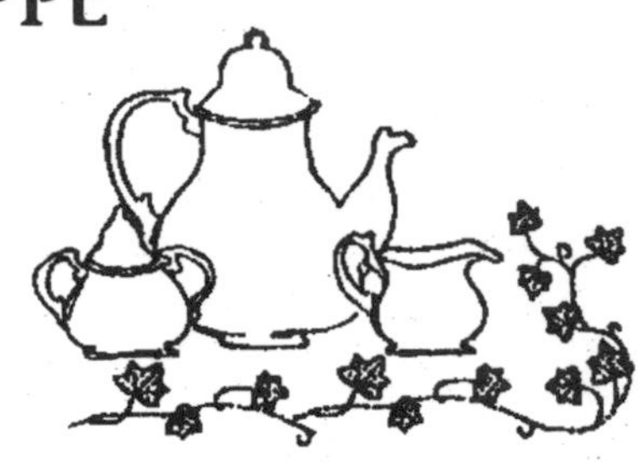

Eighteen years ago Katherine Hayes and her adult sisters vowed to carve out a little chunk of time one evening each week when they could get together and really connect over a pot of good tea. No husbands, no children, and forget those diets, this was a special evening just for them. In order to keep the time exclusively their own they often had to resort to subterfuge. Dressing up and dabbing on perfume, each lady would leave her happy home with a breezy "Gotta run, I'm off for my sorority meeting!" It even had a name. Dubbed 'Cuppa Pie Epsilon', cuppa and pie for the tea and baked goodies, "Epsilon," Katherine chuckles, "made it sound legitimately academic."

Today Katherine views those festive tea parties as practice for her bustling business venture, a delightful Victorian tea room called Pollyanna's in White Rock. This charming seaside community offers a three mile long red brick promenade along the shoreline. A stroll in the salt air is a delightful prelude to Afternoon Tea. This long narrow tea room up the hill from the beach is decorated in soothing pink and white. White capped Victorian attired servers deliver tea and treats to tables bathed in the light of Victorian hanging lamps. Priscilla curtains, Royal Albert china, and period artwork all interplay to create a cozy charm that invites you to linger.

Afternoon tea time includes a myriad of delightful choices. From the simple perfection of a scone or crumpet to a tea plate with a selection of tea sandwiches, devon cream with scone and preserves, all topped off with a French pastry; the choice is yours. Fresh homemade soups and salads, hearty meat pies and light crepes are available from the menu as well.

Katherine has graduated with honors from Cuppa Pie Epsilon, and now we're all invited to pledge her growing sisterhood of tea.

Open Monday through Thursday, 11 a.m. to 3 p.m., and Friday, Saturday, and Sunday, 11 a.m. to 7 p.m. Tea is served 10:30 a.m. to 11:30 a.m. and 2 p.m. to 3:30 p.m.

They are at the end of the gallery;
Retired to their tea and scandal.
William Congreve

SECRET GARDEN TEA COMPANY

5559 West Boulevard
Vancouver, B.C.
Phone (604) 261-3070

The fashionably eclectic neighborhood of Kerrisdale in Vancouver has a secret that you are invited to share. You are personally invited to take a few moments from your normally busy life and enter the door of the Secret Garden "where the traditions of afternoon tea are delightfully intertwined with the comforts of home."

High tea is served daily with formal tea service, fine English antique china, and fresh flowers and ivy on the three-tiered serving tray from 1:30 until closing. (Someone privy to this secret simply cannot be trusted, since it is so busy for teatime that you must make reservations 24 hours in advance now. We're sure we can trust you though, you have such an honest face.)

The room is comfortable and charming with a soft sofa that rises around you like a soft embrace and a large welcoming fireplace hearth topped with a bouquet laden mantel. Bright, homey accent pieces (many for sale) please the eye everywhere you gaze, and the selection of over 100 teas is sure to please the pickiest palate. It's like being invited to a friend's lovely home for tea, without the nagging obligatory feeling that you should volunteer to help her clean up afterwards. Go ahead, get comfy, food this tasty deserves to be savored.

Located in an area that is giving birth to interesting shopping and strolling opportunities, The Secret Garden owners Kathy Wyder and Andrea Wadman take delight in creating a special afternoon tea for you using "no mixes or artificial ingredients" whatsoever. Available for special events, showers, anniversaries and birthdays, you really should indulge yourself on occasion. Face it, you're becoming your mother anyway, so why don't you let her in on this secret? She has such an honest face.

Open daily, Monday through Wednesday, 9 a.m. to 6 p.m., Thursday through Saturday, 9 a.m. to 10 p.m., Sunday, 10 a.m. to 9 p.m.

THE SUTTON PLACE HOTEL

845 Burrard Street
Vancouver, B.C.
Phone (604) 682-5513

The Salish Indians have long seen the beauty and plenty in the area the Europeans called Vancouver. With the backdrop of dramatic mountains, they resided in peace for a couple thousand years on land that rose 38 feet above the pristine saltwater inlets and bays. The abundant land provided all they required for shelter, and food was varied and plentiful.

The first European settlers arrived a little over 130 years ago, and perhaps inspired by the plank houses the Salish built, constructed the first sawmill. Census reports show that the settlement had grown to only 2,000 inhabitants twenty years after the mill was built, but that was soon to change. From the mountains to the east, the rythmic sound of metal ringing on metal could be heard in 1886 as the final miles of track were laid for the transcontinental railroad that would forever change Vancouver. Within a couple of years the population had swelled to 27,000 as Vancouver became the western railroad terminus.

Today Vancouver has blossomed into a metropolitan area that is home to 1.5 million people, which is more than half of the entire population of British Columbia. It is the third largest city in Canada, and the fastest growing metropolitan area in North America. Enlightened urban planning has resulted in a municipality of 135 parks covering some 2,700 acres. Since no major urban freeway cuts and scars the city, you are forced to slow down, exactly like you must do to enjoy a good Afternoon Tea.

Afternoon Tea is offered at The Sutton Place Hotel (formerly Le Meridien) in the heart of the city, just a block away from popular and trendy Robson Street boutiques and eateries. (Robson Street becomes Robson Strasse west of Burrard Street which speaks to the European influence in this retail area.) Teatime at Cafe Fleuri, located in the hotel and orchestrated by Patricia Clairmont, is a soothing and tranquil experience, lightyears away from the frenzied energy of Robson. It is an excellent place to relax from sightseeing or shopping or to simply unwind between 2:30 and 5:00 p.m., Monday through Saturday.

Reminiscent of stately European manors, the hotel is furnished with period antiques, crystal chandeliers, and opulent floral displays; all the lovely Old World appeal and comfort of a fine home. A subdued elegance, without a hint of stuffiness, permeates the tea time here. From the softness of peach-toned plush wall covering and glossy white wainscoting to floral-print skirted tables, the decor inspires lingering in the casual informality. Afternoon tea here is abundant, and begins with of an array of the tastiest of English finger sandwiches, artfully presented. French pastries and the richest of warm

scones served with local berry jams and Devonshire cream follow. You choose your tea from 11 different and widely varying types which include their delicious house blend, a perfect complement to their scones - the Sutton Afternoon Blend. The service is attentive without encroaching on the most private of tea time conversation. The hotel is a favorite of well-travelled celebrities. This comes as no surprise when you view all the attention to detail and tasteful touches that Sutton Place puts into their hospitality.

As a thoughtful tribute to the rapidly-growing Asian community in Vancouver, they also offer what they call a Sutton Style Japanese Tea Ceremony, a synthesis of east and west, with a selection of three different, high quality Green Teas.

Once again, as 130 years ago, you can indulge in the abundance of Vancouver and rest assured that all your needs will be met and exceeded in the nicest possible way.

Tea is served 2:30 to 5:30 p.m., Monday through Saturday.

I suppose no person ever enjoyed with more relish
the infusion of this fragrant leaf than did Johnson.
James Boswell

SYLVIA HOTEL

1154 Gilford Street
Vancouver, B.C. V6G2P6
Phone (604) 681-9321

I know you cannot stand in the way of progress, but all of the tinted glass skyscrapers springing up in Vancouver these days make the unassuming little Sylvia Hotel all that much more beloved to me. Eight brick stories veiled in Virginia creeper create a face of simple dignity and old world charm. Located across the street from the pathways of beautiful English Bay on the south edge of Stanley Park, the Sylvia Hotel was built in 1912. It was the dream of the businessman who commissioned its construction that he would build a hotel as a legacy for each of his beloved daughters. The first, for his oldest daughter Sylvia, turned out to also be the last, as his fortune went the way of many during the Depression.

Tea is offered in the dining room daily from 4:00 to 6:00 p.m. The fresh scones, finger sandwiches and seasonal fruit are presented on attractive china to your linen covered table.

Sylvia lives in Vancouver and is in her 90s now. Having aged as gracefully as her namesake hotel, Sylvia is a regular guest for Afternoon Tea.

Tea is offered from 4:00 p.m. to 6:00 p.m. everyday. Drop-ins are welcomed.

THE TEA ROOM AT PLAZA ESCADA

757 West Hastings Street
Sinclair Centre
Vancouver, B.C.
Phone (604) 688-8558

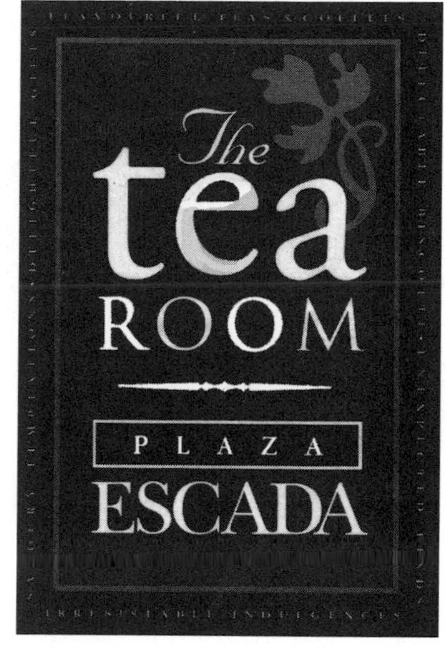

Everything about the Tea Room at Plaza Escada is Euro design-conscious, youthful, freshly modern, and pulsing with an upbeat attitude. It is, therefore, exactly what you would expect from an elite ladies fashion boutique catering to smart, self-reliant, youthful, vigorous working women of exceptionally high levels of both style and disposable income.

In keeping with the less-is-more theory, the setting at Plaza Escada's tearoom is sleek and uncluttered without being sterile. There is a no-nonsense approach to tea featuring the Republic of Tea's complete array. Since there really is no traditional Afternoon Tea here, you're free to have it anytime you want, 10:00 a.m. to closing at 6:00 p.m., Monday through Saturday. The experience is altogether refreshing. More than 40 types of tea are offered, and you can nibble delectable biscotti.

Immerse yourself in something new, imaginative and creative. Have tea at the Tea Room at Plaza Escada next time you're in downtown Vancouver.

Tea is served from 10 a.m. to 6 p.m., Monday through Saturday.

Tea is drunk to forget the din of the world.
T'ien Yiheng

TEAROOM T

2460 Heather Street
Vancouver, BC
Phone (604) 874-8320
Website: www.tealeaves.com

In 1995 fifteen youthful tea lovers (all under the age of 30) combined their many and varied talents and abundant enthusiasm and energy to create 'T'. With a mission statement to provide the public with "education, enlightenment and enchantment" through whole leaf teas from all over the world, Tearoom T is a happy celebration of cultural diversity, and a spirited forum for tea education, tea tastings and symposiums, as well as tea rituals and ceremonies.

Located in the trendy NoBo (north of Broadway) district, the idea evolved into a tea retail operation featuring more than 170 fine teas, 60 of which are always available to be served to you by the pot at simple wood tables. Assorted scones and pastries are also on hand, always presented simply in a supporting role to the star, tea.

Tea pots ranging from upmarket Italian design to the simple homely perfection of an English 'Brown Betty' line the vivid apple green shelves with hundreds of glossy black boxes of tea. Sniff jars are the olfactory treat, and the second Monday of each month a popular after-hours tea tasting by reservation is presented. In addition to a burgeoning mail order business, Tearoom T hosts popular afternoon tea dances reminiscent of the 1940s at many of the city's hotels. Details are available with a call, visit, or browse of their website.

You must marvel at the sense of direction and purpose this eclectic young group possesses. I wonder, could it just be possible that tea drinking imbues that wonderful vigor?

Open 9:30 a.m. to 7 p.m. Monday through Friday, 10 a.m. to 7:30 p.m. Saturday, and noon to 6 p.m. on Sunday.

WEDGEWOOD HOTEL

Bacchus Lounge

845 Hornby Street
Vancouver, BC
Phone (604) 689-7777

An almost constant flow of trendy and interesting people flood Robson Street daily, drifting in and out of the intimate little chic boutiques, eddying in the sidewalk cafes and ethnic eateries that define the street as Vancouver's premier shopping district. Less than a block away, the serenity and charm of an elegant boutique-style luxury hotel offers a cool, refreshing respite from this flow of humanity with a delightful Afternoon Tea in the finest European tradition.

The Wedgewood Hotel, owned and operated by Mrs. Eleni Skalbania since it was built in 1984, was created as a hospitality haven for discerning guests seeking luxurious hospitality in an intimate European atmosphere. Small by North American hotel standards with 14 floors and 94 rooms, each with a balcony, the manageable size allows a refinement of detail and personal service. This extends to the tea service in the elegance of the Bacchus Lounge as well.

The tea setting of the Bacchus Lounge recently benefited from a $1 million renovation that has imbued the room with a rich and luxurious aura. Polished cherry wood accents the burgundy and muted gold tones of the high ceilinged area. Opulent floral arrangements and antiques are warmed by the stone fireplace. Tea is served on three tiered trays, beautifully adorned, and your choice of tea is complemented by a fresh fruit compote, a variety of finger sandwiches that take full advantage of the local bounty, warm scones with cream and local preserves, tea breads or fruit cake, chocolate and assorted tea pastries.

The Wedgewood Hotel offers a refreshing eddy in the flow of life in this busy district.

Tea is offered from 2 p.m. to 4 p.m. every day. Reservations are appreciated.

WINDSOR HOUSE TEA ROOM

2540 Windsor Road
Victoria, B.C.
Phone (250) 595-3135

Locals jest that a visit to Oak Bay is so British it's like crossing behind "the Tweed Curtain." It's true that this spectacular little community unabashedly revels in its authentically British roots, after all, reminders of them abound. Even Rudyard Kipling felt at home here. While riding the free double decker bus you pass by Tudor-style shopping areas, tea rooms, crisp white cricket matches, and lovingly nurtured rose gardens. Steak and kidney pie aromas emanate from kitchen windows. Tweed-jacketed men with canes walk behind well-mannered Welsh Corgis and Jack Russells to the local pub. Cultured civility extends even to that dying art form, courteous driving.

A welcoming two story Tudor style building a block from the rocky shoreline of Oak Bay has been home to the Windsor House Tea Room for only the past five years. The air of British Empire permanence and stability it emanates bespeaks decades longer. Great taste and care have gone into the refurbishing of this old dwelling, from authentic Victorian floral patterned wallpaper and coved ceilings to the simplicity of the blue and white china service. An attractive array of gift items adorn and tempt at the same time. Lace curtains filter the sunlight through mullioned windows, and the hardwoods are polished and bright.

Their "Traditional High Tea" is offered daily from 2:30 to 5:00 p.m. as well as homemade soups, salads, and meat pies. The menu says "A good meal...a good friend...a time treasured," and the Windsor House Tea Room is a delightful place to while away an afternoon in charming surroundings.

Tea is offered everyday, 2:30 to 5:30 p.m.

THE BEST TEAROOMS OF HAWAII

Late in the 18th century winter drizzle often dampened Captain Vancouver's enthusiasm for mapping the intricate Pacific Northwest coastline. With his outdoor plans impeded by misty weather and low visibility, it's likely the good captain found his thoughts turning to sunnier climes and pineapples. Like countless Northwesterners for the next 200 years who shed their goosedown jackets and followed, Captain Vancouver pulled up anchor and headed down to the islands of Hawaii.

Honoring that fine tradition of escapism, the following section features many of the best tearooms in Hawaii. Aloha!

ASTON WAIKIKI BEACHSIDE

2452 Kalakaua Avenue
Honolulu, Oahu, Hawaii
Phone (808) 623-1030

In Hawaiian, Honolulu means "sheltered bay", a place of safety and repose. Now each weekend, in conjunction with A Special Tea Affair, the Aston Waikiki Beachside offers us that sheltered bay in the form of a Victorian Afternoon Tea.

Every Saturday and Sunday the Palm Court and the Lobby are transformed with traditional lace tablecloths, exotic floral centerpieces, and three-tiered trays presented by costumed servers. In celebration of Princess Liliuokalani's personal fascination for all things British and Queen Victoria in particular, the tea is a celebration of the link between the cultures.

Varying menus are presented which often include finger sandwiches, scones with cream and fresh preserves, and a variety of desserts.

Saturday and Sunday only, 3 p.m. to 6 p.m. with one day advance booking.

BANYAN VERANDA
at the Sheraton Moana Surf Rider

2365 Kalakaua Avenue
Honolulu, Oahu, Hawaii
Phone (808) 922-3111

Waikiki's social history is written on the faces of the landmark hotels on the shoreline. Since early this century the Moana has been a social beacon for pleasant discourse and refreshment, and an extensive restoration revived and enhanced its earlier glamour.

Family members of the big five sugar agents took tea at the Moana, perhaps sweetening their Earl Grey with the fruits of their labors. As in those more gentile times, tea is offered once again on the open veranda, beneath the spreading boughs of a shadey banyan tree in the warm sea air. Wicker furniture and fresh flowers set the tone of a bygone era, and pink clad servers in white gloves proffer tiered trays brimming with assorted tea sandwiches, warm scone with Devonshire cream and jams, pastries and cakes to accompany your tea. A rosewood scented fan is handed to each guest, to stir those lovely breezes as you take in the ocean view. As tea loving traveller Lily Yamamoto sighed, "I felt like a Southern Belle on Hawaiian time. Now when I daydream at work, I'll picture tea first then lounging on a beach."

Life is certainly sweet in Honolulu, and not all of it is because of sugar production. To immerse yourself in the sweet, soft days of another era, here is a delightful shadey spot for tea.

Tea is offered every day from 3 p.m. to 5 p.m. with reservations required.

HALEKULANI

2199 Kalia Road
Honolulu, Oahu, Hawaii
Phone (808) 923-2311

With a name that translates from Hawaiian to "house befitting heaven," you have a big clue about what's in store for you on the two mile strip of sand that constitutes Waikiki. Located on the beach, the original hotel was built in 1917, added onto stylishly in 1932, and lovingly restored in 1984 to regal opulence.

Tea is served from cane tea carts to your linen covered and flower adorned table on the veranda. Elegant and relaxing, tea on the veranda provides an gentile interlude in your vacation travels.

In addition to a variety of tea sandwiches, currant scones are served with Devonshire cream, a variety of baked goods, pastries and fruits. A comfortable tea "befitting heaven" awaits on the famous beach at Waikiki.

Tea is offered every day from 3 p.m. to 5 p.m. with no reservations required.

HAWAII PRINCE HOTEL

100 Holomoana Street
Honolulu, Oahu, Hawaii
Phone (808) 956-1111

My husband never met a yacht harbor he didn't like. The sound of the wind rattling and clanking the mast fittings is as appealing as a concerto to him. His idea of heaven includes some type of fully-equipped vessel, sleek and fast, with self-polishing brass and gleaming teak, and perpetually headed to some exotic shore under full sail where you can pick your dinner off a tree.

The Marina Front Lounge of the Hawaii Prince Hotel affords folks like Ken a glimpse of such a heaven. Not only can you watch the activity of the Alawal Yacht Harbor, but there's tea too. In the comfortable surroundings of soft pastel couches and linen covered tables, the courteous and open staff serve assorted tea sandwiches that can include shrimp, watercress, or cucumber fillings, scones with Devonshire cream, pretty petit fours, and a chocolate dipped strawberry with your tea choice. The atmosphere is relaxed and casual, comfortable and it overlooks heaven in one man's opinion.

Tea is offered every day 4 p.m. to 6 p.m. with one day advance reservation and guarantee please.

LODGE AT KOELE

Kaemoku Highway
Lanai City, Lanai, Hawaii
Phone (808) 565-7300

"Norfolk Pines?" visitors often scratch their heads as they stare up at this unexpected flora on the central plateau of Lanai. It was a New Zealander and naturalist, Geoge Munro, who on his days off from managing the Lanai Ranch, rode through the mountains planting these seedlings. Since that time in 1910, the seedlings have become statuesque at this 1,600 foot elevation, and generations of visitors have relaxed in the casual seclusion of the island.

In 1924 the entire island was purchased by pineapple baron Jim Dole for $1.1 million (about the cost of Bill Gate's garage.) Today more than a million pineapples a day are loaded on barges bound for the canneries of Oahu.

The Lodge at Koele was gently developed by the corporate successor to Jim Dole's company, Castle & Cooke, to celebrate the unique natural beauty of this "Pineapple Island." Island stone fireplace, heavy beamed ceilings and porches define the lodge, where tea is served daily in the casual setting of their Tea Room, Music Room or porch buffet style. Local coconut makes melt in your mouth macaroons, local citrus curd, light freshly baked scones, and assorted tea sandwiches are always adorned with fresh pineapple and other fruit. What could be more appropriate.

Tea is served at 3 p.m. every day, with reservations a good idea.

PRINCEVILLE HOTEL

Ka Haku Road
Princeville, Kauai, Hawaii
Phone (808) 826-9644 or (800) 826-4400

When explorer James Cook dropped anchor off the island of Kauai in 1778 he was well into his voyage of discovery. His landing clearly delineates the beginning of the western influences of this paradise of sheer cliffs, dense jungles, volcanos and beaches. One can only speculate that this brave British explorer might have relished a good strong pot of the brew that unites East and West, tea.

The North Shore region is an area rich in ancient sacred sites and unrivaled beauty, and is the location of one of the world's best resorts, the Princeville Hotel. Afternoon Tea is served at soft couches and armchairs in the living room with an unsurpassed view of Hanalei Bay, film location for South Pacific. Tea fare varies with the season, but can include traditional tea sandwiches, tea breads, pastries, fresh fruit tarts, strawberries with Grand Marnier and cream.

With the perfumed breezes blowing up from the bay mingling with the aroma of rich hot tea, Captain Cook would have felt right at home.

Tea is served everyday from 3 to 5 p.m., reservations are a must.

RITZ CARLTON KAPALUA

1 Ritz Carlton Drive
Kapalua, Maui, Hawaii
Phone (808) 669-6200

Like generations of us who shed our thermal underwear and followed, Captain George Vancouver was anxious to leave for Hawaii when winter chills hampered his mapping expeditions in the Pacific Northwest. Gaining the confidence and friendship of King Kamehameha I, he solidified the British presence in the Hawaiian Islands in the 1790s and probably enjoyed the feel of warm sand between his toes at the same time.

Set amid the dramatic scenery of craggy cliffs and sparkling blue Pacific, the Ritz Carlton Kapalua nestles like a gem in the sun. As with Ritz Carlton properties in every other of their locations, elegance, excellence and superb service are the rule. Afternoon Tea here rises to that occasion with delicate tea sandwiches, scones with cream, pastries and island fruit. There are two locations for tea. Indoors the dark panelling and loomed carpets of the Lobby Lounge provides a subdued and elegant contrast to the colorful umbrellas and blooming plants of the terrace.

Like Captain Vancouver, it's always nice to have a choice.

Tea is served daily from 2:30 to 4:30 p.m. with one day advance notice and guarantee please.

THE VOLCANO TEAPOT TEA ROOM

19-4041 Kilauea, P.O. Box 511
Volcano, Hawaii 96785
Phone (808) 967-7112

At an elevation of 3,800 feet on the side of an active volcano in Kona coffee country lies a tea room like no other.

The Volcano Teapot is a combination tea room and Bed and Breakfast housed in a restored turn of the century guest cottage in the heart of Volcano Village. Originally part of a large estate, the cottage now sits on the remaining 2.5 acres of pine trees, fruit trees, camellias, fern and native exotics. In an area where winter temperatures can reach as low as 38, and the lava flows as high as 1,000 degrees, it is an area of unexpected contrasts.

Antoinette Bullough and her husband Bill chose this setting for their charming business. Special tea events and classes are set amid the antiques, fresh flowers, four-poster bed, and soft comforters of the guest cottage warmed by the glow of a wood-burning stove. Less than a mile from the magical lava flows of Volcanoes National Park, misty rainforests, and birdwatching hotspots, the tea room is close to and cozy with the mythological home of Pele, the Goddess of Fire in Kilauea caldera. With the Goddess of Fire overseeing the preparation of tea, a visit to the Volcano Teapot Tea Room is likely to warm you from head to toe.

Call or write for schedule of upcoming tea events, or to schedule tea for yourself.

SANDWICHES & SAVORIES

TOMATO-BASIL TEA SANDWICHES

So simple and such a nice blend of fresh flavors we are indebted to our friend, Tom Caulton, for this tea sandwich and much more. Inventor, composer, computer genius, Tom is one of those people that occupies a higher mental plane than just about anyone we know.

8 slices white bread
1/2 cup ricotta cheese
Salt and pepper
1 T. your choice of Italian salad dressing
2 small ripe tomatoes, sliced
8 fresh basil leaves

Cut a circle of bread from each slice, using a round cookie cutter. Mix the ricotta cheese with salt and pepper to taste and 1 T. Italian salad dresing. Place a tomato slice on each of the four rounds, top with a basil leaf and cover with remaining round. Cut in half to yield 16 tea sandwiches.

Nutritional Analysis per Serving
Calories: 54, Total Fat: 1.9 g., Saturated Fat: .8 g.
Cholesterol: 4 mg., Carbohydrate: 7.2 g., Dietary Fiber: .5 g.
Protein: 2.0 g., Sodium: 82 mg.

PEAR AND STILTON SANDWICHES

The last day of one trip to England found us in Winchester on a chilly autumn day. Sitting by a fire in a tearoom with Pear and Stilton Sandwiches, a glass of Port, and a pot of tea refreshed us for our usual mad dash to the airport for the return flight home.

4 very thin slices honey-oat bread
1 T. butter, softened
1 ripe pear, Bosc or Anjou, halved and thinly sliced
fresh lemon juice
2 T. crumbled Stilton cheese (about 1/2 oz.)

Spread each slice of bread with the softened butter. Sprinkle the pear slices with lemon juice. Place half of the pear slices in a single layer on a slice of bread. Top with half of the crumbled cheese and a second bread slice. Repeat, using the remaining pear, cheese and bread. Trim crusts and cut into 8 finger sandwiches.

Nutritional Analysis per Serving
Calories: 68, Total Fat: 2.6 g., Saturated Fat: 1.3 g.
Cholesterol: 5 mg., Carbohydrate: 9.9 g., Dietary Fiber: 1.0 g.
Protein: 1.6 g., Sodium: 120 mg.

CUCUMBER TEA SANDWICHES

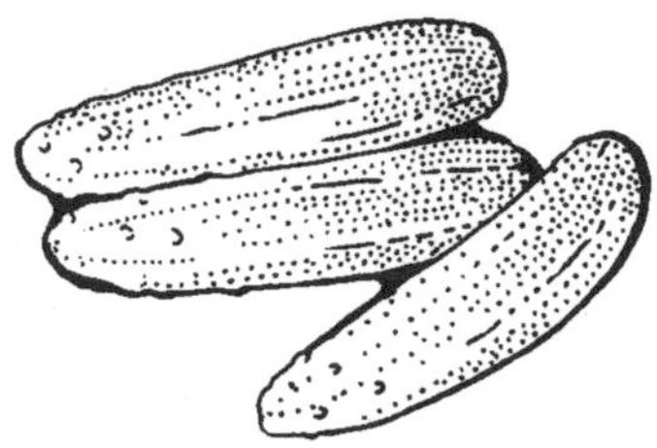

Samuel Johnson said, "A cucumber should be well sliced, and dressed with pepper and vinegar, and then thrown out, as good for nothing." My husband agrees with him, but I do not.

2 medium cucumbers, peeled, sliced thin
1 cup apple cider vinegar
1 T. sugar
salt and pepper

Fresh mint leaves
1/4 cup mayonnaise

Marinate the cucumber slices in the brine made from the vinegar, sugar, salt and pepper for at least an hour. Drain well. Remove the crusts from 6 slices of thin white bread. Spread lightly with mayonnaise. Lay four fresh mint leaves on each of 3 slices. Over the top of the mint leaves layer the drained cucumber slices. Top with the other bread slice, mayonnaise side down, and cut into four small finger sandwiches. Garnish with mint. Makes 12 tea sandwiches.

Nutritional Analysis per Serving
Calories: 77, Total Fat: 4.2 g., Saturated Fat: .7 g.
Cholesterol: 3 mg., Carbohydrate: 9 g., Dietary Fiber: .7 g.
Protein: 1.4 g., Sodium: 117 mg.

Cucumber Herb Butter Tea Sandwiches

Sir Compton McKenzie (1883-1972), in describing an English tea party, was not very charitable to the cucumber. Since I love cucumbers, I detest this quote. Ken, however, detests cucumbers and finds it fitting: "You are offered a piece of bread and butter that feels like a damp handkerchief and sometimes, when cucumber is added to it, like a wet one."

- 1 medium cucumber, peeled and salted to taste
- 4 T. butter, softened
- 1/2 T. fresh dill
- 4 thin slices of firm white bread, crusts removed

Cut the cucumber into thin slices and place them on a paper towel. Salt the cucumber lightly and cover with a paper towel. Let stand for a half hour so that any extra moisture is absorbed.

In a blender or a bowl, combine the butter and the chopped dill. Lightly spread the butter on each slice of bread, buttering all the way to the edges.

Place 9 or more cucumber slices on one slice of bread, layering them in three rows. Top with a second slice of bread. Cut the sandwich with a sharp, serrated knife diagonally to create triangles. Makes 8 finger sandwiches.

Nutritional Analysis per Serving
Calories: 89, Total Fat: 6.2 g., Saturated Fat: 3.6 g.
Cholesterol: 15 mg., Carbohydrate: 7.3 g., Dietary Fiber: .6 g.
Protein: 1.4 g., Sodium: 126 mg.

CARMELIZED WALLA WALLA SWEET AND CREAM CHEESE TEA SANDWICH

- 1 Walla Walla Sweet onion, finely chopped
- 3 tsp. butter
- 4 slices of raisin bread
- 1/4 cup cream cheese

Heat butter in skillet over medium-low heat. Add onion and cook, stirring often, about 15 to 20 minutes, until the onion is brown and carmelized. Remove from heat and allow to cool.

Spread cream cheese over bread. Spread onions over two of the slices and top with the other two slices.

Wrap and refrigerate until firm, about 15 minutes. Trim crusts, cut into four rectangles. Makes 8 tea sandwiches.

Nutritional Analysis per Serving
Calories: 77, Total Fat: 4.4 g., Saturated Fat: 2.5 g.
Cholesterol: 12 mg., Carbohydrate: 7.7 g., Dietary Fiber: .8 g.
Protein: 1.9 g., Sodium: 106 mg.

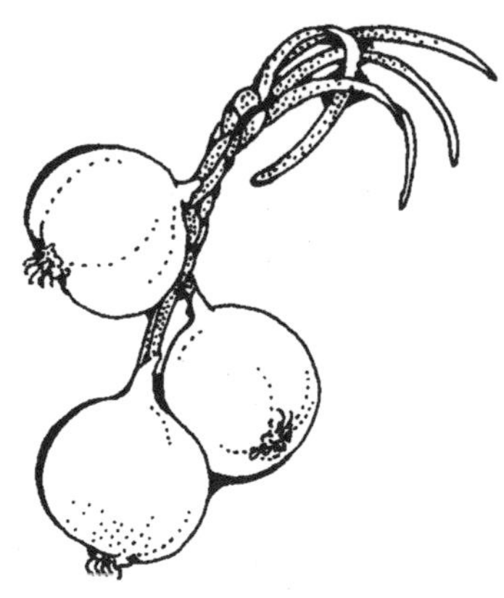

DUNGENESS CRAB AND BLACK OLIVE TEA SANDWICHES

8 oz. softened cream cheese
1/4 lb. Dungeness crabmeat
1/2 cup chopped black olives, drained
1 medium cucumber, peeled and sliced into 20 very thin slices
1 bunch fresh watercress sprigs
1 T. lemon peel
1 French baguette, sliced thin.

Beat the cream cheese until smooth, blend in the crab and olives until well mixed. Spread 1 tablespoon crab mixture onto each slice of French bread and top with cucumber slices and sprig of watercress. Top with remaining thinly sliced baguette to form a sandwich.

Makes 20 finger sandwiches.

Nutritional Analysis per Serving
Calories: 113, Total Fat: 5.1 g., Saturated Fat: 2.7 g.
Cholesterol: 17 mg., Carbohydrate: 12.8 g., Dietary Fiber: .8 g.
Protein: 4.1 g., Sodium: 219 mg.

WATERCRESS, RADISH AND CREAM CHEESE TEA SANDWICHES

1 bunch radishes (about 8 small radishes)
2 thin slices 5 grain bread
4 tsp. cream cheese
6 sprigs watercress (leaves only, no stems)
salt to taste

Wash and cut the radishes into very thin slices. Spread the cream cheese on the bread. Press 3 sprigs of watercress into the cream cheese on each slice of bread. Top each with a few slices of radish and salt lightly. Cut each slice into 4 finger sandwiches. Serve open-faced. Makes 8 tea sandwiches.

Nutritional Analysis per Serving
Calories: 27, Total Fat: 1.1 g., Saturated Fat: .6 g.
Cholesterol: 3 mg., Carbohydrate: 3.5 g., Dietary Fiber: .4 g.
Protein: .8 g., Sodium: 83 mg.

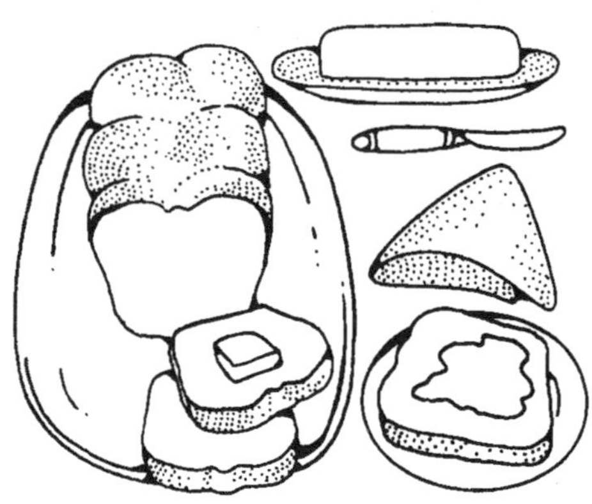

Mini-Shrimp Sandwiches

Along the Oregon coast you can get shrimp so fresh and tasty that you can find yourself trying to work them into every recipe. Here's one way to make room for them on your tea table.

- 8 oz. whipped cream cheese
- 8 oz. salad shrimp, diced
- 1 clove garlic
- 1/4 cup chopped chives
- 1/4 tsp. salt
- Freshly ground pepper
- 1 stick butter
- Juice of 1 small lemon
- 2 tsp. fresh parsley
- 20 slices thinly sliced white bread

Mix together cream cheese, shrimp, garlic, chives, salt and pepper. In a separate bowl, cream butter, adding lemon juice and parsley. Spread butter mixture on 10 slices bread, then spread on the cream cheese/shrimp mixture.

Top with the remaining bread slices and remove crusts. Cut each sandwich into 4 triangles or 4 squares.

Makes 40 tea sandwiches.

Nutritional Analysis per Serving
Calories: 80, Total Fat: 4.8 g., Saturated Fat: 2.8 g.
Cholesterol: 21 mg., Carbohydrate: 6.5 g., Dietary Fiber: .3 g.
Protein: 2.7 g., Sodium: 129 mg.

EAST INDIAN TEA SANDWICHES

When India was part of the British Empire, afternoon tea was introduced there. This recipe shows the successful blending of those cultures.

- 3/4 cup chopped cooked chicken breast
- 1/3 cup chutney
- 1/4 tsp. curry powder
- 2/3 cup mayonaisse
- 6 slices bread

Mix together and spread 3 tablespoons on each slice of bread. Trim crusts and cut into 4 equal strips.

Nutritional Analysis per Serving
Calories: 80, Total Fat: 5.8 g., Saturated Fat: 1.0 g.
Cholesterol: 8 mg., Carbohydrate: 5.0 g., Dietary Fiber: .3 g.
Protein: 2.2 g., Sodium: 83 mg.

Shepherd's Pie

Cheshire Cat - Vancouver, Washington

Here's a tasty dish for High Tea from Avril Massey of the Cheshire Cat, and a good way to use leftover mashed potatoes. This is a traditional dish of the English countryside.

1 lb. ground beef or lamb
1 large onion, diced
2 carrots, diced
1 tsp. Bisto or gravy browning
1/3 tsp. garlic salt
1-1/2 lb. cooked, mashed potatoes
2 cups medium cheddar cheese, shredded
1/2 pint water

Fry the ground meat, seasonings, and vegetables until lightly browned. Add water and gravy browning and bring to a boil then simmer lightly for 15 minutes, stir occasionally.

Transfer to an oven-proof dish, cover with the mashed potatoes and cheese and bake in a 350° F. oven about 30 minutes until golden brown.

Serves 4.

TEA NOTE

For tea service, Avril suggests a Yorkshire Red.

Nutritional Analysis per Serving
Calories: 714, Total Fat: 47.5 g., Saturated Fat: 24.4 g.
Cholesterol: 146 mg., Carbohydrate: 33.7 g., Dietary Fiber: 1.7 g.
Protein: 37.6 g., Sodium: 964 mg.

CRAB AND HERB MINI PASTIE

Tea and Tomes • Newport, Oregon

The wonderful fresh crab, abundant in our waters, makes this recipe especially tasty.

8 oz. herbed cream cheese (make it yourself or buy it at the grocers)
1/4 lb. fresh or frozen crab meat, thoroughly drained
1/4 cup black olives, drained and chopped
1 T. coarsely shredded lemon peel

2 sheets puff pastry dough - thawed

Mix together the cream cheese, crab, olives and lemon peel - set aside. Using a 2 in. round cookie cutter, cut 24 rounds from pastry. Place 1 tsp. crab filling on each round, fold over into half circle.

Using a fork crimp edges to seal. Place on an ungreased baking sheet and bake for 15 minutes at 350° F. or until golden brown. Serve warm with or without dusting of parsley over top.

Makes 24 mini pasties.

Nutritional Analysis per Serving
Calories: 168, Total Fat: 12.5 g., Saturated Fat: 3.4 g.
Cholesterol: 14 mg., Carbohydrate: 11 g., Dietary Fiber: 0 g.
Protein: 3.3 g., Sodium: 113 mg.

GARDEN PEAS AND SHRIMP ON TOAST

We've given up trying to grow peas. The rabbits find them irresistable. Fortunately good farmers' markets abound in our area.

1	stick butter, softened
1/4	lb. shelled fresh peas, rinsed
	Salt and pepper to taste
1	clove fresh garlic, minced
1/4	lb. fresh salad shrimp
8	oz. softened cream cheese
4	slices toasted bread, crusts removed
1	tsp. finely chopped dill
1	tsp. thyme

Melt 2 tablespoons butter in medium skillet. Add the peas and saute gently for about 8 minutes. Season to taste with salt and pepper, remove from heat. Allow to cool.

After the peas have cooled, add 4 tablespoons butter, garlic, and shrimp. Spread the toast with the remaining butter, the cream cheese, and top with the pea-shrimp mixture. Sprinkle with dill and thyme.

Cut into four squares or triangles. Serves 4.

Nutritional Analysis per Serving
Calories: 522, Total Fat: 44.2 g., Saturated Fat: 27.1 g.
Cholesterol: 180 mg., Carbohydrate: 18.6 g., Dietary Fiber: 2.1 g.
Protein: 14.2 g., Sodium: 602 mg.

CRAB-FILLED PUFFS

While living in Alaska for eight years, I learned to use crab in many recipes. Here is one that is a suitable and festive addition to your tea.

Crab filling:

- 1 lb. crabmeat, flaked
- 4 hard-boiled eggs, finely chopped
- 1/4 cup celery, finely chopped
- 1/4 cup onion, finely chopped
- 1 T. fresh parsley, minced
- 2 T. chili sauce
- 1-1/2 cup mayonnaise
- salt and pepper to taste

Mix all ingredients together, adding enough mayonnaise to bind. Refrigerate until shortly before serving. Fill puffs immediately prior to serving.

Puffs:

- 1 cup water
- 1/2 cup butter
- 1 cup sifted flour
- 4 eggs

Bring water to boiling, add butter. Stir until melted. Add flour, stirring briskly until dough forms a ball. Beat eggs until very thick and lemony-colored. Stir into cooled dough; blend thoroughly. Drop by teaspoonfuls onto baking sheet. Bake in preheated 400° F. oven for 15 minutes. Cool on rack.

To serve, slice and fill immediately prior to serving. Makes 24 puffs.

Nutritional Analysis per Serving
Calories: 194, Total Fat: 16.7 g., Saturated Fat: 4.6 g.
Cholesterol: 104 mg., Carbohydrate: 4.8 g., Dietary Fiber: .1 g.
Protein: 6.3 g., Sodium: 224 mg.

Chicken Salad

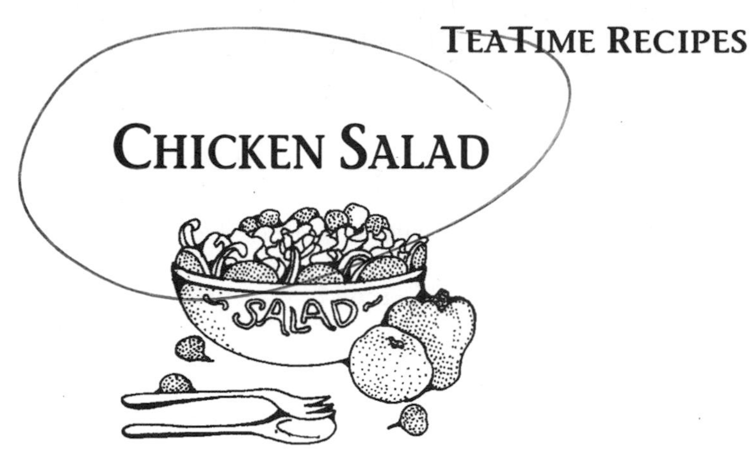

Attic Secrets • Marysville, Washington

"And we meet, with champagne and a chicken, at last."
Lady Mary Wortley Montague
"The Lover"

4 cooked chicken breasts (boneless and skinless)
1/2 cup mayonaisse
1/4 cup chopped pecans
2 T. chopped celery
1/2 tsp. onion powder
Salt and pepper to taste

Serve on lettuce or as a spread. Yields 6 servings.

Nutritional Analysis per Serving
Calories: 265, Total Fat: 18.8 g., Saturated Fat: 2.7 g.
Cholesterol: 65 mg., Carbohydrate: 1.6 g., Dietary Fiber: .4 g.
Protein: 22.1 g., Sodium: 212 mg.

CHIVE BLOSSOMS

"Blossom by blossom
The spring begins."
Algernon C. Swinburne

1 box frozen puff pastry sheets (2 sheets) thawed
1 8 oz. container soft cream cheese with chives spread
Garnishes: watercress or parsley

Bring cream cheese to room temperature. Preheat oven to 375° F. Unfold pastry and place on lightly floured surface. Roll lightly to eliminate fold lines.

Using a 2-1/2" scalloped cookie cutter, cut about 18 circles from each sheet. Gently press the pastry circles into ungreased cups of miniature muffin pans. Pastry will resemble a flower.

Fill each lined cup with about 1/2 tsp. cream cheese and bake 15 to 20 minutes. Cool slightly, remove from pan onto wire rack and top each with sprig of watercress or parsley. Makes 36.

Serve warm.

Nutritional Analysis per Serving
Calories: 281, Total Fat: 20.1 g., Saturated Fat: 3.9 g.
Cholesterol: 7 mg., Carbohydrate: 21.4 g., Dietary Fiber: 0.0 g.
Protein: 3.9 g., Sodium: 136 mg.

SCOTCH EGGS

I ate my very first Scotch Egg in Wales at a little pub in coastal Conwy. I remember looking at it and thinking "How'd they do that?" Conwy Castle, built in 1292, today houses Britain's first and most famous teapot museum. Home to more than 1,000 pots, there is also a gift shop called Char Bazaar for replicas.

2 tsp. all-purpose flour
4 hard boiled eggs, shelled
1 tsp. Worcestshire sauce
1/2 lb. bulk pork sausage
1 egg, beaten
1 cup fine dry bread crumbs
Vegetable oil for deep-frying
Parsley for garnish

Combine flour with salt and pepper in a small bowl, sprinkle over eggs. Add the Worcestshire sauce to sausage and mix well. Divide sausage into 4 equal portions and form each into a flat patty.

Place 1 of the hard boiled eggs into the center of each patty and shape the meat around the egg, covering the egg completely.

Coat the meat with the beaten egg, then roll in bread crumbs. Heat 3 inches of oil to 350° F. and gently add the meat-covered eggs. Cook for 7 or 8 minutes until crisp and golden.

Drain on paper towels and cool before slicing in half and serving, garnishing cut side with the fresh parsley.

Makes 8 halves. Serve with salad for high tea.

Nutritional Analysis per Serving (One-half egg)
Calories: 253, Total Fat: 18.9 g., Saturated Fat: 5.7 g.
Cholesterol: 152 mg., Carbohydrate: 11.2 g., Dietary Fiber: .7 g.
Protein: 8.9 g., Sodium: 330 mg.

FLINN'S OYSTER FLAN

Flinn's Tea Parlour - Albany, Oregon

"Four young oysters hurried up,
All eager for the treat;
Their coats were brushed, their faces washed,
Their shoes were clean and neat -
And this was odd, because, you know, they hadn't any feet."
Lewis Carroll, Through the Looking Glass

Rice crust:

1	cup long grain rice	2	cups water
2	eggs	1/2	cup grated Parmesan
1	T. Soy Sauce	1	tsp. white pepper
1	tsp. granulated garlic		

Cook rice and let cool, mix well with the other ingredients and press into a well greased 9 x 12 inch pan to about 1/4 to 3/8 inch thick. Place into a preheated oven at 400° F. for 10 minutes, remove and let cool.

Filling:

4 eggs well beaten with1 tsp. baking powder
1/2 cup heavy cream
6 strips bacon finely chopped
12 medium oysters, shucked
1/2 cup spring onion chopped with greens
1 cup fresh spinach finely chopped
Pinch of salt & white pepper
1 cup shredded Swiss cheese

Mix eggs, cheese, salt and pepper then pour into pan on top of crust. Cook bacon until tender. Sprinkle onion, spinach, and bacon evenly in pan. Place oysters 3 across and 4 down so they are centered when cutting. Bake at 350° F. for 30-40 minutes or until flan is set. Cut into 3-inch squares and serve warm. Makes 12 servings.

Nutritional Analysis per Serving
Calories: 195, Total Fat: 11.7 g., Saturated Fat: 6.0 g.
Cholesterol: 141 mg., Carbohydrate: 12.4 g., Dietary Fiber: .3 g.
Protein: 9.7 g., Sodium: 232 mg.

LEEK, BACON & POTATO TART

Chez Nous - Seattle, Washington

A High Tea favorite using the traditional symbol of Wales, the leek.

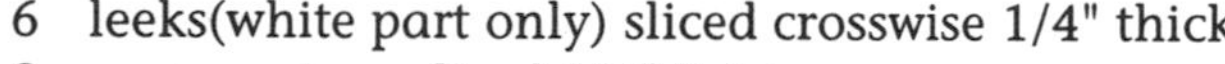

6 leeks(white part only) sliced crosswise 1/4" thick
6-8 green onions sliced 1/4" thick
5 small potatoes, boiled in skin, peeled and diced into 1/2" cubes
6 strips thick cut bacon, diced
5 garlic cloves, chopped

3 large eggs
1 1/4 cups half & half
1/2 cup Pecorino Romano Cheese, grated
1/2 cup fresh basil, chopped
3/4 tsp. dried oregano
1 tsp. salt
1/2 tsp. freshly grated black pepper
4 garlic cloves, finely crushed

Plain pastry to line a 12" fluted tart pan with removable bottom.

Spray tart pan with vegetable spray and line with the pastry bringing the pastry up the sides of the pan and cutting off the excess. Bake at 425° F. for 5 minutes.

Saute the diced bacon until brown and crispy, drain off all but 1 table-spoon of the fat, (a non-stick pan should be used if possible) and saute the leeks, onions and garlic until tender. Cover the pan if necessary to prevent it from becoming too dry.

Arrange the bacon, sauted vegetables and potatoes in the bottom of the tart pan. Combine all the custard ingredients in a bowl and mix well with a whisk and gently pour over the vegetables. Grate a little Pecorino Romano and an optional sprinkle of chopped parsley on top. Bake in the top third of the oven for approximately 30 minutes at 425° F. Check tart after 25 minutes, custard should be set and the top should be golden brown. Cook another 5-10 minutes if the center is still liquid. It is important to use a hot oven so that the pastry is well cooked, not soggy. Makes 12 servings.

Nutritional Analysis per Serving
Calories: 191, Total Fat: 7.4 g., Saturated Fat: 3.6 g.
Cholesterol: 70 mg., Carbohydrate: 25.1 g., Dietary Fiber: 3.9 g.
Protein: 8.2 g., Sodium: 338 mg.

ORIENTAL TEA HONEY RIBS

- 2 lb. pork spareribs
- 1 cup strong brewed Lapsong Souchon tea
- 1/4 cup soy sauce
- 1/2 cup honey

Place ribs in baking pan, cover, bake 425° F. for 1 hour. Pour off all fat, cut ribs into pieces. Combine tea with other ingredients. Pour over ribs and bake, uncovered, basting periodically for 30 or 40 more minutes (or until crispy brown and tender.) Serves 4.

Nutritional Analysis per Serving
Calories: 786, Total Fat: 53.6 g., Saturated Fat: 20.3 g.
Cholesterol: 177 mg., Carbohydrate: 36.3 g., Dietary Fiber: .2 g.
Protein: 39.7 g., Sodium: 1,005 mg.

Scones, Breads & Muffins

OATMEAL BREAKFAST SCONES

Scones originated in Scotland near the town of Scone which is known for much more than tea-time biscuits. For centuries Scottish rulers were crowned while seated on a large, mystical Coronation Stone, known as the "Stone of Scone." In 1296, the conquering English army under Edward I confiscated the stone in an effort to unify all Britain. The stone rested under the Coronation throne in Westminister Abbey for years but was returned to Scotland in 1997.

Prepared correctly, this authentic scone recipe will not resemble the Stone of Scone.

1 cup all-purpose flour
1 cup rolled oats
1/2 tsp. baking soda
1/2 tsp. salt
1 tsp. cream of tartar
1 T. sugar
1/4 cup shortening
1/2 cup milk

Preheat oven to 425° F. Mix together flour, oats, baking soda, salt, cream of tartar, and sugar. Add the shortening and milk, and mix with fork into a soft dough. Roll out on a floured board to 1/2 " thickness. Cut into triangles. Place on greased baking sheet, and bake for 15 minutes or until lightly browned. Serve for breakfast or tea, warm with butter and jam. Makes 8-12 scones.

Nutritional Analysis per Serving
Calories: 135, Total Fat: 6.2 g., Saturated Fat: 1.6 g.
Cholesterol: 2 mg., Carbohydrate: 17 g., Dietary Fiber: .9 g.
Protein: 3.0 g., Sodium: 70 mg.

OAK BAY SCONES

Oak Bay Beach Hotel • Victoria, B.C.

Chef Graham Plews brought this recipe to the Oak Bay Beach Hotel in 1994 from his family recipe file.

3 cups flour
1 cup sugar
2 T. baking powder
1 cup shortening
4 eggs
1 cup buttermilk

Sift dry ingredients together. Cut in shortening to a fine crumb. Beat eggs and blend with milk. Combine wet and dry ingedients

Knead dough slightly to firm up for rolling. Roll dough to 3/4" thickness and cut into 3" rounds

Bake at 375 F. for 20-30 minutes. Makes 24 scones.

Nutritional Analysis per Serving
Calories: 241, Total Fat: 10.7 g., Saturated Fat: 2.7 g.
Cholesterol: 36 mg., Carbohydrate: 32.3 g., Dietary Fiber: 0 g.
Protein: 4.3 g., Sodium: 208 mg.

CANDIED GINGER SCONES

Butchart Gardens • Victoria, B.C.

5	cups all-purpose flour
2	tsp. baking powder
1/3	cup white sugar
1-1/4	cup unsalted butter
1/2	cup candied ginger
5	large eggs
2/3	cup + 2 T. milk (2%)

Preheat oven to 350° F. Mix flour, baking powder and sugar together in a medium-sized bowl. Dice candied ginger. Using a pastry cutter, blend butter and candied ginger into flour mixture until butter is in pea sized pieces.

In a separate bowl, mix eggs and milk. Add milk mixture to flour/butter mixture and blend until combined. Place dough on a lightly floured counter and knead lightly.

Roll dough to a 1/2" thickness. Cut into 3" circles.

Place on an unfloured baking sheet and bake at 350° F. for 15 - 20 minutes, until golden brown. Makes 24.

Nutritional Analysis per Serving
Calories: 228, Total Fat: 11.7 g., Saturated Fat: 6.8 g.
Cholesterol: 76 mg., Carbohydrate: 23.2 g., Dietary Fiber: 0 g.
Protein: 4.4 g., Sodium: 49 mg.

TEA AN' TIQUES SCONES

Spokane, Washington

Owner Jackie Hayes was given this recipe by a good friend, and finds it versatile enough to change with addition of spices, fruits or cheese. Here's your chance to get creative.

- 2 cups flour
- 1 cup oats
- 1/4 cup sugar (omit if making a cheese or herb scone.)
- 1 T. baking powder
- 1/2 tsp. salt
- 1/4 tsp. cream of tarter
- 1/2 cup butter
- 1/3 cup buttermilk, cream or milk
- 2 eggs
- 1-1/2 tsp. vanilla (omit for a herb scone or substitute with extracts of almond, lemon, orange, etc.)

Combine dry ingredients and cut in butter using a pastry blender until mixture resembles coarse meal. Add remaining ingredients and blend well to form a dough.

Press into a round cake pan and bake at 425° F. for 15-18 minutes then cut into 8 wedges to serve.

Serve warm with jams, honey or a heated cream cheese for the herb or cheese scones.

Makes 8 scones.

Nutritional Analysis per Serving
Calories: 339, Total Fat: 14.4 g., Saturated Fat: 7.8 g.
Cholesterol: 84 mg., Carbohydrate: 44.2 g., Dietary Fiber: 0 g.
Protein: 8.5 g., Sodium: 413 mg.

JAMAICA MON! SCONES

Bella - Resort Street Fine Spirits & Tearoom
Baker City, Oregon

1 cup dried currants
1/4 cup rum

2 cups all-purpose flour
1 T. baking powder
2 T. sugar
1 tsp. salt

2 oz. very cold butter (1/2 stick)
Skim buttermilk to make one cup liquid (see below)
1 egg white, whisked

Preheat oven to 400° F.

Combine rum and currants in a glass bowl. Microwave for one minute on high, toss lightly to mix and set aside to cool slightly. Separate currants from remaining liquids, set both aside.

Blend together flour, baking powder, sugar and salt. Cut in butter with pastry blender or two knives until mixture resembles coarse meal. Stir in currants.

Pour remaining liquid into a one cup measuring cup. Fill with skim buttermilk and add to flour mixture. Bring dough together with fork, turn out onto lightly floured surface and coat with flour. Pat dough into a 9 – 10-inch circle. Cut dough into 8 wedges, place on parchment-lined baking sheet, brush with egg white and bake 15 minutes. Makes 8 servings.

Nutritional Analysis per Serving
Calories: 247, Total Fat: 6.1 g., Saturated Fat: 3.6 g.
Cholesterol: 16 mg., Carbohydrate: 40.8 g., Dietary Fiber: 1.2 g.
Protein: 4.5 g., Sodium: 470 mg.

Fresh Strawberry Rhubarb Scones

Wild Rose Tea Room - Redmond, Oregon

Bessie, the owner of Wild Rose, ended a letter to us about her tea room with "If there is anything special about this place it is because love built it." A lot of love goes into her scones too. Here is one of her favorites she wants to share with you.

- 3-1/4 cups flour
- 1/4 cup sugar
- 1 tsp. salt
- 1/2 tsp. cream of tartar
- 1 tsp. cinnamon
- 1 cube butter (1/2 cup)
- 1 egg
- 1/2 cup sour cream
- 2/3 cup half & half
- 1 tsp. vanilla
- 1 cup rhubarb, chopped
- 1/2 cup fresh strawberries, chopped

Combine flour, sugar, salt, cream of tartar and cinnamon in a large bowl. Cut in butter using pastry blender or two knives until mixture resembles coarse meal.

In a separate bowl whisk together egg, sour cream, half & half and vanilla.

Add liquid ingredients by small amounts to dry, stirring after each addition. Once combined, stir in the chopped rhubarb and strawberries.

Shape into 2 rounds – approximately 3/4-inch thick and cut into wedges. Bake at 375 F. for 20-25 minutes. Makes 12 servings.

Nutritional Analysis per Serving
Calories: 256, Total Fat: 11.9 g., Saturated Fat: 7.1 g.
Cholesterol: 47 mg., Carbohydrate: 32.2 g., Dietary Fiber: .4 g.
Protein: 4.9 g., Sodium: 272 mg.

CLANCY'S IRISH SCONES

Early Irish recipe modified by Dina (the wizard of scones) Clancy of Clancy's Tea Cosy

5 cups flour
1/2 cup sugar
2 tsp. baking powder
2 tsp. baking soda
1/4 cup butter (1/2 stick)
1 quart buttermilk
3/4 cup currants

In a large bowl mix together all dry ingredients. Blend in butter with pastry blender or two knives until mixture resembles coarse meal.

Toss currants with mixture. Add buttermilk 2 cups at a time, stirring gently, until consistency is that of a light dough.

Roll out on a floured board to 1/2-inch thickness and cut circles or other shapes using large cookie cutter. Bake at 400° F. for 12 to 15 minutes.

Nutritional Analysis per Serving
Calories: 157, Total Fat: 2.5 g., Saturated Fat: 1.4 g.
Cholesterol: 7 mg., Carbohydrate: 29.4 g., Dietary Fiber: .3 g.
Protein: 4.2 g., Sodium: 198 mg.

ORANGE CURRANT SCONES

Your kitchen will be prefumed with fresh and mouth-watering scents when you make these tasty scones from a recipe by my brother Greg and his wife Kris, who live on the Oregon Coast.

2	cups all-purpose flour
1-1/2	T. baking powder
1/3	cup sugar
1/2	tsp. salt
	Grated peel of 1 orange
6	T. butter
4	T. shortening
1/2	cup buttermilk
1/3	cup currants

Preheat oven to 425° F. Combine flour, baking powder, sugar, salt and orange peel. Cut in butter and shortening. Add buttermilk, stirring gently until just mixed. Fold in currants. Roll out dough 1/2-inch thick. Cut scones into triangles or use biscuit cutter. Brush with a little buttermilk and bake 15 minutes on a greased baking sheet. Makes 12 scones.

Nutritional Analysis per Scone
Calories: 202, Total Fat: 10.3 g., Saturated Fat: 4.7 g.
Cholesterol: 16 mg., Carbohydrate: 25.6 g., Dietary Fiber: .3 g.
Protein: 2.7 g., Sodium: 294 mg.

SUTTON AFTERNOON TEA SCONES

Sutton Place Hotel • Vancouver, B.C.

This recipe was brought to the Sutton Place Hotel from London, like so many other good things.

- 4 cups all purpose flour
- 1 T. baking powder
- 1/2 cup butter
- 1 cup sugar
- 3 eggs
- 7 oz. milk (7/8 cup)

Preheat oven to 400° F. In a large bowl sift the flour and baking powder together. With a pastry blender cut the butter into the mixture until it resembles coarse meal. Add the eggs and milk and mix with a fork until a soft pliable dough forms.

On a lightly floured surface roll out the dough to a 1/2" thickness. Cut out the shape with a cookie cutter. Brush the tops with an egg wash.

Heat an ungreased baking sheet in the oven until warm, place the scones on the sheet and bake near the top of the oven until they are a light golden brown about 10 to 15 minutes.

Remove the scones from the baking sheet and serve with Devonshire cream and your favorite preserves.

Makes 12 scones.

Nutritional Analysis per Serving
Calories: 390, Total Fat: 14 g., Saturated Fat: 8.1 g.
Cholesterol: 93 mg., Carbohydrate: 55.5 g., Dietary Fiber: 0 g.
Protein: 10.6 g., Sodium: 254 mg.

SWEET CREAM SCONES

Barbara Ann's Tea Room & Gift Shop • Carlton, Oregon

2 cups pastry flour
1 tsp. baking powder
2 tsp. sugar
1 tsp. salt
1 cup heavy whipping cream

In a large bowl sift together the dry ingredients, gradually add enough of the cream to form a soft dough. Knead lightly on a floured board, handling the dough gently to retain the air needed for the scones to rise. Pat out the dough to a 1" thickness and cut into rounds with a cookie cutter. Arrange on an ungreased sheet leaving 1/2" inch for rising. Chill for 10 minutes then bake at 425° F. for 10-12 minutes. Makes about 12 scones.

Nutritional Analysis per Serving
Calories: 137, Total Fat: 7.5 g., Saturated Fat: 4.6 g.
Cholesterol:27 mg., Carbohydrate: 15.5 g., Dietary Fiber: .3 g.
Protein: 1.9 g., Sodium: 216 mg.

CHILI-CHEESE SCONES

My parents, Warner and Edythe Foster, do not drink tea, and my mother only drinks one cup of coffee in the morning. This scone recipe of hers is especially good as a companion to her wonderful soups, stews and chowders.

- 1-1/2 cups all-purpose flour
- 1/4 cup yellow cornmeal
- 1 tsp. baking powder
- 1/2 tsp. crushed dried hot chiles
- 1/4 tsp. ground cumin
- 1/4 cup butter, cut in pieces
- 1/4 lb. cheddar cheese
- 1 egg
- 1/4 cup milk

Mix all dry ingredients together in a large bowl until well combined. Add butter and mix with your fingers or with a pastry cutter until coarse crumbs form.

Shred the cheese and stir it into the flour mixture. Beat egg and milk to blend, set aside 2 tablespoons of this mixture. Add the remaining egg/milk mixture to the flour mixture and stir until just moistened. Place dough on floured surface and knead 5-6 times, then pat into a 3/4" thick round approximately 6" in diameter. With a knife, cut each round not quite through to form 6 wedges. Brush with reserved egg mixture. Bake at 400° F. until golden brown, about 16 minutes. Scones are best served warm.

Nutritional Analysis per Serving
Calories: 221, Total Fat: 9.2 g., Saturated Fat: 5.2 g.
Cholesterol: 57 mg., Carbohydrate: 29.1 g., Dietary Fiber: .4 g.
Protein: 5.2 g., Sodium: 154 mg.

Lavender Biscuits

Lavender Tea House - Sherwood, Oregon

In Victorian times, friends and discreet lovers sent intricate personal messages to each other in the form of fresh or dried bouquets, with each type of flower bearing a message of emotional significance. The carnation indicated affection, the daisy was hope, violets meant faith, and the red rose, of course, to this day means love. Lavender was the flower of dedication. I anticipate that this recipe will gain a dedicated following:

1/2 cup butter
1/2 cup sugar
1 egg, beaten
1 cup flour
1 T. dried lavender flowers

Cream butter with sugar until light and fluffy, then add beaten egg. Mix in flour and dried lavender flowers.

Spoon the mixture in small dollops onto a greased baking tray and bake at 350° F. for 15-20 minutes.

Nutritional Analysis per Serving
Calories: 216, Total Fat: 12.2 g., Saturated Fat: 7.3 g.
Cholesterol: 57 mg., Carbohydrate: 24.8 g., Dietary Fiber: 0 g.
Protein: 2.5 g., Sodium: 124 mg.

TEA-THYME BISCUITS

Thyme, fresh from your own herb garden, makes this savory biscuit a treat and always reminds us of the bed and breakfast in Wales where we first tasted these.

- 4 cups flour
- 2 T. baking powder
- 1-1/2 tsp. salt
- 4 T. fresh thyme, chopped fine
- 1 cup butter
- 2 eggs
- 1 cup milk

Preheat oven to 450° F. Combine dry ingredients including the thyme. Cut the butter into them with a pastry blender. Beat the eggs with the milk and add all at once to the flour mixture. Mix just until combined. Drop heaping tablespoons onto greased cookie sheet and bake 10-12 minutes. Makes 40 small biscuits. Our hostess served these with sliced cheese and apple for a nice blend of flavors.

Nutritional Analysis per Biscuit
Calories: 40, Total Fat: 5.2 g., Saturated Fat: 3.1 g.
Cholesterol: 24 mg., Carbohydrate: 10.3 g., Dietary Fiber: .1 g.
Protein: 1.9 g., Sodium: 187 mg.

SAN JUAN ISLAND CHEESE ROLLS

"Many's the long night I've dreamed of cheese - toasted, mostly."
Robert Louis Stevenson
Treasure Island

- 1 cup milk
- 2 T. butter
- 1/8 tsp. salt
- 1/8 tsp. pepper
- 1 cup all-purpose flour
- 4 eggs
- 3/4 cup grated sharp cheddar

Preheat oven to 375° F. Combine milk, butter, salt and pepper in a pan and bring to a boil over medium heat, stirring constantly. Remove from heat, add flour and stir until mixture forms a ball. Beat in eggs until the dough is smooth, then add 1/2 cup grated cheese. Spoon equal portions into 4 well-greased 6 oz. custard cups. Cover tops with remaining cheese. Bake 45 minutes.

Makes 4 rolls.

Nutritional Analysis per Serving
Calories: 362, Total Fat: 20.1 g., Saturated Fat: 10.9 g.
Cholesterol: 258 mg., Carbohydrate: 27.6 g., Dietary Fiber: 0.0 g.
Protein: 16.8 g., Sodium: 350 mg.

ECCLES CAKES

The ovens of the village of Eccles in Lancashire, England gave birth to these traditional teatime treats.

1-3/4 cups all purpose flour
2-1/4 tsp. baking powder
1 T. sugar
1/4 tsp. salt
1/4 cup butter
2 eggs, beaten
1/3 cup half and half
2 T. currants
1 tsp. butter
2 T. sugar
Ground cinnamon

Mix together the flour, baking powder, 1 T. sugar, and salt. With a pastry blender, cut the 1/4 cup butter until the mixture resembles coarse meal. Set aside 2 tsp. of the beaten egg and mix remaining egg with the cream. Make a well in the center of the flour mixture, add egg-cream mixture and stir until just blended. Turn dough out on a lightly floured board and knead lightly (about 15 times) until dough is no longer sticky.

Roll out dough to 3/4 " thickness and using a biscuit cutter, cut 2-1/2" rounds and place them about 2" apart of greased baking sheet. Reroll scraps.

Poke a hole into the center of each round, fill with 1 tsp. currants and a pea-size dollop of butter. Pinch opposite edges of circle together in the center, enclosing currants in dough (dough will pull apart slightly while baking to form an 'X' on top.)

Brush tops of Eccles cake with reserved egg, and sprinkle with cinnamon-sugar. Bake at 450° F. for 12 minutes, or until golden. Makes 6 Eccles Cakes, which are best served freshly baked or warm.

Nutritional Analysis per Serving
Calories: 281, Total Fat: 11.8 g., Saturated Fat: 6.6 g.
Cholesterol: 98 mg., Carbohydrate: 37.6 g., Dietary Fiber: .3 g.
Protein: 6.5 g., Sodium: 336 mg.

Yes! You Can Make Your Own Crumpets!

"Teach us delight in simple things."
Rudyard Kipling

1/2 oz. dry yeast
1 tsp. sugar
3-1/2 cups warm water
4 cups all-purpose flour
2 T. baking powder
1-1/2 tsp. salt

Dissolve yeast and sugar in warm water. Add the flour, baking powder and salt. Whisk together until well blended.

Heat griddle to 450° F. Grease inside of crumpet rings (or clean tuna cans from which you have cut both the top and the bottom). Place rings on heated griddle and pour in 3/4 cup batter.

Cook until bubbles form and the top dries. Remove ring and turn the crumpet to brown lightly.

Makes 2 dozen crumpets which can later be toasted prior to serving.

Note: Many baked goods require experimentation on the part of the baker to achieve optimum results. Crumpets fall into this category. Be sure to measure ingredients carefully and watch how much batter you pour into the crumpet rings. Cooking time is also critical so be sure that griddle is hot enough and you're not letting crumpets cook too long before turning.

Nutritional Analysis per Serving
Calories: 79, Total Fat: .2 g., Saturated Fat: 0 g.
Cholesterol: 0 mg., Carbohydrate: 16.6 g., Dietary Fiber: .2 g.
Protein: 2.4 g., Sodium: 226 mg.

IRISH SODA BREAD

My great-grandfather, John Foster, immigrated from Ireland to settle in Canada. He played a fiddle, smoked a pipe, and dearly loved this Soda Bread.

3	cups flour
1/2	cup sugar
1	T. caraway seed
1	T. baking powder
1	tsp. salt
1	tsp. baking soda
3/4	lb. raisins
1-3/4	cup buttermilk
2	eggs
1	T. melted butter or margarine

Preheat oven to 350° F. Combine the flour, sugar, caraway seed, baking powder, salt, baking soda and raisins in bowl and mix well. Beat buttermilk and eggs together in a separate bowl for about 30 seconds. Add the butter or margarine, beating for 10 seconds. Stir this into the flour mixture.

Spoon the dough into a greased and floured loaf pan or cast iron skillet. Bake for about 50 minutes. Yields about 20 slices per loaf.

Nutritional Analysis per Serving
Calories: 161, Total Fat: 1.6 g., Saturated Fat: .7 g.
Cholesterol: 24 mg., Carbohydrate: 34.2 g., Dietary Fiber: .8 g.
Protein: 3.9 g., Sodium: 261 mg.

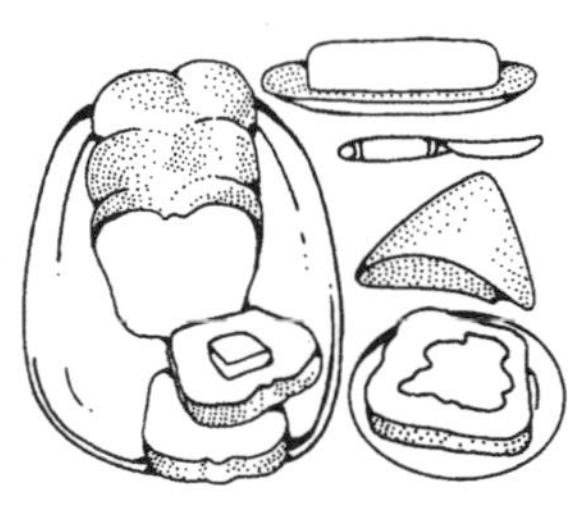

Peach Bread

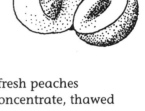

1/2 cup butter, softened
1 cup sugar
3 eggs
2-3/4 cups flour
1-1/2 tsp. baking powder
1/2 tsp. baking soda
1 tsp. salt
1-1/2 tsp. ground cinnamon
1/4 tsp. nutmeg
2 cups coarsely chopped fresh peaches
3 T. frozen orange juice concentrate, thawed
1 tsp. vanilla

Preheat oven to 350° F. Grease and flour two loaf pans. Cream butter and sugar, beating well. Add eggs one at a time, beating well after each is added.

Combine all dry ingredients and add alternately to creamed mixture with peaches, beginning and ending with dry ingredients. Stir in orange juice and vanilla.

Pour into prepared pans and bake 50 - 60 minutes until tester comes out clean. Cool 10 minutes before turning out of pans. Cool completely before slicing.

Makes 24 servings.

Nutritional Analysis per Serving
Calories: 138, Total Fat: 4.6 g., Saturated Fat: 2.6 g.
Cholesterol: 37 mg., Carbohydrate: 22 g., Dietary Fiber: .4 g.
Protein: 2.5 g., Sodium: 185 mg.

COCONUT BREAD

2-3/4 cup all-purpose flour
1-1/2 cup milk
1 cup sugar
1 egg, lightly beaten
1 T. + 1 tsp. baking powder
2 T. peanut oil
1 tsp. salt
1 tsp. coconut extract
1-1/4 cup shredded coconut, toasted and cooled

Preheat oven to 350° F. Lightly coat a loaf pan with vegetable spray. Sift flour, baking powder and salt into a medium bowl. Add toasted coconut and blend well.

Combine milk, egg, oil and extract in another bowl and mix well. Add to dry ingredients all at once, stirring briefly just until blended; do not overmix.

Turn into pan and bake approximately 1 hour or until tester comes out clean when inserted in center.

Makes 20 servings.

Nutritional Analysis per Serving
Calories: 158, Total Fat: 4.4 g., Saturated Fat: 2.5 g.
Cholesterol: 13 mg., Carbohydrate: 27 g., Dietary Fiber: .3 g.
Protein: 2.9 g., Sodium: 207 mg.

PUMPKIN BREAD

- 2 tsp. ground cinnamon
- 2 tsp. baking powder
- 1 tsp. nutmeg
- 1 tsp. baking soda
- 1 tsp. salt
- 1/2 tsp. ground cloves
- 1/4 tsp. ground ginger
- dash allspice
- 6 cups unbleached white flour
- 1 cup vegetable oil
- 1/2 cup plain yogurt
- 4 eggs
- 3 cups sugar
- 2-1/2 cups unsweetened pumpkin puree
- 1 cup chopped walnuts or pecans

Preheat oven to 350° F. In a large bowl, sift together cinnamon, baking powder, nutmeg, baking soda, salt, cloves, ginger, allspice, and flour. Set aside.

In a separate bowl, mix together the oil, eggs, yogurt, sugar, and pumpkin. Mix until smooth.

Combine the two mixtures and beat until smooth, then fold in the chopped nuts. Pour the batter into three loaf pans. Bake for 45 minutes to 1 hour. Loaves are done when they have a hollow sound when tapped. Makes three loaves that freeze well. Yields 20 slices per loaf.

Nutritional Analysis per Slice
Calories: 134, Total Fat: 5.5 g., Saturated Fat: .7 g.
Cholesterol: 14 mg., Carbohydrate: 20 g., Dietary Fiber: 1.9 g.
Protein: 2.8 g., Sodium: 75 mg.

REBECCA'S BUTTER TART MUFFINS

Secret Garden • Vancouver, B.C.

"I do like a little bit of butter to my bread!"
A. A. Milne

- 1-1/2 cups raisins
- 3/4 cup sugar
- 1/2 cup butter cut into chunks
- 2 eggs beaten
- 1/2 cup milk
- 1 tsp. vanilla
- 1/2 cup all purpose flour
- 2 tsp. baking powder
- 1 tsp. baking soda
- pinch salt
- 1/2 cup chopped walnuts or pecans
- 1/4 cup corn or maple syrup

Place raisins, sugar, butter, eggs, milk and vanilla in large heavy-bottomed saucpan. Place over medium heat and cook, stirring frequently, until mixture is hot, slightly thickened, and just beginning to bubble, about 4 to 5 minutes. Cool slightly uncovered in the refrigerator.

Preheat oven to 375° F. Grease 12 muffin cups or spray coat with cooking spray. Combine flour, baking powder, soda and salt in large mixing bowl, make a well in center and pour in warm raisin mixture, stirring until just combined. Stir in nuts until evenly mixed.

Spoon batter into muffin cups. Bake until golden and cake tester comes out clean, about 15 to 17 minutes. Remove from oven and immediately pour about one teaspoon syrup over each muffin. Cool muffins in cups about 10 minutes then remove to a rack. Best served warm. Freeze well too!

TEA NOTE
Serve with Secret Garden English Breakfast Tea.

Nutritional Analysis per Serving
Calories: 259, Total Fat: 11.8 g., Saturated Fat: 5.4 g.
Cholesterol: 57 mg., Carbohydrate: 37.5 g., Dietary Fiber: 1.0 g.
Protein: 3.8 g., Sodium: 291 mg.

Fresh Strawberry Muffins

"Doubtless God could have made a better berry [strawberry], but doubtless God never did."
William Butler
Walton, The Compleat Angler

- 1/2 cup butter, softened
- 1 cup sugar
- 2 eggs
- 2 cups flour
- 2 tsp. baking powder
- 1/4 tsp. salt
- 2/3 cup milk
- 1 tsp. grated lemon rind
- 1 cup fresh strawberries, chopped
- 1 T. cinnamon sugar

Preheat oven to 375° F. Grease or line muffin pan with paper liners. Cream butter in large bowl, gradually adding sugar and eggs, creaming until light and fluffy.

Sift together flour, baking powder and salt. Add to creamed mixture alternately with milk, beginning and ending with the dry ingredients. Stir in lemon rind and gently fold in berries.

Spoon batter into muffin pans, filling each 2/3 full. Sprinkle cinnamon sugar lightly over top of batter. Bake 15 to 18 minutes. Makes 12 muffins.

Nutritional Analysis per Serving
Calories: 236, Total Fat: 9.1 g., Saturated Fat: 5.3 g.
Cholesterol: 58 mg., Carbohydrate: 35.5 g., Dietary Fiber: .4 g.
Protein: 3.8 g., Sodium: 200 mg.

BEA BOTHELL'S EXCELLENT PIE CRUST

(because Moody Pie Crust sounds uncooperative)

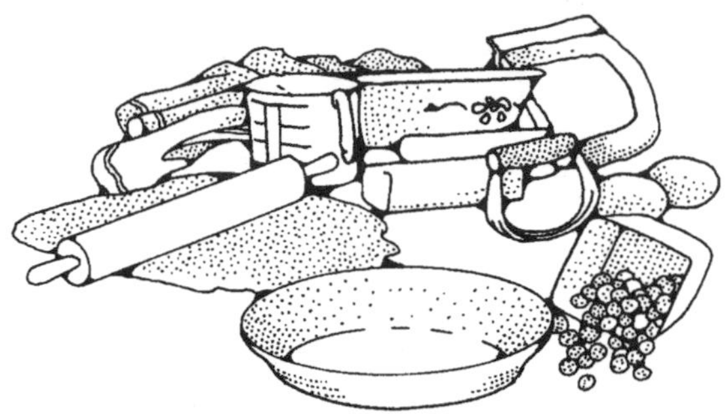

When we bought the property on Camano Island where Ken built our home, our first happy coincidence was to discover that our new next-door neighbor, Irene Moody, was from Ken's hometown, Liverpool, England! Irene's fresh blackberry pies every summer are the stuff of legends, and her pie crust is the very best we've ever had.

This pie crust recipe is from Irene's yankee husband, Pat, retired Assistant Fire Chief of Seattle, (so don't overcook it). Pat is the great-great-great-great grandson of the founder of Bothell, Washington, and this recipe originated with his great-great grandmother, so we named it after her.

- 2 cups flour
- 1/2 tsp. salt
- 1/4 tsp. baking powder
- 1 cup shortening (she uses Crisco)
- a small glass of ice water

Mix the salt and baking powder together and add to the 2 cups of flour you've placed in a bowl. Cut in 1 cup of shortening and then dive in with your hands to mix lightly until the texture is crumbly. Add ice water until the dough is the consistency to roll. Do all this quickly, because the least this dough is handled the lighter and flakier it will be. Roll on floured surface.

Makes a double crust for a 9" fruit pie.

COOKIES & BARS

BUTTER ROUNDS FILLED COOKIES

Our friend, Judy Judson Carroll, is such a good cook, that when she gets excited about a recipe, you know you better listen. Recipes flow through Judy from a myriad of sources, including her Cordon Bleu-trained daughter with whom she is co-authoring a cookbook. This one, however, originated with the mother of the mechanic who keeps her car running:

Cookie:

- 1 cup butter or margarine
- 2 cups sifted flour
- 1/3 cup heavy cream

Mix well and chill thoroughly. Roll thinly on a board dusted with a mixture of 1/2 flour and 1/2 sugar, using small amount of dough at a time. Cut into 2" circle and prick twice with a fork. Bake at 375° F. on ungreased sheet 7 to 9 minutes. Let cool on rack completely. In the meantime, make the filling:

Filling:

- 1/4 cup butter
- 3/4 cup sifted powdered sugar
- 1 egg yolk
- 1 tsp. vanilla

Do not chill the filling recipe. It's easier to spread on the cookie round when at room temperature. Sandwich a dollop of filling between two cookies rounds. Makes 36.

Nutritional Analysis per Cookie
Calories: 100, Total Fat: 7.3 g., Saturated Fat: 4.5 g.
Cholesterol: 26 mg., Carbohydrate: 7.9 g., Dietary Fiber: 0 g.
Protein: .9 g., Sodium: 65 mg.

Note: some cooks prefer not to use uncooked fresh egg products in their recipes due to risk of salmonella. Several pastuerized egg substitutes are now available to use in recipes such as this one.

GINGER SHORTBREAD

Crystallized ginger chunks make the difference in this rich shortbread.

1-1/4 cup all-purpose flour
1/3 cup sugar
1/2 cup unsalted butter, cut in pieces
3 T. crystallized ginger, chopped fine
1/2 tsp. ground ginger

Preheat oven to 325° F. In a bowl, combine the flour, both the crystallized and ground ginger, 1/4 cup of the sugar , and the butter. Crumble with your fingers and press into a firm lump with your hands.

Spread this crumbly dough in a 8" or 9" springform pan, pressing out evenly and firmly. Prick the surface with a fork. Bake about 40 minutes. Cut while warm into 8 to 12 wedges.

Sprinkle with remaining sugar, let cool, then remove the pan sides. Store in airtight container.

Nutritional Analysis per Serving
Calories: 150, Total Fat: 8.3 g., Saturated Fat: 5.1 g.
Cholesterol: 24 mg., Carbohydrate: 15.5 g., Dietary Fiber: 0 g.
Protein: 1.4 g., Sodium: 1 mg.

BROWN SUGAR SHORTBREAD

Country Cottage Cafe - Grants Pass, Oregon

1 cup unsalted butter
1 cup light brown sugar (firmly packed)
1 tsp. vanilla extract
2-1/4 cups all-purpose flour

Beat butter, brown sugar and vanilla together until fluffy, about 3 minutes. Add the flour in 4 batches and combine well after each addition. Scrape the dough into an 8-inch square pan and pat into an even layer. Prick the surface with a fork and score the top for serving sizes (do not cut all the way through).

Bake in the upper third of the oven at 350° F. for about 30 minutes or until the top is puffy and lightly browned. Makes 16 shortbreads.

Nutritional Analysis per Serving
Calories: 206, Total Fat: 12.4 g., Saturated Fat: 7.6 g.
Cholesterol: 33 mg., Carbohydrate: 22.3 g., Dietary Fiber: 0 g.
Protein: 1.9 g., Sodium: 6 mg.

WHITE SUGAR COOKIES

Tea & Other Comforts - Stanwood, Washington

Tea & Other Comforts owner Kerri Kirk got this award-winning recipe from a neighbor in Ballard when she was growing up. In the early 80s it won Best of Show in the Stanwood-Camano Island Fair. Kerri serves it as part of her Afternoon Teas, and notes "it's great for dipping!"

3/4	cup sugar
1	cup shortening
1	egg, well beaten
1	tsp. vanilla
1/2	tsp. salt
2	cups flour
1	tsp. cream of tartar
1/2	tsp. baking soda

Cream sugar and shortening well, add eggs and vanilla and beat until nice and fluffy. Sift remaining ingredients together and add to egg mixture.

Roll into balls and dip in sugar, flatten with glass or use cookie stamp, and bake 12-15 minutes at 350· F. Makes about 24 cookies.

TEA NOTE
Recommended Tea - Nilgiri Hills from Blue Willow Tea.

Nutritional Analysis per Serving
Calories: 141, Total Fat: 8.9 g., Saturated Fat: 2.2 g.
Cholesterol: 9 mg., Carbohydrate: 14.3 g., Dietary Fiber: 0 g.
Protein: 1.3 g., Sodium: 74 mg.

SCOTTISH OATMEAL COOKIES

Recently our friend Ian Clyde loaned us a marvelous vintage Scottish cookbook, written in 1929. The first page I opened and read said: "Take a sheep's head..." and that was as far as I got. Cooking has come a long way in 70 years. Thank goodness.

Ian spent 18 years on tea plantations in north India beginning in 1946, and has a wealth of fascinating insights on tea production. His wisdom been invaluable to us during our research for this book.

- 2 cups flour
- 2 cups quick cooking oats, uncooked
- 1 tsp. baking soda
- 1 tsp. baking powder
- 1-1/2 cup sugar
- 1 tsp. cinnamon
- 1/2 tsp. cloves
- 1 tsp. salt
- 2 eggs
- 1/3 cup milk
- 3/4 cup melted butter
- 1 tsp. vanilla
- 1 cup raisins

Combine all ingredients. Mix thoroughly by hand, and drop small amounts of dough from a teaspoon onto a greased cookie sheet. Bake about 10 minutes (they should not become too crisp.) Cool on a rack. Store in an airtight container, or freeze.

Nutritional Analysis per Serving
Calories: 126, Total Fat: 4.5 g., Saturated Fat: 2.6 g.
Cholesterol: 22 mg., Carbohydrate: 20.1 g., Dietary Fiber: .7 g.
Protein: 2.0 g., Sodium: 148 mg.

WILD BLACKBERRY LEMON BARS

Each summer on Camano Island the deer and I await the glorious ripening of overgrown blackberries on our neighbor's vacant property. The deer, followed by Ken with his cereal bowl, usually get there first, but there's always enough to go around.

1	cup butter, softened
3/4	cup sifted powdered sugar
2	cups all-purpose flour
4	eggs
1-1/2	cup granulated sugar
1/3	cup juice of fresh lemons
2	T. finely shredded orange peel
1/4	cup all-purpose flour
1	tsp. baking powder
1-1/2	cups fresh wild blackberries
	Powdered sugar

For Crust

Cream butter for 45 seconds to soften and add 3/4 cup powdered sugar, combining well. Add 2 cups flour, mix until combined. Press into bottom of greased 13x9x2 inch baking pan. Bake at 350° F. for 20 minutes.

For Filling

In a large mixing bowl combine granulated sugar, eggs, lemon juice, orange peel, 1/4 cup flour, and baking powder. Beat for 3 minutes until combined.

Sprinkle well-washed and drained berries over cooked crust. Pour filling over berries. Bake 350° F. for 30-35 minutes or until filling is set and lightly browned.

Cool well and cut into bars or triangles. Just before serving, sprinkle with powdered sugar for garnish. Store covered in refrigerator. Makes about 24 bars.

Nutritional Analysis per Serving
Calories: 180, Total Fat: 7.7 g., Saturated Fat: 4.7 g.
Cholesterol: 20 mg., Carbohydrate: 27.4 g., Dietary Fiber: .5 g.
Protein: 1.4 g., Sodium: 78 mg.

JAM DROP COOKIES

Every year I get at least one set of small jars of gourmet jams in interesting flavors as a gift from friends who know better than to give me traditional fruitcake. This recipe provides an excellent way to share that largesse with other friends.

2 sticks unsalted butter
1/2 cup sugar
2 egg yolks
1 T. lemon juice
2-1/4 cups all-purpose flour
1-1/2 tsp. baking powder
1/4 tsp. cinnamon
1/4 tsp. cardamom
1/4 tsp. salt
Assorted interesting jams and jellies you already have in your refrigerator.

Preheat oven to 350° F. Cream the butter and sugar. Add egg yolks and lemon juice and beat until smooth. Add all the remaining ingredients and form into a ball.

Form into small balls, approximately 1 tablespoon each, and place in miniature muffin paper cups (available at kitchen and gourmet stores). Make a thumbprint on each, and place a dollop of jam or jelly in each. Variety is the spice of life! Bake for 30 minutes or until golden.

Makes 3 dozen cookies.

Nutritional Analysis per Cookie
Calories: 85, Total Fat: 5.2 g., Saturated Fat: 3.2 g.
Cholesterol: 14 mg., Carbohydrate: 9 g., Dietary Fiber: 0 g.
Protein: .9 g., Sodium: 82 mg.

Honey Madeleines

Cathy Loendorf • Vancouver, Washington

1/4 cup butter, melted
2 eggs
1/4 cup sugar
1 T. honey
1/2 cup all-purpose flour
1/2 tsp. baking powder
(We also add a touch of fresh lemon rind for flavor)

Beat eggs with sugar until pale and thick, then stir in melted butter and honey. Sift flour and baking powder onto egg mixture, then fold in.

Spoon mixture into prepared molds and bake 10 minutes at 350° F. until light golden brown. Leave in molds 2 minutes then turn out and transfer to a wire rack to cool.

To finish, dust lightly with powered sugar. Makes about 2 dozen small Madeleines or 1 dozen large.

Can also be made in tartlet pans, if you do not have the traditional shell-shape madeleine mold pan.

Nutritional Analysis per Serving
Calories: 43, Total Fat: 2.3 g., Saturated Fat: 1.3 g.
Cholesterol: 23 mg., Carbohydrate: 4.9 g., Dietary Fiber: 0.0 g.
Protein: .8 g., Sodium: 32 mg.

CHOCOLATE CHIP MERINGUE BARS

Our dear friend Terry Dean, who helped Ken build our house, loves chocolate and Martha Stewart, in that order. I think he should send these bars to her, he just might win her over with his recipe.

1/2 cup butter
1/2 cup sugar
1/2 cup brown sugar
2 egg yolks
1 T. water
1 tsp. vanilla
2 cups flour
1/4 tsp. salt
1/4 tsp. baking soda
1 tsp. baking powder
1 12 oz. package chocolate chips
or one 12 oz. bar semi-sweet chocolate

Topping:

2 egg whites
1 cup brown sugar

Preheat oven to 350° F. Lightly grease 15" jellyroll pan.

In large bowl, cream together butter and sugars; add egg yolks, water and vanilla. Mix well. Mix together flour, salt, baking soda, and baking powder. Add to butter mixture. Pat dough into pan and sprinkle evenly with chocolate chips.

Make topping: in small bowl of mixer, beat egg whites until stiff. Gradually beat in brown sugar. Spread mixture over top of chocolate chips. Bake 20 to 25 minutes.

Cool, then cut into 24 bars.

Nutritional Analysis per Serving
Calories: 196, Total Fat: 8.5 g., Saturated Fat: 5.0 g.
Cholesterol: 28 mg., Carbohydrate: 30 g., Dietary Fiber: .8 g.
Protein: 2.2 g., Sodium: 100 mg.

DEEP DISH BROWNIES

With two cups of tea and identical Barbies standing by, my ten year old twin cousins Monica and Mimi Olsson wait almost patiently for these brownies to come out of the oven. Two of my favorite people, the girls bring these brownies and great joy to every teaparty.

3/4	cup melted margarine
1-1/2	cup sugar
1/2	cup unsweetened cocoa powder
1-1/2	tsp. vanilla
3	eggs
3/4	cup flour
1/2	tsp. baking powder
1/2	tsp. salt
6	oz. chocolate chips

"Have an adult help you," reminds Mimi. "Grandma's good at this," Monica agrees.

Blend melted margarine, cocoa, sugar and vanilla in a bowl. Add the eggs and beat well. Combine flour, baking powder and salt, and slowly add this to the egg mixture. Stir in chocolate chips. Spread in a greased 8" square pan and bake at 350° F. for 40-45 minutes (you'll know they're done when they start to pull away from the corners of the pan). Makes 16 brownies.

"The hard part is waiting for them to cool down," they both agree solemnly.

Nutritional Analysis per Serving
Calories: 241, Total Fat: 13 g., Saturated Fat: 3.9 g.
Cholesterol: 40 mg., Carbohydrate: 31.7 g., Dietary Fiber: 1.5 g.
Protein: 2.8 g., Sodium: 192 mg.

DATE BARS

That pleasant aroma emanating from the open window of the charming Cape Cod cottage nestled in the woods at the top of our hill is Nancy Cook's special date bar recipe. Tom and Nancy Cook, cultured, well-read and well-travelled, have lived in England and the Middle East. This recipe, from Nancy's mother, seems to reflect a synergy of those cultures.

3 eggs
1 cup sugar
1 cup flour
1/4 tsp. salt
1 T. baking powder
1 tsp. cocoa
1 tsp. cinnamon
1 tsp. grated lemon peel
1-1/2 cup pitted dates

1/2 cup shredded coconut

Beat eggs well, add sugar and beat until thick. Add flour, salt, baking powder, cocoa, and cinnamon, and beat until smooth. Stir in lemon peel and dates.

Bake in a shallow 9 x 13 inch pan at 350° F. for approximately 30 minutes. Remove from oven and sprinkle with coconut then bake for 2 more minutes. Cut them while they are still warm. Makes 24 date bars.

Nutritional Analysis per Serving
Calories: 101, Total Fat: 1.4 g., Saturated Fat: .8 g.
Cholesterol: 27 mg., Carbohydrate: 21.7 g., Dietary Fiber: 1.0 g.
Protein: 1.6 g., Sodium: 81 mg.

RUSSIAN TEA CAKES

1 lb. butter
8 oz. sugar
1 oz. vanilla
1-1/2 lb. flour
1/4 oz. salt
6 oz. chopped pecans

Cream butter and sugar in mixer until light and fluffy. Add vanilla and mix in.

In a separate bowl mix together flour, salt and nuts. Blend in dry ingredients with butter/sugar mixture only until incorporated.

Drop tablespoons of dough evenly spaced on a sheetpan.

Bake at 325° F. for 10 minutes only. Remove from oven, cool totally. Store in a sealed container.

Just before serving roll in powdered sugar. Makes 48.

TEA NOTE
Serve these treats with an exotic Russian Caravan tea.

Nutritional Analysis per Serving
Calories: 164, Total Fat: 10.2 g., Saturated Fat: 5.0 g.
Cholesterol: 21 mg., Carbohydrate: 16.5 g., Dietary Fiber: .3 g.
Protein: 1.8 g., Sodium: 136 mg.

BRENDA'S LEMON SQUARES

The Country Register Cafe and Tea Room • Kennewick, Washington

Crust
- 2 cups flour
- 1/2 cup powdered sugar
- 1 cup butter (softened)

Blend together and press into a small sheet pan. Bake 10 minutes at 350° F.

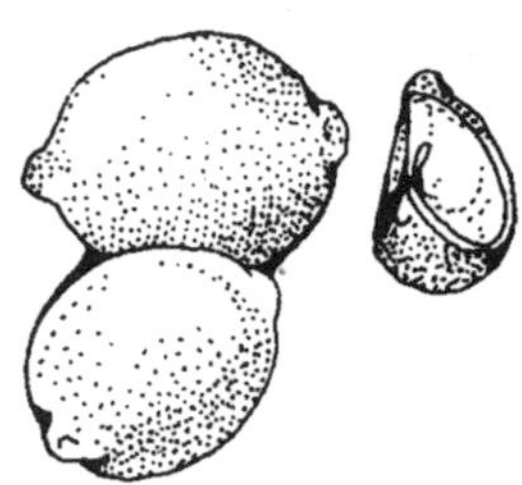

Filling
- 8 eggs
- 2 tsp. grated lemon rind
- 3 cups sugar
- 3/4 cup lemon juice
- 1 tsp. baking powder
- 1/2 cup sifted flour

Beat eggs together with lemon rind, sugar and lemon juice. Stir baking powder and flour into above mixture. Spread over crust and bake 20 to 30 minutes at 350° F. Sprinkle powdered sugar on top after bars have cooled.
36 servings

TEA NOTE
Try these tasty lemon squares with Earl Grey tea.

Nutritional Analysis per Square
Calories: 165, Total Fat: 6.2 g., Saturated Fat: 3.5 g.
Cholesterol: 61 mg., Carbohydrate: 25.6 g., Dietary Fiber: 0 g.
Protein: 2.4 g., Sodium: 76 mg.

BUTTERSCOTCH PECAN DIAMONDS

Village Tea Room • Edmonds, Washington

The favorite recipe of the Village Tea Room in Edmonds originated with Karen Giordano, noted tea expert and author who lives on Whidbey Island. This recipe appears in her book "Easy Tea Treats for Busy Tea Lovers!"

1 pkg yellow cake mix
3/4 cup shortening
2 egg yolks
1 T. milk
2 egg whites
2 T. water
1-1/4 cup ground pecans or walnuts

Preheat oven to 375° F. Combine dry cake mix, shortening, egg yolks and milk.

Spray large cookie sheet with oilspray, and line cookie sheet with waxed paper, let 2" project over sides, spray waxed paper.

Pat dough into cookie sheet (it will be thin). Beat egg whites and water slightly. Brush top of dough with egg white mixture. Press nuts evenly over the top. Bake about 15 minutes or until golden brown.

Cool 10 minutes. Have cutting board or pastry sheet ready.

Turn pan over onto board or sheet. Peel off waxed paper. Cut immediately in diagonal lines to form diamonds.

Makes about 24. Store in airtight container.

Nutritional Analysis per serving:
Calories: 194, Total Fat: 13.2 g., Saturated Fat: 2.4 g.
Cholesterol: 18 mg., Carbohydrate: 17.9 g., Dietary Fiber: .4 g.
Protein: 1.9 g., Sodium: 147 mg.

DANISH APPLE BARS

2-1/2 cup flour
1 cup margarine
1/2 tsp. salt
1 egg
2/3 cup milk
1 cup Rice Krispies
6 pared, sliced apples
3/4 cup sugar
1 tsp. cinnamon

Glaze:
1/2 cup powdered sugar,
1 tsp. vanilla
milk to moisten to drizzle consistency.

Mix until crumbly: 2-1/2 cups flour, 1 cup margarine, and 1/2 tsp. salt. Beat 1 egg yolk (save the white for later in the recipe) with 2/3 cup milk. Add to the flour mixture and knead just til mixed in. Cut the dough in half and roll one half into a rectangle and put on a cookie sheet.

Sprinkle 1 cup of crushed Rice Krsipies over this crust. On top of that arrange 6 pared, and sliced apples. Over the top of that, sprinkle a mixture of 3/4 cup sugar and 1 tsp. cinnamon.

Roll out the other half of the dough and lay over the top of the filling. Trim and pinch edges to seal as you would a pie. Brush with egg white and sprinkle with sugar. Bake at 350° F. for about 30 minutes.

As soon as it comes out of the oven, drizzle the entire top with a mixture of 1 cup powdered sugar, 1 tsp. vanilla, and just enough milk to make runny. Cut into 18 bars.

Nutritional Analysis per Serving
Calories: 287, Total Fat: 11.4 g., Saturated Fat: 2.2 g.
Cholesterol: 13 mg., Carbohydrate: 43.4 g., Dietary Fiber: 1.9 g.
Protein: 3.7 g., Sodium: 229 mg.

Cakes & Tarts

SUMMER FRUIT CAKE

Every Christmas I used to wear a button that read "Get Even. Give Fruitcake." Even if you think you hate fruitcake, this fresh fruit version will convert you.

Cake

2	cup whole wheat flour
1-1/2	cups sugar
1	tsp. baking soda
1	tsp. cinnamon
1/2	tsp. salt
1/4	tsp. baking soda
3	eggs
1/2	tsp. vanilla
3/4	cup buttermilk
1/2	cup vegetable oil
2	tsp. vanilla
2-1/2	cups fresh apricots, peaches and/or plums chopped and drained
1	cup chopped pecans
1	cup flaked coconut
1	cup raisins

Glaze

2/3 cup sugar
1/3 cup buttermilk
1/3 cup butter
2 T. light corn syrup

For the cake: Preheat oven to 350° F. Grease and flour a 9" x 13" baking dish, shaking out excess flour. Combine flour, sugar, baking soda, cinnamon and salt in medium bowl. Beat eggs, buttermilk, oil and vanilla in a large bowl. Add flour mixture to eggs and mix until smooth. Stir in remaining ingredients. Pour into baking dish and bake about 40 to 45 min. until tester inserted in center comes out clean. While cake is baking, prepare glaze.

For the glaze: Combine all ingredients except the vanilla in a saucepan and bring to a boil over medium heat. Stir 5 minutes. Remove from heat. Add vanilla and blend thoroughly. Poke entire surface of cake with toothpick. Pour glaze slowly and evenly over top. Let cool completely. Makes 15 Servings

Nutritional Analysis per Serving
Calories: 410, Total Fat: 19.4 g., Saturated Fat: 5.6 g.
Cholesterol: 54 mg., Carbohydrate: 57.9 g., Dietary Fiber: 3.8 g.
Protein: 5.5 g., Sodium: 267 mg.

BISHOP'S CAKE

There is an old Irish country superstition of "nipping the cake." This was the custom of breaking off a small piece of cake when fresh from the oven, to avert bad luck.

- 3 eggs, well beaten
- 1 cup sugar
- 1-1/2 cups flour
- 1/4 tsp. salt
- 6 oz. chocolate chips
- 2 cups coarsely chopped walnuts
- 1 cup pitted dates, cut up
- 1 cup candied cherries or maraschino cherries, halved

Preheat oven to 325° F. Grease loaf pan and line it with waxed paper; grease waxed paper. Cream together eggs and sugar, beating until thick.

Sift together flour, baking powder, and salt over the bowl of fruit, nuts and chocolate chips. Mix well. Combine with egg/sugar mixture and pour into prepared pan.

Bake for approximately 1-1/4 to 1-1/2 hours or until tester is clean. Cool on wire rack. Cake will have crusty top. Remove from pan when completely cool. Serves 12.

Nutritional Analysis per Serving
Calories: 399, Total Fat: 17.5 g., Saturated Fat: 3.7 g.
Cholesterol: 53 mg., Carbohydrate: 57.3 g., Dietary Fiber: 3.2 g.
Protein: 9.2 g., Sodium: 73 mg.

JUDITH'S SWEDISH CREAM CAKE

Judith's Tearooms and Rose Cafe • Poulsbo, Washington

Judith Goodrich ate a piece of cake in Ballard once that set her upon a quest to recreate the recipe. After eight different cakes, she created, in her own words, "cake so delicious that tears will come to your eyes when you take your first bite." This recipe is from Judith's cookbook "Favorite Recipes from Judith's."

- Yellow cake (homemade, or boxed without pudding in the mix)
- 2 T. sour cream or cream cheese
- 1/2 cup cream sherry
- dried apricots
- freshly whipped cream

Follow recipe for yellow cake and add two tablespoons of sour cream or cream cheese to the cake batter while it is mixing. Pour into prepared tube pan or angel food cake pan. Place on center rack in 350 F. oven. The cake will take anywhere from 35 to 70 minutes depending on how full your pan is. Remove and let cool for about 15 minutes.

Pour 1/2 cup cream sherry over the cake. Let it soak in and cool in the pan. Remove from the pan when completely cool and slice horizontally. Fill with freshly whipped cream and dried apricots that have been plumped with cream sherry for at least four hours.

Makes 18 servings.

Nutritional Analysis per Serving
Calories: 213, Total Fat: 10.5 g., Saturated Fat: 3.7 g.
Cholesterol: 35 mg., Carbohydrate: 26.1 g., Dietary Fiber: .4 g.
Protein: 2.6 g., Sodium: 177 mg.

TWIN MOUNTAIN BLUEBERRY TEA CAKE

The Tea Cottage - Jacksonville, Oregon

Gold miners settled into Jacksonville in the 1850s, and it was reported, "There were but few women, and most of them not angelic." That has certainly changed now with the arrival of The Tea Cottage owners, four generations of angelic women, and good cooks to boot!

- 2 cups flour
- 1 cup sugar
- 3 tsp. baking powder
- 1/4 tsp. salt
- 1/2 cup shortening
- 2 beaten eggs
- 1 cup milk
- 1-1/2 cup blueberries
- 1 cup coconut

Mix and sift together flour, sugar, baking powder, and salt, cut in shortening with a pastry blender. Combine eggs and milk, stir into dry ingredients then fold in the blueberries. Divide batter into two 9 inch layer cake pans, sprinkle coconut over top and bake at 375° F. for 25 minutes or until done. Makes 12 servings.

Nutritional Analysis per Serving
Calories: 211, Total Fat: 9.2 g., Saturated Fat: 3.5 g.
Cholesterol: 29 mg., Carbohydrate: 29.5 g., Dietary Fiber: .6 g.
Protein: 3.1 g., Sodium: 130 mg.

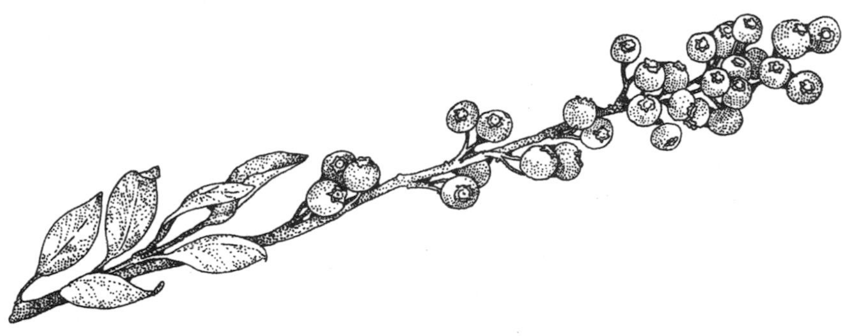

SNOHOMISH GINGER PEACH CAKE

- 2 fresh peaches
- 1/2 cup all-purpose flour
- 1 cup firmly packed dark brown sugar
- 1/2 cup shortening
- 2 eggs
- 1/2 tsp. baking soda
- 1/4 cup molasses
- 2-1/2 cup all-purpose flour, sifted
- 1 tsp. baking powder
- 1/2 tsp. allspice
- 1/2 tsp. cinnamon
- 1 tsp. ginger
- 1/2 tsp. salt
- 3/4 cup milk
- Powdered sugar

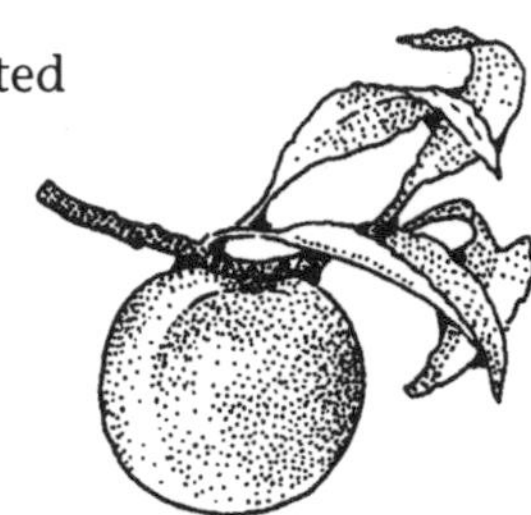

Preheat oven to 375. Place sliced peaches in bowl and sprinkle in 1 cup flour. Cream the brown sugar and shortening until fluffy, then beat in eggs. Add baking soda to the molasses and stir into sugar mixture.

Sift together the flour, baking powder, allspice, cinnamon, ginger, and salt.

Add to the creamed mixture alternating with milk until well blended.

Add peaches and pour into a greased and floured ring pan. Bake 40 minutes or until tester inserted in center comes out clean. Sprinkle with powdered sugar.

Serve with whipped cream or sour cream sweetened with a little sugar. Serves 12.

Nutritional Analysis per Serving
Calories: 263, Total Fat: 10.2 g., Saturated Fat: 2.8 g.
Cholesterol: 37 mg., Carbohydrate: 37.9 g., Dietary Fiber: .4 g.
Protein: 4.9 g., Sodium: 193 mg.

FRESH ORANGE BUTTERMILK CAKE

1 orange
1-1/2 cup sugar
1/2 cup butter
2 eggs
2 cups sifted cake flour
1/4 tsp. baking soda
1-1/2 tsp. baking powder
1/4 tsp. salt
1 cup buttermilk

Preheat oven to 350 . Grate the peel, cut orange in half, extract the juice. Add 1/2 cup sugar to the juice and peel. Stir to dissolve. Set aside.

Cream butter until light and fluffy, then add 1 cup sugar and continue to beat until light and creamy. Stir together the cake flour, baking soda, baking powder and the salt. Add these dry ingredients to the creamed mixture alternately with buttermilk, beginning and ending with the flour. Beat only to blend thoroughly. Pour into lightly greased and floured 9" square pan. Bake 30-35 min. Cool on rack 15 min. Poke holes in top of cake with handle of wooden spoon or skewer and spoon the orange juice mix over top. Slice laterally and fill with the following:

ORANGE FILLING:

1/2 cup sugar
4 T. cake flour
dash salt
1/3 cup orange juice
1-1/2 tsp. grated orange rind
3 T. lemon juice
2 T. water
1 beaten egg
2 T. butter

Combine sugar, flour, and salt in top of double boiler, add fruit juices, water, egg. Place over rapidly boiling water and cook 10 minutes, stirring occasionally. Remove from double boiler, add butter and orange rind. Cool and spread between the split layers of the Orange Buttermilk Cake. Reassemble cake. Serves 9.

Nutritional Analysis per Serving
Calories: 341, Total Fat: 11.7 g., Saturated Fat: 6.8 g.
Cholesterol: 75 mg., Carbohydrate: 55.5 g., Dietary Fiber: .8 g.
Protein: 4.5 g., Sodium: 301 mg.

APPLE-MAPLE CAKE

"Autumn evening, and the morn
When the golden mists are born."
Percy Bysshe Shelley

- 1-1/2 cups all-purpose flour
- 1 tsp. baking powder
- 1/2 tsp. baking soda
- 1/4 tsp. salt
- 1 beaten egg
- 1-1/2 cups peeled, cored, and chopped baking apple
- 1/2 cup sugar
- 1/2 cup pure maple syrup
- 1/2 cup raisins
- 1/3 cup applesauce
- 1/3 cup cooking oil
- 1-1/2 tsp. grated orange peel
- Pure maple syrup
- Whipping cream
- Sour cream

Spray 8-inch square baking pan with nonstick coating. In a bowl combine the flour, baking powder, baking soda, and the salt.

In a large bowl combine the beaten egg and the apples. Stir in sugar, 1/2 cup maple syrup, raisins, applesauce and orange peel. Add the dry ingredients and stir until just combined. Spread better in the prepared pan.

Bake at 350° F. for 40 to 45 minutes or until toothpick comes out clean. Brush the warm cake with additional maple syrup and cool slightly. Serve warm or at room temperature with Maple Cream. Makes 9 servings.

Maple Cream - In a chilled mixing bowl beat 1/2 cup whipping cream on medium speed until stiff peaks form. Stir together 1/2 cup sour cream and 1/4 cup pure maple syrup and fold into whipped cream. Serve immediately.

Nutritional Analysis per Serving
Calories: 394, Total Fat: 16.6 g., Saturated Fat: 5.9 g.
Cholesterol: 47 mg., Carbohydrate: 59.9 g., Dietary Fiber: 1.2 g.
Protein: 3.9 g., Sodium: 192 mg.

MANGO UPSIDE-DOWN CAKE

3 ripe mangos, peeled
1/2 cup unsalted butter + 1/3 cup
3/4 cup light brown sugar
1/4 tsp. cardamon
1/2 cup rum + 1 tsp.
1-2/3 cups flour
2 tsp. baking powder
pinch of salt
2/3 cup sugar
2 eggs
2/3 cup milk

Cut mangos in strips 1" wide, 3" or 4" long. Melt 1/2 cup butter in a skillet over medium heat. Add mangoes and sprinkle brown sugar and cardamon over top. Cook, stirring gently about 5 minutes. Remove mango with slotted spoon and place aside. Continue to cook the sugar mixture until it gets syrupy, about 5 min. Remove from heat and add rum.

Arrange a single layer of the mango in a starburst pattern in an 8" cake pan. Add enough of the syrup to cover mangoes. Set aside.

Heat oven to 350° F. Sift together flour, baking powder, and salt. Set aside.

Cream another 1/3 cup butter with sugar. Beat in remaining 1 tsp. rum and eggs until fluffy. Add flour mixture and milk gradually, beat until smooth.

Spread batter over fruit in cakepan and bake until golden brown 35-40 minutes. Cool on rack for a full 30 minutes before inverting onto cake plate. Serves 12.

Nutritional Analysis per Serving
Calories: 425, Total Fat: 15.4 g., Saturated Fat: 9.0 g.
Cholesterol: 74 mg., Carbohydrate: 61.5 g., Dietary Fiber: .9 g.
Protein: 6.2 g., Sodium: 85 mg.

PINA COLADA CAKE

Serve at your Cinco de Mayo Tea!

3 cups flour
1 tsp. baking soda
1 tsp. salt
1 tsp. cinnamon

2 cups sugar

1-1/2 cups vegetable oil
3 large eggs, lightly beaten
1 8 oz. can crushed pineapple with the liquid
2 cups mashed bananas (about 5 bananas)

3-1/2 oz. flaked coconut
1-1/2 tsp. vanilla

Preheat oven to 350° F. Butter and flour 10" tube pan with removable bottom.

In large bowl sift together first 4 ingredients; add sugar and combine well. In another bowl, combine next 4 ingredients; add to dry ingredients, and stir until just combined. Stir in coconut and vanilla.

Pour into prepared pan and bake 1 hour 10 min. to 1 hour 20 minute or until tester comes out clean. Cool cake on wire rack 15 minutes, then remove from pan.

18 servings.

Nutritional Analysis per Serving
Calories: 400, Total Fat: 21.3 g., Saturated Fat: 4.2 g.
Cholesterol: 35 mg., Carbohydrate: 50.4 g., Dietary Fiber: 1.2 g.
Protein: 3.7 g., Sodium: 214 mg.

APRICOT BRANDY POUND CAKE

"My experience convinced me that tea was better than brandy."
Theodore Roosevelt

- 1 cup butter
- 3 cups sugar
- 6 eggs
- 3 cups flour
- 1/4 tsp. baking soda
- 1/2 tsp. salt
- 1 cup sour cream
- 1/2 tsp. rum extract
- 1 tsp. orange extract
- 1/2 tsp. almond extract
- 1/2 tsp. lemon extract
- 1 tsp. vanilla
- 1/2 cup apricot brandy

Preheat oven to 325° F. Grease and flour a 9" or 10" tube pan. Cream the butter and sugar thoroughly in large bowl. Add eggs one at a time, beating well after each addition.

Sift together flour, soda, and salt three times. Combine sour cream, flavorings and brandy. Add dry ingredients, alternately with sour cream mixture, to butter/sugar/ egg mixture, beginning and ending with dry ingredients.

Pour into prepared pan; bake 60 - 70 minutes.

Cool 15-20 minutes before removing from pan.

Makes 18 servings

Nutritional Analysis per Serving
Calories: 365, Total Fat: 14.7 g., Saturated Fat: 8.5 g.
Cholesterol: 104 mg., Carbohydrate: 50 g., Dietary Fiber: 0.0 g.
Protein: 4.7 g., Sodium: 208 mg.

PEAR WALNUT CAKE

The Pewter Pot • Cashmere, Washington

The upper Wenatchee Valley, where Cashmere is located, is one of the world's premier pear-growing regions. This is one of The Pewter Pot's favorite recipes for pears.

- 2 cups flour
- 1 tsp. cinnamon
- 1 tsp. baking soda
- 1/2 tsp. nutmeg
- 1/2 tsp. salt

- 1/2 cup vegetable oil
- 1-1/2 cups brown sugar
- 3 eggs
- 1/4 cup water
- 1 tsp. vanilla extract
- 3 ripe pears, cored and diced with peel on (use Bartlett, d'Anjou, or Bosc pears)

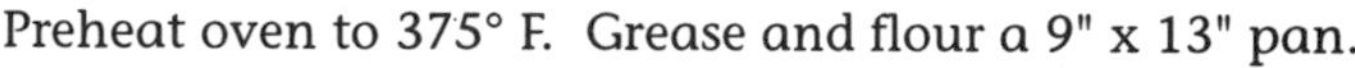

Preheat oven to 375° F. Grease and flour a 9" x 13" pan.

Stir together dry ingredients and set aside. Cream the oil with the sugar and eggs until light and fluffy. Add the water and vanilla and mix well. Stir in dry ingredients.

Add the pears and pour the batter into the prepared pan. Bake for 45 to 55 minutes. Cover with foil if the cake gets too brown during baking. Serve warm with whipped cream or ice cream. Serves 12.

Nutritional Analysis per Serving
Calories: 269, Total Fat: 10.7 g., Saturated Fat: 1.5 g.
Cholesterol: 53 mg., Carbohydrate: 40.2 g., Dietary Fiber: 1.1 g.
Protein: 3.9 g., Sodium: 217 mg.

VIENNESE TART

British Pantry • Redmond, Washington

1 lb. butter.
4 oz. powdered sugar.
12 oz. all-purpose flour.
4 oz. corn flour.
1 tsp. vanilla.
pinch salt.
raspberry, strawberry or apricot jam.
optional food coloring.

Prepare your favorite sweet short pastry. Line tart tins or foil. For a variety, pipe or drop from a teaspoon approximately 1/2 teaspoon of raspberry, strawberry or apricot jam on the pastry.

Prepare filling; whip together the butter and powdered sugar for 3 minutes - until light and fluffy. Sift the all-purpose and corn flour together and add pinch of salt. Slowly add to butter mixture, blend well and then whip for 2 minutes. The texture should be smooth and light similar to thick frosting.

Blend in 1 teaspoon vanilla and any coloring you may wish to add (pink or yellow). Place mixture in a piping bag with star tube and pipe over the jam on the pastry in a circular motion. Bake at 400° F. for about 15 minutes, cool and dust with powdered sugar. Makes 24 tarts.

TEA NOTE:
Mavis Redman of the British Pantry provided this recipe to us from her father's recipe file. She recommends a pot of Darjeeling or Ceylon blend as the perfect accompaniment.

Nutritional Analysis per Serving
Calories: 231, Total Fat: 15.7 g., Saturated Fat: 9.6 g.
Cholesterol: 41 mg., Carbohydrate: 21.3 g., Dietary Fiber: .7 g.
Protein: 2.0 g., Sodium: 158 mg.

VALERIE'S NAKED APPLE PIE

No, my pal Valerie's not naked when she makes this. At least I don't think she is. The pie doesn't have a crust so it's sort of, well, nude. You can apply a little whipped cream in the interest of modesty. A former business partner and forever friend, Valerie Herlocker and her husband Lance are moving from metro Seattle to Camano Island next year. We can't wait to peek in her kitchen window and see what she wears when she bakes this.

1	egg
1/2	cup brown sugar, firmly packed
1/2	cup granulated sugar
1	tsp. vanilla
	pinch of salt
1/2	cup flour
2 or 3	medium sized apples, sliced
1/2	cup coarsely chopped pecans

In a bowl, beat the egg and add the sugars, vanilla and salt. Sift flour and baking powder into egg mixture. Add the apples and nuts. Spread into a greased 9-inch baking pan and bake at 350° F. for 30 minutes or until apples are cooked. Serve warm. Serves 8.

Nutritional Analysis per Serving
Calories: 193, Total Fat: 5.4 g., Saturated Fat: .6 g.
Cholesterol: 27 mg., Carbohydrate: 35.8 g., Dietary Fiber: 1.4 g.
Protein: 2.2 g., Sodium: 28 mg.

Lemon Custard with Almond Tartlett

Piccadilly Circus - Snohomish, Washington

Custard:

	zest and juice 6 of lemons (about 1 cup)
2	eggs
1-1/2	cups sugar
1/2 to 1	cup butter

Zest and squeeze 6 lemons, place all the ingredients except the butter into a bowl over a double boiler. Whisk together until smooth, add in the butter and cook slowly until the butter is melted, then periodically whisk until thickened. Cover and chill.

Cookie:

1	cup butter
3/4	cup sugar
3	eggs
1	tsp. almond extract
1-1/2	cups all-purpose flour
1	cup finely ground blanched almonds

Soften the butter and whisk with the sugar until creamed. Add the eggs and extract and whisk in completely. Fold in the flour and almonds. Flatten little balls of dough on parchment and bake at 350° F. until golden, about 10 minutes.

When the cookies have cooled, pipe or spoon a dollop of the custard on top, garnish with a colorful slice of fresh strawberry, sprig of mint, or orange zest. 36 servings.

TEA NOTE:
Recommended tea is Taylor's Yorkshire Gold or Darjeeling.

Nutritional Analysis per Serving
Calories: 168, Total Fat: 10.4 g., Saturated Fat: 5.1 g.
Cholesterol: 50 mg., Carbohydrate: 17.3 g., Dietary Fiber: .3 g.
Protein: 2.3 g., Sodium: 87 mg.

PARISIAN FRUIT TART

Tea & Crumpets - Shelton, Washington

Tea & Crumpets' owner Connie Holman grew up in Louisiana Cajun country and learned to cook with the bold flavor influences of that culture. This dramatic tart is eye-pleasing as well as delicious.

3 T. cornstarch
1/8 tsp. salt
1-1/4 cups sugar
1 cup light cream
1 cup milk, scalded
3 egg yolks
1 tsp. pure vanilla extract

1/2 cup heavy cream, whipped

1/2 cup water
1 tsp. lemon juice
2 cups sliced peaches, blueberries, nectarines, apricots, or other fruit in season

Make or buy a 9" tart shell. Set aside until completely cooled.

In the top of a double boiler mix cornstarch, salt and 1/4 cup of sugar. Mix in the light cream then hot milk, place over hot water and cook, stirring until thickened. Cook 10 minutes longer stirring occasionally. Beat egg yolks in bowl, gradually add the hot cream mixture, stir, return to double boiler and cook for 2 minutes. Remove from heat, stir in vanilla and cool completely. Fold in whipped cream and pour into the tart shell. Cook remaining sugar, water and lemon juice for 5 minutes. Add the fruit, cook 5 minutes then remove the fruit with slotted spoon and chill. Cook the remaining syrup in pan for 10 minutes or until very thick, cool 10 minutes. Arrange chilled fruit over cream mixture and brush with syrup. Chill thoroughly. Makes 12 servings.

Nutritional Analysis per Serving
Calories: 239, Total Fat: 9.6 g., Saturated Fat: 5.5 g.
Cholesterol: 83 mg., Carbohydrate: 35.8 g., Dietary Fiber: .6 g.
Protein: 3.4 g., Sodium: 136 mg.

FRESH NECTARINE TART

Ken's youngest daughter Mandy Lewis is a dental hygienist in New Zealand. That doesn't keep her from having a sweet tooth. Here's her recipe.

Crust:
- 1-1/4 cup flour
- 1/4 tsp. salt
- 1/2 cup butter, cut in chunks
- 2 T. sour cream
- 4 large ripe nectarines, peeled and thinly sliced.

Custard:
- 4 T. sour cream
- 1 cup sugar
- 1/4 cup flour
- 1/4 tsp. salt
- 1/4 tsp. almond extract
- 1/4 tsp. mace
- 3 egg yolks

Preheat oven to 375° F.

To make crust, place butter chunks in food processor fitted with steel blade. Pour flour, salt, and 2 tablespoons sour cream over butter and process until mixture is crumbly. Press mixture into bottom of greased 9" tart pan with removable bottom. Bake 20 minutes or until lightly golden. Arrange nectarine slices over crust in concentric circles overlapping slightly for a petal design.

To make the custard, combine remaining sour cream, sugar, flour, salt, almond extract, mace and egg yolks in processor and process 5 to 10 seconds or until blended. Pour over nectarines.

Bake 35 to 40 minutes or until firm. Cool on wire rack. When completely cooled, remove sides of tart pan. Serve at room temperature, but store in refrigerator. 18 Servings

Nutritional Analysis per Serving
Calories: 161, Total Fat: 7.2 g., Saturated Fat: 4.1 g.
Cholesterol: 51 mg., Carbohydrate: 22.9 g., Dietary Fiber: .5 g.
Protein: 2.0 g., Sodium: 115 mg.

TINY PECAN PIES

Jacque and Bob Chase are the new owners of The Homespun Market in LaConner, Washington. She's even a gourmet cook . . .

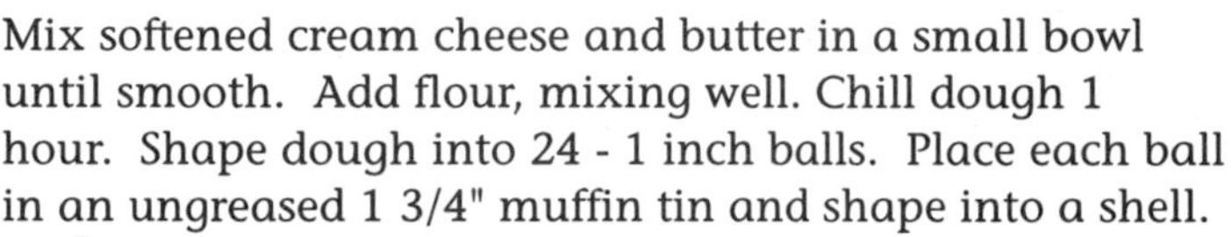

24 Pastry Shells:
1/2 cup butter or margarine
3 oz. soft cream cheese
1 cup flour

Mix softened cream cheese and butter in a small bowl until smooth. Add flour, mixing well. Chill dough 1 hour. Shape dough into 24 - 1 inch balls. Place each ball in an ungreased 1 3/4" muffin tin and shape into a shell.

Filling:
3/4 cup brown sugar firmly packed
pinch salt
1 T. butter
1 tsp. vanilla
1 egg
2/3 cup chopped pecans

Combine brown sugar, butter, egg, salt and vanilla in a mixing bowl. Beat at medium speed with an electric mixer until smooth. Layer 1/2 teaspoon of chopped pecans in bottom of each pastry shell. Add 1 teaspoon of filling and 1/2 teaspoon of pecans. Bake in 325° F. oven for 25 minutes.

Yield: 24 Tiny Pies.

Nutritional Analysis per Serving
Calories: 109, Total Fat: 7.8 g., Saturated Fat: 3.7 g.
Cholesterol: 24 mg., Carbohydrate: 9.1 g., Dietary Fiber: .2 g.
Protein: 1.3 g., Sodium: 69 mg.

TEA TIME SWEETS

JUDITH'S NORWEGIAN RICE PUDDING

Judith's Tearooms and Rose Cafe • Poulsbo, Washington

Judith Goodrich, owner of Judith's Tearooms and Rose Cafe in Poulsbo, has patrons who make the trip to Poulsbo just to have this " light and truly Norwegian pudding."

1-1/2 cups rice
4 cups water
1 tsp. salt

1/2 cup sugar
1 T. cinnamon
1 T. vanilla
2 cups raspberries or lingonberries
1 pint heavy whipping cream
1 T. sugar

Bring water and salt to a boil. Add rice and boil for 10 minutes. Reduce heat and simmer 10 minutes more. Set aside When cooled, gently stir in sugar, cinnamon and vanilla. Refrigerate.

Whip fresh heavy cream with just a little sugar. Set aside. If fresh berries are in season, use them, but if using frozen berries, take as much care as possible to not crush the fruit. Do not add sugar to the berries. The blend of tart and sweet is what makes this a special treat.

Just before assembling, fold the whipped cream into the rice porridge. Using wine glasses, layer the pudding with the berries and continue layering. Top with a dollop of whipped cream. Makes approximately 10 servings.

Nutritional Analysis per Serving
Calories: 324, Total Fat: 18 g., Saturated Fat: 11 g.
Cholesterol: 65 mg., Carbohydrate: 38.3 g., Dietary Fiber: 2.4 g.
Protein: 3.2 g., Sodium: 236 mg.

Marysville White-Chocolate Strawberries

1 pint (2 cups) fresh strawberries
6 oz. white chocolate

Wash and pat dry the berries. Leave the hulls on. Melt white chocolate in top of double boiler over hot water (not boiling). Holding strawberries by the stem, dip about 2/3 of each berry into chocolate. Let excess drip off, then set strawberry on a baking sheet. Repeat for all berries, chill for 1/2 hour or until chocolate is solid. Serve chilled. Makes about 12 dipped strawberries.

Nutritional Analysis per Dipped Strawberry
Calories: 116, Total Fat: 5.4 g., Saturated Fat: 2.9 g.
Cholesterol: 0 mg., Carbohydrate: 18.9 g., Dietary Fiber: 4.2 g.
Protein: 1.5 g., Sodium: 4 mg.

ANNIE'S BREAD PUDDING

Annie Fenwick's Tea Room • Gresham, Oregon

"Like the word itself, pudding is quietly unassuming and soothing . . . [it has] an honesty and dignity all its own."
Jennifer Wilkinson
Traditional Home Magazine

- 4 cups cubed, buttered bread
- 2 cups milk, scalded
- 1/2 cup sugar
- 2 eggs slightly beaten
- 1/4 tsp. salt
- 1 tsp. cinnamon
- Zest of 1 lemon
- 1 tsp. lemon extract
- 2 tsp. almond extract
- 1/2 cup raisins (optional)

Place buttered bread in oven proof dish. Blend remaining ingredients and pour over bread cubes. Place dish in pan of water 1" deep. Bake 40-45 minutes, or until silver knife comes out clean.

Serve warm with "Toriani" butterscotch syrup and whipped cream. Makes 12 servings.

Nutritional Analysis per Serving
Calories: 261, Total Fat: 5.5 g., Saturated Fat: 2.6 g.
Cholesterol: 46 mg., Carbohydrate: 45.8 g., Dietary Fiber: .4 g.
Protein: 7 g., Sodium: 731 mg.

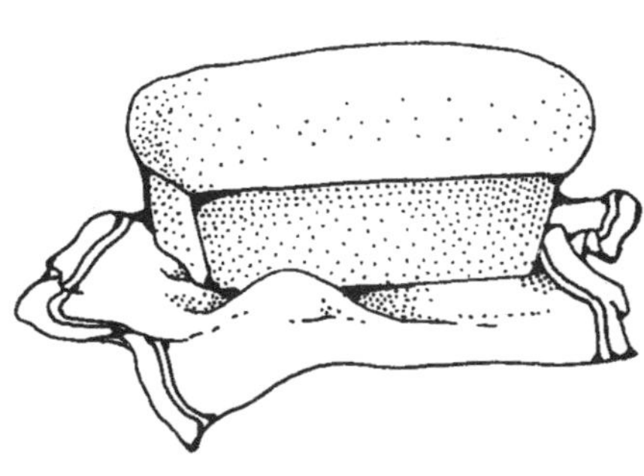

JENNY'S NEW ZEALAND PAVLOVA

Pavlova was a tea treat originally created in Australia at the turn of the century as a tribute to the touring Russian ballerina of that name. This recipe was adapted by Ken's oldest daughter, Jenny Lewis, a school vice-principal in Auckland, New Zealand:

- 6 egg whites
- 2 cups extra-fine sugar (available at specialty British markets, but simple to make by processing regular granulated sugar a few seconds in your blender)
- 1-1/2 tsp. white vinegar
- 1-1/2 tsp. vanilla
- 1 T. cornstarch
- 2 cups whipping cream
- Fresh fruit in season, kiwis and strawberries are especially nice

In a metal bowl, beat egg whites to stiff peaks. Add one tablespoon sugar at a time until all has been added and the egg whites are glossy (15-20 minutes) Fold in vanilla, vinegar and cornstarch.

Preheat oven to 300° F. Line baking sheet with foil. Butter the foil and outline a 7" circle. Heap the egg mixture onto the circle, molding the sides higher with a slight depression in the center.

Place on bottom rack and bake 45 minutes. Turn off the heat and leave until oven is cool. Meanwhile whip the cream and set aside. Remove the egg meringue from oven and top with the whipped cream and sliced kiwis, strawberries, blueberries, blackberries or any combination of fresh fruit. Serve immediately. Makes 6 servings.

Nutritional Analysis per Serving
Calories: 555, Total Fat: 29.4 g., Saturated Fat: 18.3 g.
Cholesterol: 109 mg., Carbohydrate: 70.6 g., Dietary Fiber: .2 g.
Protein: 5.1 g., Sodium: 85 mg.

APRICOT BAKED PEARS

"What beautiful fruit! I love fruit when it's expensive."
Sir Arthur Wing Pinero
The Second Mrs. Tanqueray

Local pears are good even though they're not expensive, and this is particularly wonderful on a chilly evening.

1/3 cup apricot jam
1/4 cup orange juice
4 medium pears, halved, peeled and cored
Whipped cream (optional)
Ground nutmeg (optional)

In a baking dish, stir together the jam and the orange juice. Place pears in dish, cut side down; spoon sauce over top. Bake covered, at 350° F. for 25 to 30 minutes (or until tender).

Serve warm in individual dessert dish. Spoon sauce over pears. If desired, top with whipped cream and sprinkle with nutmeg. Makes 4 servings.

Nutritional Analysis per Serving
Calories: 218, Total Fat: 6 g., Saturated Fat: 3.3 g.
Cholesterol: 19 mg., Carbohydrate: 44.3 g., Dietary Fiber: 4.3 g.
Protein: 1.2 g., Sodium: 16 mg.

KIKO'S GREEN TEA ICE CREAM

The green tea flavor is very refreshing. This easy dessert ice cream does not require an ice cream freezer to prepare.

1	qt. heavy cream
1	pint milk
1-1/2	cup sugar
1	heaping tsp. Mattcha (or grind any good green tea into a powder)

Mix the cream, sugar and milk in a large bowl until the sugar dissolves. Place the dry green tea in a measuring cup and add enough warm water to measure 3/4 cup. Mix the tea and water into a thin paste. Add this to the cream, milk, and sugar mixture. Place in the freezer until the mixture is frozen about an inch from the sides all around and slushy in the center. Scoop into blender and blend until smooth, about 2 minutes. Return it to the freezer until completely frozen. Makes 12 servings.

Nutritional Analysis per Serving
Calories: 317, Total Fat: 21.3 g., Saturated Fat: 13.2 g.
Cholesterol: 75 mg., Carbohydrate: 29.9 g., Dietary Fiber: 0.0 g.
Protein: 3.3 g., Sodium: 51 mg.

SWEET SPICED PECANS

I think when "visions of sugarplums danced in their heads" these festive Sweet Spiced Pecans were doing the Macarena too.

- 1 cup sugar
- 1-1/2 T. ground cinnamon
- 1 tsp. ground cloves
- 1 tsp. salt
- 1 tsp. ground ginger
- 1/2 tsp. ground nutmeg
- 1 egg white
- 1 T. cold water
- 1 pound pecans

Preheat oven to 250° F. Butter a large jelly roll pan.

Mix together thoroughly all dry ingredients. (May be done in food processor.) Beat egg white with cold water until frothy but not stiff. Add spiced sugar mixture and stir well. Add nuts; stir well to coat.

Spread nuts in pan, place in oven and bake for 1 hour, stirring to separate every 15 to 20 minutes. Remove from oven when dry and toasty.

Cool. Store in airtight container. Makes 16 one ounce servings.

Nutritional Analysis per Serving
Calories: 242, Total Fat: 19.3 g., Saturated Fat: 1.6 g.
Cholesterol: 0 mg., Carbohydrate: 18.4 g., Dietary Fiber: 2.6 g.
Protein: 2.5 g., Sodium: 138 mg.

Grand Marnier Chocolate Truffles

Ken grew up in Liverpool, England, where every dessert is referred to as "pudding" and still ends a meal with the hopeful query "What's for puddin', luv?" These are far better than puddin' . . .

- 8 oz. plain, but high quality, milk chocolate bar (we like Cadbury's)
- 2 -3 T. whipping cream
- 2 T. Grand Marnier liqueur
- 1 egg, slightly beaten
- 3/4 tsp. grated orange rind
- 2 T. unsalted butter

Coatings: cocoa, finely chopped nuts, chocolate sprinkles, or coconut

Melt chocolate over low heat in double boiler. Warm up the whipping cream and stir it into the chocolate. Remove from heat and immediately add the liqueur. Whisk in egg, orange rind and butter until the mixture is smooth. Refrigerate for 2 hours, until it is firm. Using a melon scoop or teaspoon, scoop out chocolate and roll into balls. Roll in the coating you choose. Refrigerate immediately, or freeze. Makes about 2 dozen truffles.

Nutritional Analysis per Serving
Calories: 75, Total Fat: 5.1 g., Saturated Fat: 2.8 g.
Cholesterol: 15 mg., Carbohydrate: 6.3 g., Dietary Fiber: .4 g.
Protein: 1.2 g., Sodium: 11 mg.

THE CONNAUGHT HOTEL'S TRIFLE

Conceived as a London residence for the landed gentry, this dignified hotel was built in 1897 and named in honor of Queen Victoria's third son.

Sponge:	5	eggs.
	2/3	cup sugar.
	1	cup all-purpose flour.
Syrup:	3	T. water.
	3	T.sugar.
	3	T. dry sherry
	1	T. rum
Custard:	2	egg yolks.
	1	egg.
	1/4	cup sugar.
	1	T. cornstarch.
	1-1/2	cup milk
	1	cup black currant or cherry jelly.
Whipped Cream:	1	cup whipping cream.
	1	T. sugar.
	1	T. sifted sugar powder.
	1	T. vanilla.
	1	cup fresh raspberries.
	1/4	cup toasted sliced almonds.
	1/4	cup chopped pistachio nuts.

For sponge cake; Grease and lightly flour a 9x9x2 inch baking pan.

In a large mixing bowl, beat the 5 eggs with an electric mixer on high speed for about 4 minutes or until thick. Gradually add the 2/3 cup of sugar; beat at medium speed for 4-5 minutes or until light and fluffy. Fold in the flour. Turn batter into prepared pan. Bake in a 350° F. oven for 20 minutes or until top springs pack when touched lightly. Remove and cool in pan on a wire rack for 10 minutes. Remove from pan and cool completely.

Meanwhile, for syrup; Place 3 tablespoons water and 3 tablespoons sugar in a small saucepan. Bring to boil, remove from heat, stir in the sherry and rum. Cool to room temperature.

For custard; Beat together the yolks and one egg, set aside. In a medium saucepan stir together the1/4 cup sugar and the cornstarch. Stir in milk. Cook and stir over medium heat until thickened and bubbly. Cook and stir for 2 minutes more. Remove from heat. Gradually stir about half of the hot mixture into the beaten egg mixture. Return all of the egg mixture to the saucepan. Cook and stir until nearly bubbly, but do not boil. Reduce heat, cook and stir 2 minutes more. Remove from heat and cool slightly.

When cake is cool, split in half horizontally. Spread the cut side of the bottom layer with the jelly. Replace the top layer of the cake. Cut the cake into 3/4-inch cubes. Place the cake cubes in a 2- 3 quart glass bowl. Pour the cooled syrup over the cake cubes. Pour warm custard over all. Cover and chill.

Just before serving, place the whipping cream, one table-spoon sugar, powdered sugar, and vanilla in a medium mixing bowl.

Beat with an electric mixer until stiff peaks form, smooth over top of trifle and garnish with the almonds and pisachio nuts topping them with the fresh raspberries and sprigs of mint. Yields about 24 servings.

Nutritional Analysis per Serving
Calories: 182, Total Fat: 7.4 g., Saturated Fat: 3.3 g.
Cholesterol: 87 mg., Carbohydrate: 25.8 g., Dietary Fiber: .8 g.
Protein: 3.7 g., Sodium: 33 mg.

WHOOPIE PIES

"Precisely," Claire nodded when I yelled "Whoopie!" as she unveiled a plate of decadent chocolate sandwich cookies with light dreamy filling and flourished it under my nose. Claire and husband Kim Winget, youthful retirees from the San Francisco Bay area, moved to our Camano Island hill last year and brought with them much joy and energy to the neighborhood.

Cookies:

- 1/3 cup vegetable shortening
- 1 cup sugar
- 1 egg
- 2 cups sifted all-purpose flour
- 1/2 cup unsweetened cocoa powder
- 1/4 tsp. salt
- 1/2 cup buttermilk
- 1 tsp. vanilla
- 1 tsp. baking soda dissolved in 1/2 cup of water.

Filling:

- 3/4 cup shortening
- 6 T. (heaped) marshmallow cream
- 1 cup powdered sugar
- 1 tsp. vanilla
- 1/4 cup milk (approx.)

Cream shortening until light and add sugar gradually, beat in egg. Sift flour, cocoa and salt. Combine buttermilk and vanilla. Add sifted dry ingredients to creamed mixture alternately with buttermilk-vanilla combination, beginning and ending with dry ingredients. Beat in baking soda-water solution. (Mixture will be more the consistency of thick batter than a cookie dough.) Drop by rounded teaspoon-fulls onto well- greased cookie sheets, spaced about 1-1/2 inches apart keeping cookie size and shape as uniform as possible.

Bake in 400° F. oven 7-8 minutes, or until a finger pressed in the center of a cookie leaves a print that springs back slowly. Remove at once to wire racks to cool.

Prepare filling by beating the shortening, marshmallow creme, vanilla, and sugar; adding milk until filling is a good spreading consistency. Sandwich cookies together with filling and enjoy.

Makes 36 Whoopies.

Nutritional Analysis per Serving
Calories: 126, Total Fat: 6.6 g., Saturated Fat: 2.0 g.
Cholesterol: 7 mg., Carbohydrate: 16.1 g., Dietary Fiber: .4 g.
Protein: 1.3 g., Sodium: 57 mg.

FROZEN MOCK FRANGOS

During a meeting last year of the local fire department auxiliary, the "Fireflies," a plate of light, cool treats caused quite a buzz. We have Terry Drinkwine to thank for this refreshing recipe.

Graham Cracker or Vanilla Wafer cookie crumbs
1/2 cup butter or margarine
2 cups powdered sugar
4 ozs. unsweetened solid chocolate, melted
4 eggs
1 T. Creme de Menthe or peppermint flavoring.
2 tsp. vanilla.

Cover the bottom of small foil cups with Graham Cracker or Vanilla Wafer crumbs.

Beat butter or margarine and powdered sugar until light. Add melted chocolate then eggs, beat well. Add peppermint flavoring or Creme de Menthe and vanilla and mix well.

Fill cups and put in freezer until frozen solid, (about 1 hour). Garnish with dollops of whipped cream, top with half maraschino cherry and freeze until serving time.

Makes 48 desserts.

Nutritional Analysis per Serving
Calories: 126, Total Fat: 3.8 g., Saturated Fat: 2.1 g.
Cholesterol: 23 mg., Carbohydrate: 7.2 g., Dietary Fiber: .4 g.
Protein: .9 g., Sodium: 36 mg.

THEME TEAS

All too often, those of us who did not grow up with Afternoon Tea develop some misconceptions about it. Fostered by Masterpiece Theater and fueled by supermarket gothic romance novels, an Afternoon Tea could indeed be envisioned as intimidating with an oh-so-proper protocol and stodgy ritual altogether alien to our Northwest lifestyle. But as you will learn firsthand by visiting the tearooms in this book, tea simply is not stiff, uncomfortable, or rigidly formal at all.

Teas can be the perfect backdrop for any festive event, whether it be the return of the hummingbirds in spring or a bridal shower, a child's birthday or announcing an engagement, teas are always appropriate and fun. In an era where alcohol has fallen from favor, a tea setting can even provide a millenium alternative to cocktail parties that is healthy, sane and civil.

We have presented some of our favorite theme teas throughout the book (see the index under "theme teas"). Additionally, we would like to offer the following list of events and excuses to gather friends and loved ones to enjoy some taste treats and a good cuppa. Cheers!

MORE IDEAS FOR THEME TEAS

Children's Teas:

Teddy Bear Tea

Mad Hatter's Tea

Easter Bunny Tea

Fourth of July Tea

Four-Legged Friend Tea

Gingerbread Tea

Grown-Up Teas:

Valentine's Day Tea

St. Patrick's Day Tea

Graduation Tea

Bridal Tea

Baby Shower Tea

Harvest Tea

Angel Tea

SPREADS & CONDIMENTS

APPLE GINGER CHUTNEY

When my grandparents lived on the cold plains of Alberta, my grandmother longed to live somewhere that she could grow apple trees. She found that place in subsequent homes in British Columbia and Washington, and here is her tangy chutney.

- 4 large Granny Smith apples, peeled, cored, and chopped
- 2 cups minced onion
- 1-1/2 cups cider vinegar
- 1-1/2 cups firmly packed brown sugar
- 1 cup golden raisins
- 1/4 cup minced peeled fresh ginger root
- 1 red bell pepper, minced
- 3/4 tsp. dry mustard
- 3/4 tsp. salt
- 1/2 tsp. dried hot red pepper flakes

In large saucepan combine the apples, onion, vinegar, brown sugar, raisins, ginger root, bell pepper, mustard, salt, and the red pepper flakes. Bring the mixture to a boil, stirring, and cook over moderate heat, stirring occasionally for 40 minutes, or until it has thickened. Spoon into glass jars with tight-fitting lids or seal in freezer bags. This chutney keeps, covered and chilled, for 2 weeks. Makes about 6 cups (24 - 2 oz. servings).

Nutritional Analysis per Serving
Calories: 69, Total Fat: .1 g., Saturated Fat: 0 g.
Cholesterol: 0 mg., Carbohydrate: 18.1 g., Dietary Fiber: .9 g.
Protein: .4 g., Sodium: 121 mg.

AUNT MARWAYNE'S PLUM CHUTNEY

"Try this chutney spread thinly on a tea sandwich of turkey or chicken, with a little bit of mayonnaise," says my aunt, the astrologer, Marwayne Leipzig.

- 8 cups (pitted, cut up) ripe blue Italian plums
- 2 cups raisins
- 1 cup brown sugar
- 1 cup onion, chopped
- 1/2 cup vinegar
- 10 cloves of garlic, minced
- 8 T. mustard seed
- 2 T. chopped ginger
- 1/2 tsp. cayenne pepper

In a pot over medium-low heat, cook all the ingredients for about an hour.

Freeze in small freezer-safe containers, or spoon into hot jelly jars and seal the same way you would when putting up jam or jelly. Yields about 60 servings

Nutritional Analysis per Serving
Calories: 44, Total Fat: .6 g., Saturated Fat: 0 g.
Cholesterol: 0 mg., Carbohydrate: 10 g., Dietary Fiber: .7 g.
Protein: .8 g., Sodium: 12 mg.

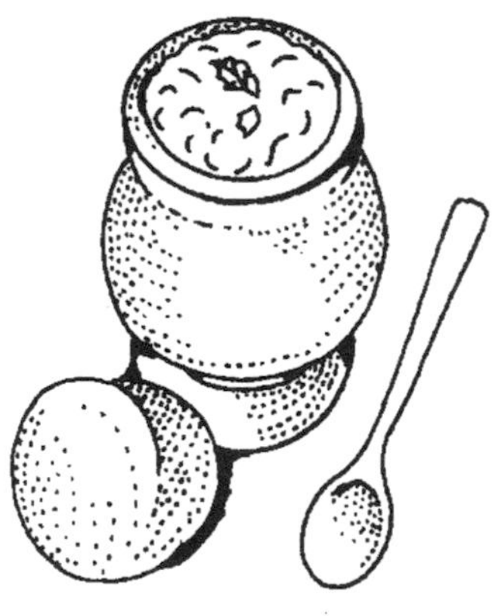

CALICO CREAM CHEESE

Pomeroy House • Yacolt, Washington

A colorful, fresh tasting sandwich spread.

Combine in a medium bowl;

8 oz. cream cheese softened
1/4 green pepper chopped into 1/4" cubes
1/4 yellow or orange pepper chopped into 1/4" cubes
1/4 red pepper chopped into 1/4" cubes
1 T grated onion
1/4 tsp. anchovy paste
salt and pepper to taste

Generously spead filling on party rye bread and garnish with fresh dill sprigs.

Nutritional Analysis per two-tablespoon serving
Calories: 51, Total Fat: 5 g., Saturated Fat: 3.1 g.
Cholesterol: 16 mg., Carbohydrate: .7 g., Dietary Fiber: .1 g.
Protein: 1.1 g., Sodium: 78 mg.

QUEEN MARY'S LEMON CURD

Queen Mary • Seattle, Washington

This recipe is from England where it has graced the Greengo family tea tables for at least four generations. It's now a favorite with patrons of Queen Mary.

10 egg yolks
13 oz. fresh lemon juice
1/2 teaspoon salt
1 packet of gelatin
1 lb., 2 oz. granulated sugar
1/2 lb. butter
peel of 4 lemons

Combine egg yolks, sugar and lemon juice in heavy-bottom saucepan and stir until almost boiling. Over medium heat whisk in the rest of the ingredients.

Bloom gelatin in cold water, dissolve over low heat and add to hot mixture, stir to incorporate. Strain.

Yields about 40 servings.

TEA NOTE:
The suggested tea to complement is Earl Grey or Queen Victoria blend.

Nutritional Analysis per Serving
Calories: 108, Total Fat: 5.9 g., Saturated Fat: 3.3 g.
Cholesterol: 66 mg., Carbohydrate: 14.2 g., Dietary Fiber: .3 g.
Protein: .9 g., Sodium: 76 mg.

CHAMPAGNE JELLY

Angelina's French Country Tea Parlour - Aurora, Oregon

Angelina's owners Marilyn and Angela offer this delicious Champagne Jelly with their heart-shaped ginger lemon scones.

- 4 cups sugar
- 1 cup white grape juice
- 1 cup brut Champagne
- 1/4 tsp. citric acid
- 3 oz. pouch liquid pectin

In a deep saucepan combine sugar, grape juice, Champagne, and citric acid. Cook, stirring constantly over medium high heat, until it comes to a full boil that cannot be stirred down.

Add pectin and again cook stirring to a full boil once more, boil for one minute. Remove from heat and skim off foam.

TEA NOTE
Recommended Tea: Angelina's own signature French blend.

Nutritional Analysis per 2 ounce Serving
Calories: 186, Total Fat: 0 g., Saturated Fat: 0 g.
Cholesterol: 0 mg., Carbohydrate: 46.1 g., Dietary Fiber: 0 g.
Protein: .1 g., Sodium: 9 mg.

LEMON CURD

The Country Tea Garden • Selah, Washington

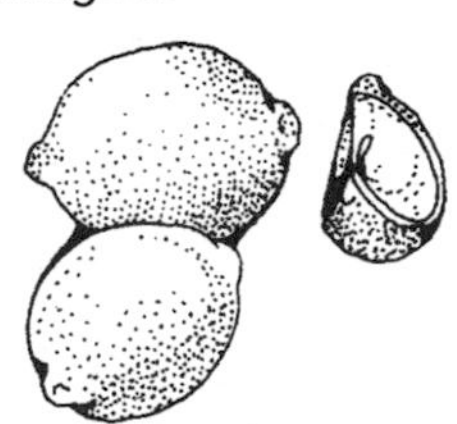

- 5 eggs
- 1 cup sugar
- 2/3 cup lemon juice
- 1/2 cup real butter (1 stick)
- lemon peel (optional)

Blend eggs, sugar and juice in a blender on high while melting butter, add melted butter into mixture while blending.

Cook over a medium low heat stirring constantly until the mixture thickens enough to mound. Pour into containers and cool.

Serve with scones and Devonshire cream.

Nutritional Analysis per 2 ounce serving
Calories: 166, Total Fat: 9.7 g., Saturated Fat: 5.4 g.
Cholesterol: 109 mg., Carbohydrate: 18.1 g., Dietary Fiber: .1 g.
Protein: 2.7 g., Sodium: 104 mg.

POMEGRANATE SYRUP

Creative PossibiliTEAS - Aurora, Oregon

Creative PossibiliTEAS owner Jane Blackman loves the beauty of pomegranates. "It's like playing with rubies," she muses. Jane suggests wearing an old apron and keeping a damp cloth handy for wipe ups when working with her favorite fruit. She serves this ruby red syrup in an elegant crystal decanter tied with a pink ribbon for added flair. While Jane favors it in a high quality Ceylon tea it can flavor any tea, and is especially yummy in iced teas.

Remove seeds from one large pomegranate (or 2 small). Be sure to remove the membrane. Simmer seeds in one cup of water in microwave or on stove top until seeds are expanded, (or you can grind the seeds in a processor before cooking for more essence from the seed.) Drain liquid from seeds. While still warm, add one or two cups of sugar to the juice. Cover and chill overnight. Use to sweeten tea. Cover unused syrup and keep refrigerated.

Beverages

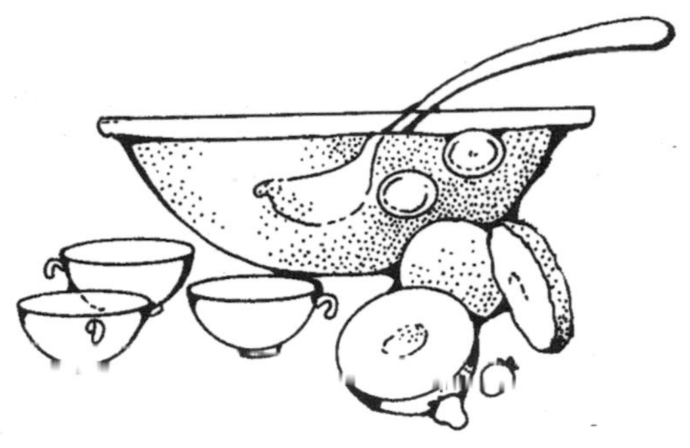

LEMONADE COOLER

Village Tea Room • Edmonds, Washington

8 tea bags
3 quarts boiling water
3/4 cup sugar
1 (12 oz.) can lemonade
Lemon slices
Mint
1 (32 oz.) bottle ginger ale, chilled

Place tea bags in boiling water and steep 10 minutes. remove tea bags. Add sugar and stir until desolved. Add lemonade and chill.

Just before serving add ginger ale. Garnish with mint sprig. Yield 16 cups.

ORIGINAL CHAI

Here is just one version of Chai made from the original spices and other ingredients. Experiment with your own:

1 quart milk
1 tsp. cinnamon
1/2 tsp. cardamom
1/2 tsp. fresh ginger, peeled and minced
1/2 tsp. cloves
10 tsp. honey
8 tsp. black tea
2 tsp. vanilla

Add cinnamon, cardamom, ginger, cloves to milk in saucepan. Simmer for 45 minutes, stirring occasionally. Remove from heat and add honey and vanilla. Boil 1 quart of water, pour into teapot in which you have already placed 8 tsp. of a good quality black tea. Allow to steep for 5 minutes. Blend the prepared tea with the hot spiced milk mixture and aerate by pouring between two containers. Strain and serve. Store in your refrigerator and reheat or serve chilled. (Try serving this chilled instead of an after dinner liqueur for a real eye-opener.)

Glossary of Tea Terms

A

Agony of the leaves - Tea tasters expression descriptive of the unfolding of the leaves when boiling water is applied.

Assam - High grade tea grown in Assam Province in Northeast India.

Aroma - Denotes that both the tea leaf and infusion have one of a certain number of smells which are highly valued. Such aroma is connected with flavor and is highly fragrant.

Autumnal teas - Term applied to India and Formosa teas, meaning teas touched with cool weather.

B

Biscuity - A pleasant aroma associated with a well-fired Assam

Black tea - Any tea that has been thoroughly fermented before being fired as opposed to green or Oolong tea.

Blend - A mixture of different growths.

Body - A liquor having both fullness and strength as opposed to a thin liquor.

Bright - Sparkling red liquor. Denotes good tea which has life as opposed to a dull looking infused leaf or liquor.

Brisk - "live" not flat liquor. Usually of pungent character.

C

Caffeine content - In a cup of tea, less than 1 grain; in a cup of coffee, 1.5 grain.

Ch'a - (Char)(Chai) Chinese. Tea.

Color - Color of liquor which varies from country to country and district to district.

D

Darjeeling - The finest and most delicately flavored of the Indian teas. Grown chiefly in the Himalayan Mountains at elevations ranging from 2,500 to 6,500 feet.

E

Even - Tea leaf which is true to grade and consisting of pieces of roughly equal size. When applied to infused leaf it is usually combined with bright and coppery.

F

Fermented (black) tea - Chinese refer to black tea as "hong Cha" or "Red tea" because when it is brewed it takes on a reddish-orange color. More popular often among Westerners than Chinese. Often used to make specialty blends with the addition of Jasmine blossoms or spices.

Full - Strong tea, without bitterness, having color and substance as opposed to thin and empty.

G

Garden - Used interchangeably with "plantation" in some tea countries, but usually referrind to an estate unit.

Garden mark - The mark put on tea chests by the estate to identify its particular product.

Goddess - A semi fermented tea. Has a stern taste and is credited as an aid to digestion.

Green tea - Tea leaves that have been sterilized either in live steam, hot air, or hot pans, whereby fermentation is prevented, and then rolled and dried.

H

Handkerchief tea - From the island of Formosa. It gets its name from the fact that Chinese tea growers bring down from their little gardens or farms verry tippy teas, often of the highest quality, in large silk handkerchiefs.

I

Ichiban-Cha - Japanese for "first tea," or first plucking.

M

Malty - Slightly high-fired tea, like Keemun

Mature - No flatness or rawness.

Monster - Dutch for "sample."

N

Nose - The aroma of tea.

Oolong - From the Chinese wu-lung meaning "black dragon." A semi femented tea of fine quality, hand rolled and fired in baskets over pits containing red-hot charcoal. Originally shipped principally from Guanzhou and Amoy in China, the production of Oolong was introduced more than a century ago to Taiwan.

Sappy - Full juicy liquor.

Scented tea - Made in China and Taiwan by introducing jasmine, gardenia, or yulan blossoms during the firing and packing process.

Self drinking - In tea tasting, a tea is said to "stand-up" when it holds its original color and flavor.

Smoky - Tasting of smoke, used interchangeably with the term "tarry."

Standing up - In tea tasting, a tea is said to "stand-up" when it holds its original color and flavor.

Stand out - Liquor above the average.

Stewy - Soft liquor, lacking point.

Strength - Thick liquor, pungent and brisk.

Sweet - A light, not undesirable liquor.

Tea - Tea is the tender leaves, leaf, buds, and tender internodes of different varieties of Thea sinesis prepared and cured by recognized methods of manufacture.

Tip - The bud leaf of the tea plant.

Tippy tea - Teas with white or golden tips. (See handkerchief tea.)

Well twisted - Leaf which is tightly rolled or twisted which is indicative of ideally withered tea.

TEA SUPPLIERS

Barnes & Watson Fine Teas
1319 Dexter Avenue N. #30
Seattle, WA 98109

Blue Willow Tea
911 E. Pike, Suite #204
Seattle, WA 98122

C.B.I. / Xanadu Teas
2181 N.W. Nicolai St.
Portland, OR 97210

Camellia Tea Company
P.O. Box 8310
Metairie, LA 70011-8310

Celestial Seasonings
4600 Sleepytime Dr.
Boulder, CO 80301

Crabtree & Evelyn, Ltd.
Box 167
Woodstock Hill, CT 06284

East India Tea
1481 - Third St.
San Francisco, CA 94107

East Indies Co.
7 Keystone Dr.
Lebanon, PA 17042

Eastern Shore Tea
550 Main St.
Church Hill, MD 21623

Eden Tea
701 Tecumseh Road
Clinton, MI 49236

First Colony Tea
204-222 West 22nd St.
P.O. Box 11005
Norfolk, VA 23517

Fortnum & Mason Ltd.
Piccadilly, London
England W1A 1ER

Fox Mountian Farm
1600 Chippewa St.
New Orleans, LA 70130

Golden Moon Tea
P.O. Box 1646
Woodinville, WA 98072

Grace Tea Company
50 W. 17th
New York, NY 10011

Harney & Sons Fine Teas
P.O. Box 638
Salisbury, CT 06068

Kinnells Scottish Teas
P.O. Box 1283
Edmonds, WA 98020

Lindsay's Teas
380 Swift Ave. Suite 10
South San Francisco, CA 94080

Market Spice Tea
85-A Pike Place
Seattle, WA 98101

McNulty's
109 Christopher St.
New York, NY 10014

Peet's Coffee, Tea, & Spice
2124 Vine St.
Berkeley, CA 94708

The Republic of Tea
8 Digital Dr. Suite 100
Novato, CA 94949

TEA SUPPLIERS

Royal Gardens Tea
P.O. Box 2390
Fort Bragg, CA 95437

Schapira's Coffee & Tea
Box 327 Factory Lane
Pine Plains, NY 12567

Simpson and Vail
53 Park Place
New York, NY 10007

Stash Tea
P.O. Box 910
Portland, OR 97207

Stone Rose Naturals
P.O. Box 30814
Seattle, WA 98103

Tazo Teas
P.O. Box 66
Portland, OR 97207

Tea Association of the USA *
Tea Council of the USA
230 Park Avenue
New York, NY 10169

The Tea Club
1715 N. Burling St.
Chicago, IL 60614

Tea to You
3712 N. Broadway/Box 471
Chicago, IL 60613

Todd & Holland Tea Merchants
417 Lathrop Avenue
River Forest, IL 60305

Water and Leaves
380 Swift Ave. #6
So. San Francisco, CA 94080

Yogi Tea
8401 Santa Monica Blvd
W. Hollywood, CA 90069

Many of the tea rooms listed in this book are also excellent sources for teas and teatime accessories.

* Supply tea information only

TEA ROOM INDEX

TEA ROOM INDEX

RECIPE INDEX

RECIPE INDEX

TEA ROOMS ANTICIPATING OPENING IN 1998

In addition to superlative hospitality skills, the new tea room owner needs patience, attention to detail, nerves of steel, and funding. Building Departments, Health Departments, Leasing Agents, Contractors and Bank Loan Officers are just a few of the hurdles being leaped by several businesses anticipating opening a new tea room (or adding Afternoon Tea to a menu). Look for these tea rooms to open in 1998 if all goes well for them, and we sincerely hope it does:

Brambleberry Cottage, N. 122 Argonne - C, Spokane, WA 99212

Cafe Chalet, 511 Front St., Lynden, WA 98264

Carnelian Rose Tea Room, 14813 NE Salmon Cr. Ave., Vanc., WA 98686

Celestial Treasures, 135 Spring St. E. Unit B, Friday Harbor, WA 98250

Coffee Europa, 30406 Pacific Highway S., Federal Way, WA 98003

Dutch Mothers, 405 Front St., Lynden, WA 98264

Englishry, 1220 Central, Bellingham, WA 98226

Flying Cats, 114 Chance a la Mer N.E., Ocean Shores, wA 98569

For Heaven's Sake, 1950 Keene Road, Building S, Queensgate Victorian Village, Richland, WA 99352

Gingko Tea Room, Redmond Town Center, Redmond, WA 98052

Liberty House B & B, 514 Liberty, The Dalles, OR 97058

Magnolia House, 2211 Crestline, Coeur d' Alene, ID 83814

My Favorite Things, 209 E. Highway 2, Old Town, ID 83822

Tea & Tomes, 716 N.W. Beach, Newport, OR 97365

Whims & Wishes, 780 Long St., Sweet Home, OR 97386

Wits End Bookstore & Tea Shop, 770 N. 34th, Seattle, WA 98103

TeaTime in the Northwest

Report Form

Tea is quietly blossoming in the Northwest with many new tearooms opening each month. If you discover a new tea room, or know of an old favorite that was not included in ***Teatime in the Northwest***, please take a minute to let us know so that future editions will reflect the growth and diversity of the region's tea culture. If you have comments about any of the tea rooms listed in ***Teatime in the Northwest***, we would be interested in your experiences and opinions.

Name of new tea room or establishment

____

Address ______________________________________

____

Phone ____

Comments _____________________________________

____

____

Comments about tea rooms listed in TeaTime in the Northwest

____

____

____

Signed _______________________________________

Your Name and Address __________________________

____

Thank you for your input!

Please send to: Sharon & Ken Foster-Lewis
298 W. Parkside Dr.
Camano Island, WA 98292